CHUCK NORRIS

BLACK BELT PATRIOTISM

HOW TO REAWAKEN AMERICA

FIDELIS BOOKS

NASHVILLE, TENNESSEE

ISBN: 978-0-8054-6436-8

Fidelis Books, an imprint of B&H Publishing Group
Nashville, Tennessee

Hardback version published by Regnery Publishing, Inc.,
Washington, DC.

Dewey Decimal Classification: 323
Subject Heading: PATRIOTISM \ CITIZENSHIP \
CHRISTIAN LIFE

Unless otherwise noted, Scripture quotations are from the
Holy Bible, New International Version, copyright © 1973,
1978, 1984 by International Bible Society.

1 2 3 4 5 6 7 8 • 14 13 12 11 10

Dedication

I would like to dedicate this book to two groups.

First and foremost, to my family. To my wife and best friend, Gena, for her unconditional love and dedication to me, and for the countless hours she spends in assisting me in a myriad of ways in life. There are not enough words or space to thank you my love for all you do. And to my seven children (Michael, Dina, Eric, Kelley, Tim, and our twins Dakota and Danilee) and ten grandchildren (Gabi, Dante, Hannah, Camrynn, Chloe, Max, Greta, Eli, Chantz, and Dustin), for providing me the joys of fathering and grandfathering, and constantly reminding me to keep having fun in life. I dedicate this book to you all because it is for you that I joined the culture wars in hope of leaving you the legacy of a better America.

Secondly and similarly I dedicate this book to the generation of Millennials, the young men and women between the ages of eighteen and twenty-nine, to whom we will leave the America we've been handed. It is my wish and prayer that *Black Belt Patriotism* will inspire you to rise up and bear the baton of our Founders' America. You are the generational hope that the America of yesteryear can be reawakened and still be the America of tomorrow.

Contents

INTRODUCTION 1

CHAPTER ONE
One Nation, Divided, and Without a Clue 13

CHAPTER TWO
Go Back to Go Forward 25

CHAPTER THREE
Stop America's Nightmare of Debt 47

CHAPTER FOUR
Secure and Protect Our Borders 73

CHAPTER FIVE
From Here to Eternity 93

CHAPTER SIX
Reclaim the Value of Human Life 111

CHAPTER SEVEN
Calling All Millennials! 127

CHAPTER EIGHT
Honor and Care for the Family 159

CHAPTER NINE
Be Fit for the Fight...................................... 177

CHAPTER TEN
Reawaken the American Dream........................... 205

    Acknowledgments 221

    Special Acknowledgment 223

    Appendices

        The Declaration of Independence 225

        The Constitution of the United States 229

        The Ten Commandments....................... 243

    Notes... 245

    Index 273

★ ★ ★

A Response to America's Economic Recession and Washington's Excessive Spending Solutions

A BOOK NEEDED MORE NOW THAN EVER

I AM VERY GRATEFUL that the first edition of *Black Belt Patriotism* reached #14 on the *New York Times Best Seller List*. However, I truly believe this updated and expanded paperback edition is even more relevant and timely than when it was first published a year-and-a-half ago.

The eight original issues and solutions I address in the book, which I know can reawaken the American dream as our Founders understood it, are under more assault now than ever before. They are the very seams in the tapestry of our country that are being unwoven with more fervor and intentionality today than even a few years ago.

Since this book was released in September 2008, our country has a new president and a Democratic majority in Washington. For better or worse, we have new leadership and a new direction for America. It's a kinder and gentler Washington, to whom the global war on terror has turned into an "Overseas Contingency Operation."[1] It's a softer and relational Washington, with whom international bonds are more important than national borders and boundaries.[2] It's a more secular Washington, which says that the country is no longer a "Christian nation."[3] It's a more liberal Washington, which has enacted more left-leaning legislation in its first year than any previous administration.[4] It's a more generous Washington, from whom handouts, bailouts, and borrowing are granted and given at record-breaking political speed.

BIG GOVERNMENT: AMERICA'S ONLY REMEDY?

What is most disheartening about America's present political milieu is that those in Washington seem to be convinced that more and bigger government is America's primary solution. Even Obama emphatically declared early in his presidency that "only government"[5] is our savior. But that is the fundamental flaw with his administration and in his political motivation—and it is symptomatic of an entire generation that has been conditioned to believe government is the remedy for just about every societal illness.

In trying to fix the economy, they have buried future generations in trillions of dollars more debt while only growing government control over our lives. Instead of minimizing the roles of government as America's Founders advised, the federal government is supersizing nearly every stratum of its power, influence, and far-reaching tentacles into local communities across the nation. That is partially why, at town hall meetings, in publications, and on blogs, the passion and wisdom of experts and patriots are again bubbling to a boil in an attempt to stop political abuse and redirect political currents. But the mainstream media has often overlooked and even suppressed their opposition to Obama, opting instead for favorable stories that support the one they helped elect into office.[6]

One good example of that came this past year when the *New York Times* missed the opportunity to publish a great op-ed letter[7] to President Obama from Lou Pritchett,[8] a former vice president of Procter & Gamble who worked for that company for thirty-six years until his retirement in 1989. So I thought I'd give his letter a little press here and then add a few more thoughts of my own.

Mr. Pritchett confirmed via Snopes[9] that he was the author of the open letter to President Obama: "I did write the 'you scare me' letter. I sent it to the *NY Times* but they never acknowledged or published it."

I think you'll readily see why no left-leaning newspaper would run it.

Dear President Obama:

You are the thirteenth President under whom I have lived and unlike any of the others, you truly scare me.

You scare me because after months of exposure, I know nothing about you.

You scare me because I do not know how you paid for your expensive Ivy League education and your upscale lifestyle and housing with no visible signs of support.

You scare me because you did not spend the formative years of youth growing up in America and culturally you are not an American.

You scare me because you have never run a company or met a payroll.

You scare me because you have never had military experience, thus don't understand it at its core.

You scare me because you lack humility and "class," always blaming others.

You scare me because for over half your life you have aligned yourself with radical extremists who hate America and you refuse to publicly denounce these radicals who wish to see America fail.

You scare me because you are a cheerleader for the "blame America" crowd and deliver this message abroad.

You scare me because you want to change America to a European style country where the government sector dominates instead of the private sector.

You scare me because you want to replace our health care system with a government controlled one.

You scare me because you prefer "wind mills" to responsibly capitalizing on our own vast oil, coal, and shale reserves.

You scare me because you want to kill the American capitalist goose that lays the golden egg which provides the highest standard of living in the world.

You scare me because you have begun to use "extortion" tactics against certain banks and corporations.

You scare me because your own political party shrinks from challenging you on your wild and irresponsible spending proposals.

You scare me because you will not openly listen to or even consider opposing points of view from intelligent people.

You scare me because you falsely believe that you are both omnipotent and omniscient.

You scare me because the media gives you a free pass on everything you do.

You scare me because you demonize and want to silence the Limbaughs, Hannitys, O'Reillys, and Becks who offer opposing, conservative points of view.

You scare me because you prefer controlling over governing.

Finally, you scare me because if you serve a second term I will probably not feel safe in writing a similar letter in eight years.

Lou Pritchett

Thank you, Mr. Pritchett, for your love for America, your honesty and willingness to risk your reputation by speaking up to this administration.

Now let me add a few of my own fears to yours.

President Obama:

You scare me because so many amazing corporate and American leaders like Lou Pritchett say things about you like: "You scare me."

You scare me because, after you initiate more government borrowing and bailouts than all presidents combined, you require Congress to follow a system that is "pay-as-you-go."[10]

You scare me because you really do believe that going into massive amounts of debt can remedy our economy in the long run.

You scare me because you repeatedly still play the blame game with the Bush administration but never blame the Clinton administration, even though they were responsible for the Fannie Mae and Freddie Mac subprime fiasco via the proliferation of loans to low income unqualified borrowers.

You scare me because you buy and run banking, automobile, and soon health industries with taxpayers' money but refuse to call it socialism.

You scare me because your actions don't reflect the federal governmental constraints and fiscally prudent principles of our Founding Fathers and Constitution.

You scare me because you promise to lead from the center but drive hard and fast to the left.

You scare me because you claim to be a fighter for minorities and the Constitutional promises of life, liberty, and the pursuit of happiness, yet what greater minority can be defended than those in the womb, against whom you have already enacted more pro-abortion-related laws than anyone since Roe v. Wade?[11]

You scare me because you promise to defend the U.S. against all potential enemies, yet you pacify those who harbor terrorists, fight for the rights of combative detainees, and enable the enemies of Israel.

You scare me because you deny America's Judeo-Christian heritage before other countries of the world,[12] espousing "the promise of a secular nation"[13] during an age in which religious revisionism is already on the rise.[14]

You scare me because your media team (including the mainstream media) will seek to label as radical, quarantine socially, or in some way penalize any opposing conservative voices (like conservative talk-show hosts, news agencies, columnists, or fellow actors like Jon Voight).[15]

You scare me because, as we've all watched over your first year in office, you can get away with all these things mentioned above and the mainstream media and most of the public will continue to hail you as king.

You scare me because your media team will not address or diminish in any way your deification before the world, epitomized by the editor of Newsweek *who stated on MSNBC's*

Chris Matthews's show, "I mean, in a way Obama's standing above the country, above the world. He's sort of God."[16] (How much scarier can it get than representative statements like that in a republic that once stood for equity among political powers and a government "by the people and for the people"?)

How much more will Americans take? When will enough be enough?

AN ENCOURAGEMENT FROM A POWER GREATER THAN ME

Since this book's first printing, America has also experienced the greatest recession since the Great Depression. Wall Street bottomed out. And Main Street has suffered monumentally. A plethora of companies and corporations across the nation filed for bankruptcy, leaving some cities like ghost towns. Simultaneously, the country has incurred massive amounts of debt through the federal government's attempts to try and rescue our economy, literally selling America via its indebtedness to countries like China and universally depreciating the value of the dollar. But most heart-wrenching of all, millions have lost their jobs, homes, and livelihoods.

Of course not everyone is personally responsible for their financial woes. Millions have lost their jobs, retirements, and livelihoods because of the crash of the market, particular industries, or local property values. I genuinely feel for those who have suffered through the toughest of economic times over the past couple years. That is why I want to offer an encouragement from someone much greater than me.

No, I'm not talking about God, though he definitely needs to be a part of America's solution (that's chapter 5). I am talking about my eighty-eight-year-old mother. Her family lived through the Great Depression in rural Oklahoma when she was a young child and she remembers what her family and neighbors did to get through those tough times.

Like so many her age, my mother has lived with grace, optimism and courage, despite facing some of life's greatest difficulties. She almost died at birth and again at ten years of age. She lived in and through some of the hardest hit places of the Great Depression, spending most of her life below the poverty level. She endured a perilous relationship with an alcoholic and mentally abusive husband (my father), who served in World War II and suffered irreparably from post-traumatic stress and the devil in the bottle. She single-handedly raised three boys, only to suffer the loss of her second son to the Vietnam War. She survived cancer, was a widow twice over, and has outlived all eight of her siblings. What's amazing is that, through it all, I can't recall hearing Mom complain once. That is so typical of her generation and they are to be commended for it.

This past year in my syndicated column, "An eighty-seven-year-old's economic survivor guide," I shared verbatim what my mother had to say to those who are facing economic and other hardships relating to the recession. It became one of my most popular columns—no doubt because of her simplicity and wisdom.

Prior to big government handouts, here are three practices her generation did to not only survive but thrive through adversity— pearls of wisdom often overlooked in our time as a part of the solution. My mother shared:

- "Be an integral part of a local community. Today people are much more alone, much more isolated. We used to be close with our neighbors. If one person had a bigger or better garden or orchard, they shared the vegetables and fruits with others in need. Society has shifted from caring for one another to being dependent upon government aid and welfare. That is why so many today trust in government to deliver them. They've forgotten an America that used to rally around one another in smaller clusters, called neighborhoods and communities. We even took care of one another's health care concerns—an alternative that Washington is completely overlooking. We must rekindle those local communal fires and relearn the power of that age-old commandment, 'Love thy neighbor.'"

■ "Help someone else. We never quit helping others back then. Today, too many people are consumed with their own problems and only helping themselves. 'What's in it for me?' is the question most are asking. But back then, it was, 'What can I do to help my neighbor too?' I love Rick Warren's book *The Purpose Driven Life*, and especially his thought, 'We were created for community, designed to be a blessing to others.' Most of all, helping others gets our minds off of our problems and puts things into better perspective. There is nothing like helping someone else to help ourselves get through tough times."

■ "Lean upon God for help and strength. We didn't just have each other to lean on, but we had God too. We all attended church and belonged to a faith community. Church was the hub of society, the community core and rallying point. Today people turn to government the way we used to turn to churches. It's been that way ever since Herbert Hoover's alleged promise of a 'chicken in every pot' and President Roosevelt's New Deal. Too many have abandoned faith and community. We trust in government and money more than God. And maybe that's a reason why we're in this economic pickle."

Tell me America wouldn't be better off if more lived by those three principles? If we want to encourage the next generation, indeed help them to be one of America's greatest generations too, then we must rekindle, encourage, and equip them to implement these ways of succeeding.

In Tom Brokaw's book *The Greatest Generation*, he explains why my mother's generation which survived the Great Depression and fought in World War II and rebuilt the postwar world deserves that title and our continued thanks:

> They won the war; they saved the world. They came home to joyous and short-lived celebrations and immediately began the task of rebuilding their lives and the world they wanted. They married in record numbers and gave birth to another distinctive generation, the Baby Boomers. A grateful nation made it possible for more of them to attend college than any society had ever educated, anywhere. They gave the world new science, literature, art, industry, and economic strength unparalleled in the long curve of history.[17]

The Greatest Generation is a tough generation. Anyone who knows someone in that age bracket knows just how tough they are. They deserve our thanks and praise. But they also deserve more than that. They deserve our respect and remembrance of the America they built for us. We need to learn from their values and mimic their faithfulness. We need to carry forward the America they handed us and not drop that baton and forget it in the sands of time.

I'm certain that if the generations today could connect with and learn from the Greatest Generation of yesteryear, the America of tomorrow would be a better and brighter place. With their wisdom, we all could experience what Isaac Newton experienced when he said, "If I have seen further, it is by standing on the shoulders of giants."

AMERICA: REAWAKEN!

While doing another interview on Glenn Beck's radio show in 2008,[16] he told me someone asked him, "Do you really believe that there is going to be trouble in the future?" And he answered, "If this country starts to spiral out of control and Mexico melts down or whatever, if it really starts to spiral out of control, before America allows a country to become a totalitarian country (which it would have under I think the Republicans as well in this situation; they were taking us to the same place, just slower), Americans won't stand for it. There will be parts of the country that will rise up."

Then Glenn asked me and his listening audience, "And where's that going to come from?" He answered his own question, "Texas, it's going to come from Texas. Do you agree with that Chuck?"

I replied, "Oh yeah!" Definitely. That is why I quipped the tongue-and-cheek response to our wayward federal government, "I may run for president of Texas."

That need may be a reality sooner than we think. If not me, someone someday may again be running for president of the Lone Star state, if the state of the union continues to turn into the enemy of the state.

I'm reminded of the part in the movie, *Shawshank Redemption*, in which Tim Robbin's character had been in prison for decades as an innocent man. As he came to the end of his ropes, he told an inmate friend and lifer played by Morgan Freeman, "The way I see it, you better get busy livin' or get busy dying." That's also true for patriots across America.

I'm tired of watching our country being torn to shreds by those who think the answer is more government debt and more government control. I'm tired of being in bondage to a tax system that robs U.S. citizens like the King of England did before the Revolution. I'm tired of watching our sovereignty being sold by loans and loose borders. And I will not sit back and merely watch this decay and degradation of the U.S. and then hand it to my children and grandchildren to deal with. That is why I've committed the rest of my life to help Old Glory rise again to her heights of splendor.

In 2009 the Alamo celebrated its 173rd commemoration, when on March 6, 1836, Texans under Col. William B. Travis were overcome by the Mexican army after a two-week siege at the Alamo in San Antonio. But they didn't go down without a hell-of-a-fight, as those roughly 145 Texans fought to their dying breaths against more than two thousand Mexican forces under General Santa Anna. (Casualties in the battle were 189 Texans vs. about 1,600 Mexicans.) They lost that battle but would provide the inspiration to win the war. Their fighting spirit rallied the new found republic and still does to this day. So when you think all is lost in America, remember the Alamo!

Sam Houston put it well, when he gave the marching orders, "We view ourselves on the eve of battle. We are nerved for the contest, and must conquer or perish. It is vain to look for present aid: none is at hand. We must now act or abandon all hope! Rally to the standard, and be no longer the scoff of mercenary tongues! Be men, be free men, that your children may bless their father's name."

If you're ready to keep fighting that good fight, then I invite you to turn the pages and let me lay out the battle and restoration plans for America.

★ ★ ★

One Nation, Divided, and Without a Clue

I LOVE AMERICA—always have, always will. But even the most patriotic among us will confess that America seems to have lost its way. As a people, we seem more divided than ever before. Switch on the television and it's clear we've lost our moral compass. Our economy, once celebrated as a guarantor of freedom and prosperity, now seems corrupted by greed, materialism, and uncertainty. Other countries that used to envy us now despise us. We seem to have lost not only our sense of ourselves but of our place in the world.

I don't claim to be a scholar. I'm not a sociologist or a political scientist. I am just a concerned citizen who is extremely worried, as I'm sure most of you are, about the direction our country is heading. I have watched our country change—and, unfortunately, not for the better. When I was in school in the 1950s, what the teacher said to do, you did. No questions asked. The teacher was in charge, not the students. We would never think about being disrespectful, much less attacking a teacher. Boy has that changed now!

In the 1960s I watched prayer taken out of the schools. I watched the baby-boomer generation rebel with the slogans, "If it feels good, do it," and "Don't trust anyone over thirty." They are now middle-aged parents. And while many of them have come to see the error of their ways, their permissiveness has rubbed off on their children, who have pushed the edge of promiscuity and liberal living that much further. The feel-good concept of the 1960s was drugs and sex, which has morphed into total unbridled licentiousness in an unfortunate downward spiral that is taking our culture in a direction that no sane person should want it to go. It is time for America to wake up and change this course.

I don't believe in whining. I'm an optimist and I believe we can do better. I have outlined below the major problems I think our country faces and in every chapter in this book I'll also provide what seem to me to be practical, real-world solutions we can either do ourselves or pressure our politicians into doing (making them do the jobs we elected them to do).

I also believe the first step in fixing the mess we're in is recognizing how we got here. And that means looking back before we can move forward. We need to learn from the past, from history, and most especially from the example of our Founding Fathers. I love American history and over the last few years I've gained a greater appreciation for our Founding Fathers. I, like many of you, went through much of my life with conservative beliefs, but really on the basis of instinct, experience, and common sense rather than with a philosophical grounding, beyond knowing a few guiding quotes from the Founders. Studying and researching more of America's heritage has helped me gain a whole new appreciation for the Founders' lives and opened my eyes to their old solutions for our new problems. I'll outline what those are and how I think we can achieve them.

The first step is to pick our battles. I've narrowed it down to what I think are the eight most important challenges we face as a country and as a people. And they start with remembering who we are.

NO NATIONAL LEGACY

America's first major problem is we have forgotten our roots. Too many of us don't know or don't feel connected to those who founded our country.

In 2007 a national survey commissioned by the U.S. Mint[1] found that only 30 percent of Americans knew Thomas Jefferson was our third president and only 7 percent could name the first four presidents in order. If you're a part of the 93 percent, they were George Washington, John Adams, Thomas Jefferson, and James Madison. The fact is most Americans don't have a clue why our Founders created this country, what principles motivated them, or why they framed our Constitution the way they did.

As citizens of this great country, we need to renew our understanding of the Declaration of Independence and the Constitution. We need to go back and study the debates between the Federalists and the Anti-Federalists. We need to examine other important documents of our history, like the Articles of Confederation, the Bill of Rights, and the Northwest Ordinance. We need to sit down and learn all the important American history we should have learned in school—and probably didn't.

You might not have thought it mattered then. But you have to understand that it matters now. If Americans don't know their constitutional history, they won't care, or even acknowledge, that our constitution of liberty is being transformed into a charter for big government, which is exactly what has happened over a period of decades. You know that old saying, "too many cooks in the kitchen"? That's how I feel about our representatives in Congress. There are too many cooks in the kitchen (535 to be exact), and what they've cooked is inedible. I've seen them scream and squabble at each other until they had to have a "time out," just like kids in grammar school. Another way to see federal government is like an octopus with its tentacles overreaching and overextending into every facet of society. Clearly the government we have today is not the government outlined in the Constitution. It's grown far beyond the limits the Constitution sets—and as a result we are facing dangers from which the Constitution's Framers tried to protect us.

The Framers set out a path for us and we've strayed from it. And the first thing any rational man does when he's lost his way is to look at a map. If you think, as I do, that America has taken a wrong turn, studying America's history is the first step to helping us find our way back.

NO CONTROL OVER SPENDING

America's second major problem is debt.

On January 1, 1791, during George Washington's second year as president, the national debt was about 75 million dollars.[2] On September 30, 2007, the government estimated the balance owed was now more than 9 trillion dollars.[3] In 2009, it grew to 11 trillion dollars. The nonprofit, nonpartisan Institute for Truth in Accounting calculates the actual national deficit is closer to a staggering 56 trillion dollars.[4] Even at 9 trillion, that means to eliminate the national debt would require every American to pay roughly $30,000 each. Of course, that's not going to happen, especially since the average American has almost the same income-debt ratio as the federal government.

Often not highlighted, but equally alarming, is our trade deficit, which has ballooned over the past decade. The *Wall Street Journal* recently reported:

> In just 15 years, our annual trade deficit has mushroomed to over $800 billion from $38 billion in 1993. With Mexico, our trade surplus evolved into a $90.7 billion trade deficit. With China, our trade deficit jumped to $250 billion today from about $22 billion. President George H. W. Bush once estimated that a $1 billion trade deficit represents 13,000 lost jobs. Do the math.[5]

According to the Federal Reserve, the total U.S. consumer (installment) debt reached $2.46 trillion in June 2007. Credit cards account for roughly $800 billion of that amount.[6] Of course those levels of consumer debt are not helped by a recessive housing and stock market or staggering oil and gas prices.

To be in debt is to sacrifice your freedom and independence and give someone else power over you. Do we think we can continue to experience freedom politically and even personally, when our private and national debts loom over us like the king of England once did? Debt is bondage, plain and simple.

After the Revolutionary War, America's Founders were well aware of the need to avoid further debt. Thomas Jefferson wrote in 1816, "To preserve our independence, we must not let our rulers load us with perpetual debt."[7] Jefferson's administration (1801–1809) actually reduced the national debt by roughly $26 million, despite fighting a war with the Barbary Pirates and making the Louisiana Purchase.[8] We need to rediscover the Founders' sense of fiscal prudence.

NOT ENOUGH BORDER CONTROL

America's third major problem is that our government has failed to enforce our nation's borders. While the Border Patrol and the Department of Homeland Security have started making some progress, it is slow, late, and not enough. Our borders, ports, and airports remain nearly open runways for illegal immigrants, drug cartels, gunrunners, and potential terrorists. There is still a dire shortage of Border Patrol officers, and the Homeland Security Department is still trying to fill last year's 138 vacancies in high-level jobs—an employment crisis that it called "a critical homeland security issue that demands immediate attention."[9]

Unfortunately the possible creation of a North American Union (with Canada and Mexico) and the so-called NAFTA Superhighways will, if they happen, only make these problems worse.

Enforcing our borders is about more than law enforcement. It's about preserving our nationhood as Americans and it's about national security. I believe threats of terror remain real an imminent. It is simply irresponsible to leave our borders unguarded, our national security unprotected, and our border laws unenforced.

Our Founders knew about terrorism from the Barbary pirates. Our nation's borders were often dangerous places. And the Founders struggled to find a balance between welcoming the poor, the downtrodden, and the persecuted, with preserving what they knew to be a unique American nation, united by a common language and culture. Before becoming our fourth president, James Madison challenged Congress on February 3, 1790, that when "considering the advantages that may result from an easy mode of naturalization, we ought also to consider the cautions necessary to guard against abuses."[10] In a later chapter we'll look at some of our Founders' recommendations regarding immigration, as well as my own recommendations for the illegal immigration problems.

NO MORAL COMPASS

America's fourth major problem is that we've lost our moral compass. Our moral absolutes have turned into absolute mush.

In 2005, a national survey by sociologist George Barna[11] concluded that 65 percent of Americans now believe that moral truth depends on circumstances; only 35 percent believe that moral truth is absolute and unchanging.

In a previous study,[12] Barna noted that most people today base their morality on feelings. Brad Pitt, who I'm sure is a great guy, spoke for this majority when he said, "I have a hard time with morals. All I know is what feels right. What's more important to me is being honest about who you are. Morals I get a little hung up on."[13] You know the phrase, "If it feels good, do it."

But that was not the outlook that shaped the beginning of our nation. The motto of the Founders was closer to: "Do what is right." And they defined what was right in terms of their inherited Christian culture. Before the Constitution, each of the American colonies codified into law every one of the Ten Commandments, and many of them even had state-established churches.[14] Every one of the colonies firmly established that its laws and customs were based on the Judeo-Christian faith of the colonists. It was fundamental to American ideas of freedom that it was right to submit to the will of God but wrong to submit to the will of tyrants. They knew that freedom could exist only among a moral people, because only a moral people could carry its responsibilities. That is why John Adams said in a letter to the Massachusetts Militia, "We have no government armed with power capable of contending with human passions unbridled by morality and religion. Avarice, ambition, revenge, or gallantry, would break the strongest cords of our Constitution as a whale goes through a net. Our Constitution was made only for a religious and moral people. It is wholly inadequate for the government of any other." And it is why George Washington warned in his farewell address about the danger of supposing "that morality can be maintained without religion."

But too many of us have supposed just that. Prayer has been banned from our schools. The Ten Commandments have been sandblasted from our public buildings. The ACLU makes a living trying to get courts to ban religion—especially Christianity—from any public forum.

But if we want to restore America as our Founders meant it to be, we need to start with the first principles they started from. We need to restore our sense of civility, morality, and responsibility.

NOT ENOUGH VALUE FOR HUMAN LIFE

America's fifth major problem is that we've devalued human life. Even those among the Founders who were deists believed that humans were the highest creation of God. That is why we find the words in the Declaration of Independence, "We hold these truths to be self-evident, that all men are created equal, that they are endowed by their Creator with certain unalienable Rights, that among these are Life, Liberty and the pursuit of Happiness." Inherent within those words is a declaration of human value that would destroy slavery and that should protect every one of us, from the senior citizen in the rest home to the baby in the womb, regardless of race or sex.

Unfortunately this appraisal of human worth has been lost in time. Extreme Darwinists deny that human beings have any more rights, or are any more important, than animals. Atheists deny that there is any Creator who could give value to human life. And in the 1973 landmark case *Roe v. Wade,* the Supreme Court ruled that life could be terminated in the womb. More than a million babies a year have been sacrificed on the altar of that Supreme Court ruling, which is as ludicrous as was the Supreme Court's ruling in *Dred Scott v. Sandford* in 1857, which upheld slavery.

Fortunately *Dred Scott* was overturned, though it took a terrible war and the loss of 620,000 lives to do it. *Roe v. Wade* has not been overturned and inevitably it has set a precedent for every new devaluation of life, including the movement to legalize euthanasia and suicide. Once again we need to heed the words of Thomas Jefferson, who wrote in 1809, "The care of human life and happiness, and not their destruction, is the first and only legitimate object of good government."[15]

NO FUTURE FOR THE CHILDREN

Our sixth major problem is that we are failing our children. Whenever a culture decays, children bear the brunt. When sexual promiscuity, pornography, and easy divorce are accepted, children are the ones affected the most. Whenever a culture devalues life, children are the ones who grow up without hope or aspiration. Whenever a culture drives out religion from the public sphere, children are the ones forced to grow up in a society immersed in perverse values: a world where gangster rappers are heroes, where greed and gluttony are good, where immorality thrives, or is tolerated, or even encouraged.

We all know that when it comes to this nation's moral health, as measured by our children, we're in bad shape: juvenile crime has skyrocketed (48 percent in just the last eleven years), at least one out of every four kids is overweight or obese, and our teen pregnancy rate is a national scandal (such as the group of girls who had a pact to get pregnant, and seventeen of them did, at the high school in Gloucester, Massachusetts). We're so used to reading the news about declining test scores, rising illegitimacy rates, and an epidemic of sexually transmitted diseases among ever younger Americans that we've come to ignore it. But it's safe to say our Founding Fathers could never have imagined such rampant degradation. In fact, in 1787 Ben Franklin wrote a pamphlet titled "Information to those who would remove to America," which noted that "bad examples [of] youth are more rare in America, which must be a comfortable consideration to parents." Can you picture a politician saying that about our youth today?

NO TRADITIONAL FAMILY VALUES

America's seventh major problem is the dissolution of the family—not just through divorce and dead-beat dads, but through the erosion of the most basic social institution of all: marriage. Today, living together is generally accepted and even glorified by many celebrities. And who suffers because of these transient relationships? Everyone—especially the children. In 1940 fewer than four babies out of a hundred were born to unmarried women. Today, 40 percent are.[16] Sixty-three percent of American children under age five are in some form of day care every week, living life apart from their parents.[17]

Thirty-six percent of parents worry that their total family income won't be enough to meet the bills.[18] Nearly half of America's labor force is women and of course many of these women are mothers.[19]

Seventy-seven percent of children between the ages of five and thir-teen are designated as "latchkey kids,"[20] which means, essentially, they have part-time parents. These are kids who are alone for hours every week and they spend much of that time watching television, playing video games, and surfing the Internet. Technology has become our national babysitter—and as we know, much of that technology likes to shock and titillate with bloody violence and sexual content.

If the traditional family is collapsing, it's also being threatened by groups that want to redefine it out of existence. Times were not always this complicated for families. Though the Founders weathered their own particular family trials in Early America, they treasured marriage and were committed husbands and fathers. And they realized that no other success could compen-sate for failure at home. I believe we should do the same.

NO MIGHT TO FIGHT

America's eighth major problem is apathy: physical, mental, and spiritual. According to the World Health Organization[21] and the Centers for Disease Control and Prevention,[22] childhood and teen obesity in the U.S. has tripled over the last thirty years. They also report one-third of adults are now obese, with another third being overweight. According to their data, those numbers have "increased sharply for both adults and children"[23] since the 1970s.

Compared to other countries, Americans eat much larger por-tions. We eat to get full—other cultures often eat for health rea-sons. We live to eat, while they eat to live. Given all the serious diseases linked to being overweight, we need, as my good friend Governor Mike Huckabee put it, to stop digging our graves with a knife and fork. I ask you: How can we expect to fight a culture war when we can't even win a war against consumption?

Our Founders worked hard. They ate well. They knew noth-ing of processed foods like ours. Many were hunters and farmers. They raised livestock, harvested crops, and planted gardens and orchards from which they gathered fresh fruits and vegetables. The Founders knew—it is common sense—the importance of staying strong and fit. With no automobiles, their primary mode of transportation was their feet (another great solution for our gas crisis!). But they certainly didn't expect to micromanage our diets by creating a Food and Drug Administration or a United States Department of Agriculture. As Thomas Jefferson quipped, "Was the government to prescribe to us our medicine and diet, our bodies would be in such keeping as our souls are now."[24]

The bottom line is that it is up to each of us to maintain our bodies and our minds. The Founders had the mental, physical, and spiritual tenacity to start a nation. We need that same tenacity to restore it.

EIGHT INSURMOUNTABLE FOES?

Americans are facing perilous times. And we still long for a hero or heroes to come and save the day. I truly believe those cultural heroes are you and me. I also believe that, just as any martial arts champion knows, the only way we are going to win is to face one fight at a time. As my friend Bruce Lee once said, "A fight is not won by one punch or kick. Either learn to endure or hire a bodyguard."

As a martial arts fighter, I realized I had to possess the inner strength to stare down the impossible: to face giant opponents, often alone, in order to become six-time world middleweight karate champion. Many times I fought opponents who were stronger and faster than me. I knew in order to win, I had to study the weaknesses of my opponents, visualize my victory, and believe I could win. The same is true for us in this culture war.

It doesn't take many people to foster a revolution. Jesus did it with twelve disciples. George Washington did it with his few suffering troops at Valley Forge. And we can do it today. We can set a new direction for America with people like you and me, who through our efforts in our communities and at the ballot box and in our personal lives can make this country everything it should be, everything our nation's Founders wanted it to be. America has fallen asleep at the wheel and it's time for her to wake up before it's too late. It's up to us; and this book is my way of showing where we can start.

★ ★ ★

CHAPTER TWO

Go Back to Go Forward

A FEW YEARS BACK an editor at the *New York Times* wrote, "The Founding Fathers were paranoid hypocrites and ungrateful malcontents."[1] He's not alone. Many liberals in media and higher education share his sentiments, labeling our Founding Fathers as racists, bigots, chauvinists, and charlatans, among other things. This is not only ungrateful—it's wrong. As Samuel Adams said in 1771, "Let us first see it prov'd that they were mistakes. 'Till then we must hold ourselves obliged to them for sentiments transmitted to us so worthy of their character, and so important to our security."[2] It's their contributions, not their character flaws, that we should be highlighting. Thomas G. West, professor of politics at the University of Dallas, rightly acknowledged our Founders' worth in his excellent book *Vindicating the Founders* by pointing out that they "set up a government that did what no democracy had ever done before: It combined majority rule with effective protection for minority rights. It enabled a larger number of men and women to live in prosperity and liberty than any other nation has ever done."[3]

Of course, the Founders weren't perfect, but they were far better than what many in the media make them out to be. We know that most of the Founders regarded slavery as a wrong that would have to be addressed. They knew that equal rights applied to all: men and women, black and white. They did not achieve all they wanted, but what they did achieve was miraculous. That miracle is our heritage. As Joseph Ellis stated in his narrative masterpiece, *Founding Brothers*, the Constitutional Convention should be called "the miracle of Philadelphia."[4] America's Founding Fathers gave us a framework to build and improve our Republic. But we can't do that unless we know who they were, what they stood for, and what they achieved. To restore America, we need to reclaim our past and learn from it. It is only by turning back and examining the past, according to Thomas Jefferson, that we will be able "to judge the future; it will avail [us] of the experience of other times and other nations; it will qualify [us] as judges of the actions and designs of men; it will enable [us] to know ambition under every disguise it may assume; and knowing it, to defeat its views."[5]

Unfortunately those who want to reconstruct our constitutional government, redefine our founding documents, and revise our history according to their ideological whims are being allowed to do just that because of the apathy of too many well-meaning Americans. If we don't care about our past, if we don't learn our history, if we don't cherish the Constitution and the principles of the Declaration of Independence, then America will be robbed of its rightful future. The first thing we need to do to restore America is to insist that our government officials abide by the origin of those founding documents and that they rightly interpret their tenets. If, like most people, you're a little rusty on the origin of those founding documents, here's a quick primer on what our government was meant to be—and should be.

RECONSTRUCTING AMERICA'S GOVERNMENT

In 1776, by an act of the Second Continental Congress,[6] the original thirteen colonies of North America adopted a Declaration of Independence, dissolving their relations with England. America would be a confederation of independent countries ("states"). In 1777 the Articles of Confederation (our first constitution and governing document) was written and adopted by the Second Continental Congress, though not ratified until 1781. The Federalists soon recognized the deficiencies in the Articles of Confederation, so they called for a constitutional convention in Philadelphia in 1787. By the end of their four-month convention, the United States Constitution was adopted, though not completely ratified until 1790. It has been amended twenty-seven times since (the first ten amendments constitute the Bill of Rights).

The whole point of the Constitution is to provide a framework for our government, to set its rules, and to protect our rights by limiting government power. The Constitution requires that the president[7] and members of Congress "be bound by Oath or Affirmation to support this constitution." In other words, every elected member of the federal government is accountable for abiding by the Constitution. We the people must hold them accountable. But how many of us hold our elected leaders to account? And how far have we allowed the federal government and federal courts to take powers the Constitution doesn't give them? When we do, we let them rob us of our own freedom and of the right to self-determination our forefathers wanted us to have.

Tragically government is hanging onto the Constitution by threads. Despite the fact the U.S. government is supposed to find its very identity and procedures for operation in this founding document, governing officials through the decades have progressively strayed from obedience to it. Judge Andrew P. Napolitano, in his government-shattering book *Constitutional Chaos*, outlines hundreds of examples from our courts to congressional halls of how the government has not upheld the oath of office to the Constitution, all of its articles and amendments. Napolitano's work is a shocking unveiling that exposes the depth and breadth of constitutional corruptions. And let there be no doubt about this: they will continue to increase until we counteract them and speak up!

It is well known I supported Governor Mike Huckabee for the Republican nomination for president in 2008. But I also admire the way Congressman Ron Paul, another candidate for the Republican nomination, stood up for the Constitution. In Congress, Ron Paul, a former obstetrician-gynecologist and a fellow Texan, is known as "Dr. No" for consistently voting against unconstitutional legislation—sometimes alone.

When government robs us of our freedom, of course, it dresses up its action in words that make it sound commendable. Who, for instance, could be opposed to laws against "hate crimes"? But Paul was one of the few truthtellers to remind us that so-called "hate crimes" legislation is really just anti-freedom of speech legislation, prohibited by the First Amendment.

As Congressman Paul pointed out, "Hate crime laws not only violate the First Amendment, they also violate the Tenth Amendment. Under the United States Constitution, there are only three federal crimes: piracy, treason, and counterfeiting. All other criminal matters are left to the individual states. Any federal legislation dealing with criminal matters not related to these three issues usurps state authority over criminal law and takes a step toward turning the states into mere administrative units of the federal government."[8]

He's right, but how often do we hear such honesty from our elected members of Congress? The longer this constitutional chaos continues—and it has been accelerating for decades—the less our country resembles the America our Founding Fathers created and wanted us to have. And it is going to take we the people, to hold our governing officials accountable. That is what our Founders expected and admonished.

Patrick Henry said, "The Constitution is not an instrument for the government to restrain the people, it is an instrument for the people to restrain the government—lest it come to dominate our lives and interests." Please, read this great quote again. Patrick Henry gave us our marching orders: we need to restrain our government to abide by the Constitution.

We must remind every government official, from the White House to our local school boards, that they must either conform and serve in accordance with the Constitution (federal and state), or we, the people, will follow the Founders' prescription to remedy bad government. That remedy is found in the Declaration of Independence, and it sends shivers up my spine every time I read it:

> That whenever any Form of Government becomes destructive of these ends [man's unalienable rights to life, liberty, and the pursuit of happiness], it is the Right of the People to alter or to abolish it, and to institute new Government, laying its foundation on such principles and organizing its powers in such form, as to them shall seem most likely to effect their Safety and Happiness. . . . But when a long train of abuses and usurpations, pursuing invariably the same Object evinces a design to reduce them under absolute Despotism, it is their right, it is their duty, to throw off such Government, and to provide new Guards for their future security.

I still think political corruption (and an even more equitable representation) might be dealt with someday by reducing the size of Congress. I understand bi-cameral legislatures. But the fact is we always have as a last resort the reduction of the size of Congress—and hence a greater control over our Representatives. The Constitution requires two Senators per state and at least one representative (with a maximum of one per thirty thousand people). Through time, Congress has established one representative per nine hundred thousand—nothing sacred about that number.

While more Congressmen might seem like the answer, I believe fewer is. Our Founders honestly wrestled with whether the number of representatives should represent a certain number of people or a specific area of people (since regions often represented a collective persuasion—like, for example, in some of the southern or Midwest states). When America grows in such a way that ten or so more liberal coastal states basically sway national elections, or when more densely populated urban areas dominate rural counties in state elections, I think we need to rehash the arguments of old and what the term *representative* truly means.

Let me illustrate it this way: if California represents a larger liberal voice with its fifty-three representatives, how fair is it that the total populations of seven states (Alaska, Delaware, Montana, North Dakota, South Dakota, Vermont, and Wyoming—each with only one representative)[9] can in no way out vote the liberal stream of California? On the other hand, these seven states prove my very point: they each have only one representative, who represents the entire state—and if they don't like what that representative is doing for them nationally, they can easily make the changes. The U.S. doesn't need a new reapportionment act to raise the number of representatives, but a return to the Constitution to reduce the number of representatives in pursuit of creating more equitable regions or districts.

REDEFINING AMERICA'S FOUNDING DOCUMENTS

It greatly alarms me that Americans' constitutional right to freedom of speech is being squeezed out of our culture.

One of the geniuses of America's Founding Fathers was to provide and secure the firm foundation in the First Amendment: "Congress shall make no law respecting an establishment of religion, or prohibiting the free exercise thereof; or abridging the freedom of speech, or of the press; or the right of the people peaceably to assemble, and to petition the Government for a redress of grievances."

Several years ago I remember watching then *20/20* correspondent Diane Sawyer interview Saddam Hussein, dictator of Iraq. She was respectfully confronting him for atrocities and executions as punishments for people merely speaking a word against him, his rule, or his politics. Surprisingly naïve of America's constitutional basis, Saddam asked, "Well, what happens to those who speak against your president?" (His rhetorical question was clearly expecting that such speech was also a crime in the U.S. and punishable by law.) Shocked by his sheer ignorance of the U.S., and somewhat at a loss for words herself, Diane quipped back in answering his question, "They host television talk shows!" Saddam's facial expression revealed that he was totally confused by her answer.

Sounds so far out, doesn't it? Offensive speech being punishable by law? But it might not be that far off for America, especially if the course of our right for freedom of speech continues on its present track—a path of progressive restrictions, both from our government and our culture.

Limiting free speech is not just happening through legal ends, but through social avenues as well. It was tragic to watch this past year at the White House correspondents' dinner[10] how the present administration provided the platform, then laughed at a parade of mean-spirited, cruel jokes that made fun of Rush Limbaugh's history of addiction to painkillers, wished him kidney failure, and suggested he might have been the twentieth hijacker involved in 9/11. Is that even funny? Despite that I believe even this offensive language is protected by the First Amendment, is it the type of belittling humor we should expect at a White House function? When the federal government seeks to silence their critics through intimidation and social demise, have they not failed to properly lead a blended nation and uphold the heart of the Constitution? Mark my words that the reinstitution of the Fairness Doctrine,[11] which will subject talk radio among other media to government regulation, is right around the corner.

Government isn't the only one restricting free speech. This past year we witnessed many in our culture clamping down on this basic American right, as former Miss California and Miss U.S.A. runner-up, Carrie Prejean, gave her honest opinion to a question during the Miss U.S.A. pageant. As a result of her speaking freely about her personal convictions, she's been persecuted for her opinion, lost her crown, and even received death threats from those who oppose her.[12]

Whatever one believes about the boundaries of marriage or how one feels about scanty modeling photos is far secondary to Miss Prejean being culturally harassed and persecuted on account of her merely speaking her honest opinion about traditional marriage,[13] *especially* in response to a question asked by a judge during a beauty pageant. As she said in her press conference with Donald Trump, "This shouldn't happen in America!"[14] That is absolutely the truth.

There seems to be a double-standard when it comes to free speech in society: shall certain camps be expected not to offend while others are free to do so? If the First Amendment is not also there to protect anyone's offensive speech, then what type of speech is it protecting? And if it protects even unpleasant and distasteful speech as well, yet our culture remains intolerant of offensive speech, then have we not abandoned the First Amendment?

I don't care what your cause is. I don't care what your mission is. I don't care what the issue is. I don't care what your beliefs are. It is every American citizen's Constitutional right to speak freely, without fear of repercussion. It's simply un-American and unconstitutional to impede, harass, threaten, or persecute anyone who is guilty of nothing more than sharing their opinion or even exercising their right to vote. This is America—not Saddam's Iraq!

Our Founders cry out from their graves and heaven for us to remember what they established—a nation free from tyranny and oppression. Thomas Jefferson was particularly passionate and eloquent at this point with these words now indelibly inscribed on the memorial in Washington named after him. Whether to the dominance of religious sectarianism or the prohibition of free speech, his words apply: "I have sworn upon the altar of God eternal hostility toward any tyranny over the mind of men."[15] So have I. Have you?

America, when free speech is restricted or punished, we can be certain we've drifted from our roots. Isn't it time we returned home to the Constitution? Don't just fight for your freedom of speech—fight for others.

This past year I shot (no pun intended) an NRA public service announcement, in which I fought for our Second Amendment rights too by saying, "If some thug breaks into my home, I can use my roundhouse kick. But I prefer he look down the barrel of my gun."[16]

The reason I was so adamant in that PSA is because there has been some movement in our country to move away from our Second Amendment rights. More and more, this pillar of American life and liberty is being attacked and abandoned, not only out of sheer bias but ignorance of our Founders, the Revolutionary period and our Constitution. Instead, it has become the target of cultural jokes and is often regarded as biased lifestyle components of "rednecks" and rural citizens.

Even President Obama's partiality became evident on the campaign trail in April of 2008. You might recall, at a private California fundraiser, when he addressed the economic hardships of those in Pennsylvania. He quipped, "You go into some of these small towns in Pennsylvania, and like a lot of small towns in the Midwest, the jobs have been gone now for 25 years and nothing's replaced them. . . . And it's not surprising then they get bitter, they cling to guns or religion . . . as a way to explain their frustrations."[17]

And with new Supreme Court Justice Sonia Sotomayor's narrow view of the Second Amendment and two more justices likely on the edge of retirement, the over 90 million firearm bearers in this country have a right to be concerned. No wonder some are calling the gun issue the "New Abortion."[18]

In 2008, the Supreme Court wrangled over the question: Should it allow private citizens or only public servants ("state militias") "to keep and bear arms"?[19] In 2009, concerning a case out of Chicago, the Justices agreed to rule on whether the Second Amendment gives Americans a constitutional right to keep and bear arms that is enforceable against local and state gun laws.[20]

Is someone joking? Could the twenty-seven words of the Second Amendment be any clearer? "A well regulated Militia, being necessary to the security of a free State, the right *of the people* to keep and bear arms, shall not be infringed." (Italics mine)

Just because Washington, D.C., had a pistol problem (with their ban on handguns from 1976–2008,[21] during which time the murder rate actually increased[22]), the Supreme Court and the federal government shouldn't penalize the rest of the country by resetting national precedent based upon a biased Constitutional interpretation.

The Bill of Rights either encompasses the privileges of every citizen in every amendment or none at all. During the Revolutionary period, even other contemporaneous state gun laws[23] aligned with that federal measure. As Chief Justice John Roberts asked, "If it is limited to state militias, why would they say 'the right of the people'?[24] What is reasonable about a total ban on possession?"[25]

Thomas Jefferson similarly wrote near the end of his life in 1823: "On every question of construction (of the Constitution) let us carry ourselves back to the time when the Constitution was adopted, recollect the spirit manifested in the debates, and instead of trying what meaning may be squeezed out of the text, or invented against it, conform to the probable one in which it was passed."[26]

The clear interpretation of the Second Amendment provided the basis for Jefferson to offer this encouragement to his nephew

Peter Carr, "Let your gun therefore be your constant companion of your walks."[27] That same clear interpretation also forever establishes "the right of the people to keep and bear arms, [and it] shall not be infringed." As George Washington stated, "Firearms are second only to the Constitution in importance; they are the peoples' liberty's teeth."

Again Jefferson said, "A Bill of Rights is what the people are entitled to against every government, and what no just government should refuse, or rest on inference."[28] Luckily, we have a Bill of Rights. But the threats against it are constant and growing. The wording of the Bill of Rights is not ambiguous. But people who want to expand the power of government keep chipping away, modifying, and replacing what it actually says.

Look again at the First Amendment. Liberals would have you believe it establishes a "separation of church and state." But that phrase appears nowhere in the First Amendment, which actually reads: "Congress shall make no law respecting an establishment of religion, or prohibiting the free exercise thereof; or abridging the freedom of speech, or of the press; or the right of the people peaceably to assemble, and to petition the government for a redress of grievances."

The phrase "the separation of Church and State" actually comes from a letter Thomas Jefferson wrote in 1802 to the Danbury Baptists. He told them that no particular Christian denomination was going to have a monopoly in government. His words, "a wall of separation between Church and State," were not written to remove all religious practice from government or civic settings, but to prohibit the domination and even legislation of religious sectarianism. The Danbury Baptists had written to Thomas Jefferson seeking reassurance that their religious liberty would be guaranteed, not that religious expression on public grounds would be banned.

Proof that Jefferson was not trying to rid government of religious (specifically Christian) influence comes from the fact that he endorsed using government buildings for church meetings, signed a treaty with the Kaskaskia Indians that allotted federal money to support the building of a Catholic church and to pay the salary of the church's priests, and repeatedly renewed legislation that gave land to the United Brethren to help their missionary activities among the Indians.

Some might be completely surprised to discover that just two days after Jefferson wrote his famous letter citing the "wall of separation between Church and State," he attended church in the place where he always had as president: the U.S. Capitol. The very seat of our nation's government was used for sacred purposes. As the Library of Congress[29] notes, "It is no exaggeration to say that on Sundays in Washington during the administrations of Thomas Jefferson (1801–1809) and of James Madison (1809–1817) the state became the church."

Does that sound like someone who was trying to create an impenetrable wall of separation between church and state? If all the American Civil Liberties Union (ACLU) said about the First Amendment were true, Jefferson would flunk their religious-state separation test. Liberal groups like the ACLU don't want Americans to know that, for the Founders, Judeo-Christian belief and practice and government administration and policy were not separated at all. Denominational tests for public office were prohibited, but the idea that Judeo-Christian ideas and practices had to be kept separate from government would have struck them as ridiculous because the very basis for the Founders' ideas were rights that were endowed upon all of us by our Creator.

The ACLU and like-minded groups are not preserving First Amendment rights; they are perverting the meaning of the Establishment Clause (which was to prevent the creation of a national church like the Church of England) to deny the Free Exercise Clause (which preserves our rights to worship as we want, privately and publicly). Both clauses were intended to safeguard religious liberty, not to circumscribe its practice. The Framers were seeking to guarantee a freedom *of* religion, not a freedom *from* religion.

As Judge Roy Moore of Alabama reminded his readers, "The issue was addressed 150 years ago when the Senate Judiciary Committee, while considering the congressional chaplaincy, said, '[The Founders] had no fear or jealousy of religion itself, nor did they wish to see us an irreligious people; they did not intend to prohibit a just expression of religious devotion by the legislators of the nation, even in their public character as legislators; they did not intend to spread over all the public authorities and the whole public action of the nation the dead and revolting spectacle of atheistical apathy.'"[30] Yet groups like the ACLU are spreading that "revolting spectacle of atheistical apathy" across our land, and in doing so they are not only changing our laws but revising our history. Two examples recently came to my attention through my pastor, Todd DuBord, and Lake Almanor Community Church.[31]

REVISING AMERICA'S HISTORY

In 2007 Pastor Todd and the members of his small, rural, northern California church, had a huge national impact, reversing aggressive and blatant historical revisionism at two major national landmarks: the Jamestown Settlement in Virginia and the Washington Monument in Washington, D.C.

Every year tens of thousands of students in busloads from across the country come to these landmarks to learn about America's origins and history. But as Pastor Todd discovered, they were consciously being denied the truth.

In 2006 he was part of a church group taking an American heritage tour of the East Coast. They were visiting the Jamestown Settlement,[32] which is a replica of the first English colony in America in 1607 (thirteen years before the pilgrims reached Plymouth). As they were touring the settlement, a tour guide repeatedly told the group that the primary purpose of the English colonization was "to make money." Pastor Todd told me the guide would ask them to repeat those three words several times like a mantra: "to make money." A few from the group winced at that statement, because it didn't coincide with the history they remembered. Another eyebrow-raising statement came when they toured a replica of the church built in the center of the settlement. They noticed three plaques hung behind the pulpit: the Lord's Prayer, the Ten Commandments, and the Apostles' Creed. Pastor Todd asked the guide about them. She replied that she was "not allowed" to identify the plaques as anything more than "religious."[33]

Being the inquisitive sort, Pastor Todd dug into the history of Jamestown.[34] He discovered, among other things, that the colony's charter, issued by King James in 1606, listed as the settlement's primary purpose the "propagating of Christian religion to such people as yet live in darkness and miserable ignorance of the true knowledge and worship of God." To leave out the colony's Christian purpose, to downplay the role of Christianity in the colony's life, is to misrepresent history. Unfortunately, as we all know, these sorts of politically correct omissions are shockingly routine—not only at our nation's historic landmarks but in our public schools.

But Pastor Todd and his church were not going to let this matter rest. They did what we all need to do: they got involved to make change happen. They began a letter-writing campaign of protest, including a letter to the governor of Virginia. Pastor Todd wrote articles about how history was being misrepresented at Jamestown. That led to his doing dozens of radio interviews on the subject. Like any good fighter, he didn't content himself with a few good rounds or a few good punches. He knew he had to fight until the referee held up his fist in victory.

Eight months after his visit, Pastor Todd received a phone call from an executive with the Jamestown Foundation. The executive was tart at first but warmed up after Pastor Todd assured him that his goal was not to create trouble or controversy, but to help the Foundation present the most accurate history of the Settlement.

Their conversation led to a meeting of the Jamestown Settlement historians, who confessed that Pastor Todd's research was correct. The eventual result was a memorandum[35] sent to all of Jamestown's museum program assistants, asking them to present "a more comprehensive picture" of the Jamestown colony's mission. In particular, they should teach visitors on the guided tours that the "first motivation mentioned in the 1606 charter is to spread the Christian religion."

From the Jamestown Settlement's guides to their Web site, you will now hear the truth about American history because a small group of people in rural Northern California refused to give up our national origins to secular progressivism. (I also commend the Jamestown Settlement's administrators, who demonstrated a willingness and openness to accept the importance of accurate history, even if it is not politically correct.)

Coincidentally, in 2007 Pastor Todd was thrown into controversy again when he and a tour group visited the Washington Monument.[36] On December 6, 1884, an aluminum capstone weighing 100 ounces (the largest in that day) was placed on the very top of the Washington Monument, completing its long-delayed construction. On the National Park Service Web site, it describes what is etched on the capstone: The west face read: "Corner Stone laid on bed of foundation, July 4, 1848. First stone at height of 152 feet laid August 7, 1880. Capstone set December 6, 1884"; and the east face read "LAUS DEO" [Praise be to God]. The north and south faces contained names of the commission and the key men in the work of completion. Although weather-beaten, the inscription is still visible.

You can see how times have changed. When the builders added the capstone to the tallest structure in Washington, D.C., honoring our first president and the founding of this nation, they thought nothing more appropriate than to include the Latin inscription "Praise be to God." Imagine trying to have such an inscription put on a government building today. In fact, today the pressure is to cover up such inscriptions. Because the capstone is not visible to the naked eye (at 555 feet up), the National Park Service created a replica some years back and placed it inside the monument, on the second floor from the top, as part of an elaborate display about the history of the capstone. But what Pastor Todd and his tour group couldn't see on the replica was the inscription *Laus Deo*. They examined the three sides of the capstone replica (the fourth was pressed up against the wall), trying to read the small print. They read the larger wall display, and there was nothing mentioned about it there, either. Pastor Todd went back to the replica and pressed his head against the wall to see down the hidden side of the replica. There it was, barely visible to the naked eye. When he asked one of the National Park Service representatives why the replica was pushed up against the wall so tight that you couldn't easily see the inscription, her response was interesting. She said simply, "This isn't a conspiracy."

As he did with his questions on Jamestown, Pastor Todd researched the history of the capstone replica. He discovered two photos of the replica,[37] one from 2000 and the other from 2007. He noticed that not only was the replica away from the wall in 2000, so that all four sides could be seen, but that the display sign for the capstone said:

APEX OF THE MONUMENT
Reproduction

The builders searched for an appropriate metal for the apex that would not tarnish and would act as a lightning rod. *They chose one of the rarest metals of the time, aluminum. The casting was inscribed with the phrase, Laus Deo, (Praise be to God).*

In 2007, the small sign was changed to eliminate the last sentence:

CAP OF THE MONUMENT
Reproduction
The builders searched for appropriate metal for the cap that
would not tarnish and would act as a lightning rod. *They chose
one of the rarest metals of the time—aluminum.*

In other words, sometime between 2000 and 2007, the National
Park Service took action to hide the inscription at the top of the
Washington Monument. Pastor Todd mounted another campaign
to get the truth out: with letters, articles, and interviews, which
led to the National Park Service correcting the display. Just five
days after *World Net Daily*[38] broke the news online, the National
Park Service had received hundreds of thousands of e-mails about
this monumental omission. At the same time FOX News had a
live broadcast at the Washington Monument, during which their
reporter discovered the display sign for the capstone replica had
already been mysteriously replaced—complete with a new explanation of Laus Deo![39]

The erasing of our history is nearing epidemic proportions in
this country. And the Jamestown Settlement and Washington
Monument are only two examples. If you recall, both of these
revisionist episodes were running during the same season (first
part of 2007) when the U.S. Mint "accidentally" left "In God We
Trust" off the new presidential dollar coins. And how many more
examples like this exist that haven't been detected yet?

Omitting the Almighty from culture seems to be *in vogue* these
days. What a grave tragedy it is how religious revisionism has
come even to the very seat of our nation's government—the
Capitol and the White House.

In mid-2007 the Architect of the Capitol removed any mention
of God from the flag-folding ceremonies at veterans' funerals
and earlier attempted to remove "God" from congressional flag
certificates.

Religious revisionism has even come to the doors of 1600
Pennsylvania Avenue in D.C., as our own president denied our

country's Judeo-Christian heritage and make up when he spoke in Turkey on April 6, 2009: "We do not consider ourselves a Christian nation."[40]

I'm a fighter for the freedoms of speech and religion. They are our Constitutional rights, what the First Amendment is all about. But those freedoms don't give secularists, atheists, or even our president the entitlement to eliminate or revise America's religious heritage.

One last example can be seen this past year in atheists' attempts to eliminate God in the new $621 million taxpayer-provided Capitol Visitors Center (CVC) in Washington, D.C.[41]

In July of 2009, the House and Senate both passed identical resolutions,[42] approving the engravings of the National Motto ("In God We Trust") and the Pledge of Allegiance in prominent places in the CVC—a 580,000 square feet facility under the Capitol where 15,500 guests visit each day.[43]

Spearheading the measures were leaders like Daniel Lungren (R-Ca.), Congressman Randy Forbes (R-Va.), and Senator Jim DeMint (R-S.C.), whom have also drawn attention to the oversight of religious heritage in the CVC. The *YouTube* video of Congressman Forbes addressing the House on this matter ("Our Judeo-Christian Nation"[44]) has received to date more than 2.5 million hits, making it one of the most widely viewed floor speeches in YouTube history. Some of the nineteen omissions and inaccuracies in the CVC can also be seen on the Senator's YouTube posting "War on God."[45]

Forget for a moment the fact that the national motto is on all our currency. Forget for a moment the fact that the pledge is recited every day in a myriad of settings across this land. Forget for a moment the fact the Capitol is exceedingly rich in religious history and usage, including how it was used for church services all the way up through the Civil War—in 1867 the Capitol was the largest church in Washington with two thousand people attending weekly.[46]

How could anyone have anything against the engraving of our nation's motto, which is above the Speaker's rostrum in the House of Representatives? How could anyone have anything against the Pledge of Allegiance, which has been recited each day since its inception in both Houses of Congress?

Engraving the motto and pledge in the CVC sounds so basic and reasonable, doesn't it? Apparently not to the Freedom from Religion Foundation, the nation's largest group of atheists and agnostics, who filed suit in an effort to prevent the engraving of "In God We Trust" and the Pledge of Allegiance within the CVC.

The Freedom from Religion Foundation sought to sue to prevent these engravings because, they say, that "both the motto and the words 'under God' in the pledge were adopted during the Cold War as anti-communism measures. Engraving them at the entrance to the U.S. Capitol would discriminate against those who do not practice religion and unfairly promote a Judeo-Christian perspective."[47] (I guess that also transforms our currency with "In God We Trust" on them into Christian tracts?) How preposterous!

Some members of Congress who supported the measure have denounced the lawsuit as ludicrous.[48] Representative Steve King (R-Iowa) said, "This lawsuit is another attempt by liberal activists to rewrite history and deny that America's Judeo-Christian heritage is an essential foundation stone of our great nation." Representative Daniel Lungren (R-Ca.) said he was expecting a lawsuit but called the claims "patently absurd." And Congressman Forbes recently stated in an official memo from his offices:

"This lawsuit sheds light on the lengths that a small minority will take to remove our nation's faith history from this generation and future generations of Americans. I, along with many Members of the Congressional Prayer Caucus, intend to fight this unabashed and dangerous effort to silence our nation's history. Truly even our Pledge of Allegiance and our national

motto are not spared from these efforts. Our Declaration of
Independence states that our rights are 'endowed by our
Creator.' If the plaintiffs in this lawsuit are successful, they will
succeed not only in removing the history for which our fathers
and Founders sacrificed so much, but also in removing the very
source our Founders believed provided our rights to life, liberty
and the pursuit of happiness."

So, could the lawsuit by the Freedom from Religion Foundation prevail and prevent the engravings in the CVC? Mark my
words: If a few liberal judges get the case and we the people do
nothing, it will. And then that precedent will be used to extend
their next argument that our national motto "In God We Trust"
is unconstitutional.

Though the lawsuit is still pending. I'm glad to announce that
permission to proceed with the engravings of the National Motto
and Pledge on the Walls of the CVC was grated. Nevertheless,
I am still encouraging Americans to write[49] or call[50] the Architect
of the Capitol's Office and also their representatives[51] to remind
them that you, the taxpayer, paid for that $621 million facility
and that you think some corner of its 580,000 square feet deserves
to be dedicated to a permanent display of the Capitol's rich religious history.

Atheists might not be found in every foxhole, but the bunker
called the Capitol Visitors Center has a couple in there right now.
I think it's time Americans let them know the motto and pledge
are not only at the heart of our country, but that whitewashing
God from the walls of history is actually an unfair promotion of
atheism and an injustice to all that is America.

Is it merely coincidental that so many acts of revisionism have
occurred over the last couple years at governmental and historical
sites? Is it merely coincidental that the more modern memorials
in Washington (like the Roosevelt and WWII memorials) bear virtually no religious inscriptions at all, while all the former ones
do? Is it merely coincidental that the new CVC is the next

fighting ground to erase any display of America's Judeo-Christian heritage?

The point is that this sort of censorship of our Judeo-Christian and American heritage is going on all the time—and for the sake of our children, our culture, and the truth, we need to be on the historical alert! Be observant. Read your children's textbooks (your tax dollars are paying for them), walk through museums, visit historic landmarks, watch history shows on television, and you'll see that the corruption of our national memory is much worse than you thought. That's why we need to get involved the way Pastor Todd and members of his congregation did. Always remember that we, the people, have the power to make positive change. Our forefathers did it and they would expect us to do the same.

★ ★ ★

CHAPTER THREE

Stop America's Nightmare of Debt

A FEW YEARS AGO I was watching a television special titled *Greed*. John Stossel was its host, and the entire program was based on one premise: maybe greed is good. At one point in the program John, acting as the adversary of greed, talked to Ted Turner, who dismissed criticism of greed, saying, "Oh greed, greed, greed, everyone is greedy."

"It's not destructive?"

"A certain amount of it is probably healthy."

Stossel ended the program with the words, "Greed is a productive force." Or, as I once heard Donald Trump say, "The point is that you can't be too greedy."

Times have changed. When I was growing up, most people believed the biblical teaching that "the love of money is the root of all evil."[1] Today, people believe, as George Bernard Shaw once put it, that "the lack of money is the root of all evil."[2]

Don't get me wrong. I'm not against being wealthy (obviously). But I am against making money into a god. Money is not more important than family, or children, or God. To date, money has never truly satisfied a soul, as any biography of a wealthy person could tell you. Sure, like infidelity and drugs, it brings some momentary pleasure. But, in the end, greed needs to be fed like a lion—and the lion breeds and becomes a pride of lions. I know. Believe me I know. I've felt their claws and been bitten by their destructive teeth. Years ago it nearly devoured me until I learned the hard way how to tame the money monster.

Greed is not good. It is destructive. It is ripping apart marriages, families, communities, and this nation. Why is government spending out of control? Greed. Why do we as individuals and as a nation keep falling deeper into a pit of debt? Greed. We need, we want, and we have to have it. We can't afford it, but we can't say no. So we charge it, deferring the penalty.

You've probably seen the bumper sticker, "Whoever dies with the most toys wins." Unfortunately a lot of people believe that. They define their lives by their possessions. They judge their success in terms of how much and how fast they accumulate things. It's an attitude you'll find as much among Wall Street bankers as among drug-dealing street thugs, Hollywood actors, and real estate agents. It's everywhere. So maybe it's no surprise that we're drowning in debt, and unless we change our habits, we could actually be bankrupted by our prosperity.

I'm not an economist or a financial counselor, but I am a businessman and have learned much from my financial successes and failures. I can't solve all of America's fiscal woes, but some don't take a master's degree in business administration to figure out. There's one financial principle we can all understand: you shouldn't spend more than you earn.

ONE NATION UNDER DEBT

Our economy is in shambles. The Stock Market has tanked. The dollar has lost half its value against the Euro. Americans are losing their homes to mortgage foreclosures at an alarming rate. Unemployment has reached double digits in many counties and states across the nation. We seem more and more dependent on imports for our energy and manufactured goods. We're consuming, but what are we producing? One thing we're producing is bigger government—which is part of the problem, not the cure.

As a country we're $11 trillion dollars in debt.[3] And Washington's only solution seems to be to make more loans and print more money. The federal government is constantly telling the American people to borrow, spend, borrow, spend, and nothing about living within their means. The Democratic Congress tries to save every financial institution, rather than to allow the reasonable death of some under a diminishing supply and demand. Our presidents repeatedly try to jumpstart the last and highest revolution of the credit merry-go-round by refilling the gas tanks of financial institutions for one more go-round. But why? To lend out to those who are already maxed out on monthly payments? Or is it the unemployed who are now suppose to borrow the big bucks? We must quit bailing out what we've borrowed.

It's official. Government spending is out of control. And it's not merely a Democrat or a Republican problem. Both have contributed to the demise of our nation.

Washington's most recent financial spiral started with the Bush Wall Street bailout (TARP) of $700 billion (what I call new debt #1). But then it continued under President Obama, who pushed for the next $787 billion stimulus bill (debt #2). And that wasn't enough either. Then they tried the $410 billion omnibus spending bill (with 9,000 earmarks—60 percent Democrat and 40 percent Republican in origin),[4] which like the others was railroaded through Congress (debt #3). Then President Obama informed us that another $634 billion would be required for a down payment for universal health care[5] (debt #4), and so on. All of that doesn't include other economic stimuli needed on the government horizon, as Representative Daniel Inouye (D-Hawaii), chairman of the Senate Appropriations Committee, noted when he called the mammoth $787 billion spending bill "stimulus No. 1."

To add insult to injury, Washington passed a $3.6 (nearly $4 trillion) dollar budget proposal for 2010, despite that the White House projected a 2009 budget shortfall of $1.5 trillion—triple the $455 billion in 2008.[6] Even liberal media predicted that Obama's spending would "leave a string of deficits dwarfing any in the nation's history."[7] And they were right.

On January 1, 1791, during George Washington's second year as president, the national debt was about $75 million.[8] Today, our national debt stands at about $11 trillion.[9] The official government estimates forecast that will be double over the next decade.[10] The White House has projected a cumulative $9 trillion deficit between 2010 and 2019, while the Congressional Budget Office estimates a more optimistic deficit as $7.1 trillion based upon higher revenues as Bush tax cuts expire. Washington's out-of-control spending could turn the nation's already-staggering $11 trillion debt into an astronomical $20 trillion.

Unfortunately, Ronald Reagan was right, "Government's view of the economy could be summed up in a few short phrases: If it moves, tax it. If it keeps moving, regulate it. And if it stops moving, subsidize it."

But when the receipts don't cover the outlays, it should be a sign we're in trouble. When the government, year after year, digs itself deeper and deeper into debt, someone needs to be held accountable to fix the system. When government wasted $100 million a year on minting pennies that cost $1.26 each and nickels that cost 7.7 cents each to make, we have already admitted that our government is clueless and the worst run business in the world.[11] When taxpayers are forced to pay $100 million for an earth-monitoring satellite that never launched into space and costs an additional $1 million a year to store,[12] someone is making ludicrous financial decisions in Washington, D.C.

It has been estimated by watchdog organizations that the government wastes nearly $1 trillion dollars *every year*.[13] That is a staggering amount, especially when one considers the annual federal budget is nearly $4 trillion. Yet, to date, I've never heard one government official confess he or she is a bad money manager. The system is broken, but our government bureaucrats have no incentive to fix it. Who holds them accountable? Congress?

Congress is where the wasteful spending starts. It's up to we the people, not only to demand change and elect people who promise it, but to hold them accountable.

Of course the federal government isn't the only one bordering on bankruptcy. Many state governments have gigantic financial problems, if not always with deficit spending, then with corruption—the stories you read in your newspaper every day, if you have the stomach for it. The Center for Public Integrity recently gave a grade to each of the fifty states for how well legislators followed financial-disclosure laws. Out of one hundred points, most states were at sixty-five. In school, that would earn you a D, and that's really what we have: D-grade government.[14]

And we know the reasons. You can list them on your fingers: pork-barrel spending, lobbyists, special interest groups, corrupt corporations, government-induced dependency on federal and state programs, and deficit spending, and the list goes on.

AMERICANS: OUT OF CONTROL TOO?

Not only is our government spending recklessly, they're trying to encourage us to do the same. The Federal Reserve Board has repeatedly cut interest rates[15] in hopes of easing the strain in the credit markets and jumpstarting the economy (though of course one effect of this is to further weaken the dollar, possibly fuel inflation and discourage saving). Moreover, the federal government has decided to send taxpayers "economic stimulus checks." The federal government hopes you'll start spending again—real soon.[16] But instead of these false incentives and short-term, desperate attempts at fixes, what if Congress did something really helpful, like dramatically cutting the size of government or cutting taxes, so people can save and invest?

Like I said before, government is out of control. But the sad fact is that so are too many Americans. A big catalyst for both was during the Clinton era, in 1999, when Fannie Mae and

Freddie Mac extended their consumer credit wings to bring into the fold just about anyone who wanted to buy a car or own a home. Credit cards were approved without applying and prolifrated in every mailbox across the nation, dozens of times over, including to students. And consumer loans were given to everyone from criminals to illegals. Anyone could get business or car loans, gold cards, and equity lines of credit. Remember? "No credit? Bad credit? No problem!"

So most borrowed and bought, borrowed and bought, and borrowed and bought, until we created a consumer black hole that was spiraling out of control, drawing nearly everyone and everything into it and could only be satisfied by a colossal and continuous river of credit. Most Americans maximized their credit and super-sized their limits, until their payments easily outweighed their incomes and then it all began to implode. But how long did we think we could maintain the credit charade?

The late financial guru Larry Burkett prophesied almost twenty years ago in his book, *The Coming Economic Earthquake*,[17] that an impending economic calamity was coming upon the U.S. unless a drastic effort was made to curb massive federal spending and the soaring deficit. Larry was right. He gave one basic principle to avoid the future market meltdown: "Don't be a slave to debt! Get out of debt!"[18] Larry is still right today.

There are only two things that are going to get us out of this particular financial mess, and "only Americans" (not "only government," as Obama has proclaimed) can implement those solutions. Both come down to one word: restraint. We must restrain our government and we must restrain ourselves. Feeding the money monster will not reduce its size—it will perpetuate the problem. We must tame the money monster. We must return it to its cage. We must return to a time when we put a bridle on the spending of government and our homes. We've got to simplify our lives. We've got to learn to be happier with less. We've got to get out of debt.

TAMING THE MONEY MONSTER

The old entertainment columnist Earl Wilson once said, "If you think nobody cares if you're alive, try missing a couple of car payments." That's attention you don't need, but it's attention that increasing numbers of Americans are finding hard to avoid. The answer? Well, one part of it, as radio talk-show host and FOX's financial strategist Dave Ramsey puts it, is not to be a "slave to the credit card companies."[19] If you're in debt bondage now, you obviously need to get out of it—setting up a strict plan to pay off your debts—and not go back.

I've come to appreciate the sound advice of Dave Ramsey, not only for his printed resources but for the wealth of information on his Web site.[20] He even has some information on how to help your kids make wise financial decisions.[21] Begin by educating yourself. Go to Dave's Web site and read the sections on "Myths and Truths of Personal Finance."[22] Some of his advice might surprise you. For instance, before you start paying off your debts, set up a $1,000 emergency fund, because an "emergency" is often the first thing to derail your plan to pay off debt; pay off your debts using the snowball strategy, paying off the little things first and working your way up; and even while you're working to pay off debt, set up a budget so you can start doing what you should've already done: saving and investing.

Reducing your debt increases your freedom. Thomas Jefferson advised both government and citizens to "put off buying anything until we have the money to pay for it."[23] Or as the Good Book admonishes: "Owe no debt to anyone, except the continuing debt to love."[24]

IN HAMILTON WE TRUST?

After the Revolutionary War, the United States was born but broke. We were in need of some wizards of commerce to set our financial house in order.

In their book *Financial Founding Fathers: The Men Who Made America Rich*,[25] authors Robert Wright and David Cowen show how nine men created the American financial system. Two of them are household names: Alexander Hamilton (the first secretary of the treasury) and Andrew Jackson (the seventh president of the United States). The other seven are not: Tench Coxe, Albert Gallatin, Thomas Willing, Robert Morris, William Duer, Nicholas Biddle, and Stephen Girard. These men understood that financial prosperity was as important as the Constitution in securing America's future. To that end they created a central bank, a monetary system, financial agencies, and a framework for trade, investment, and debt.

As the first secretary of the treasury, Alexander Hamilton made three major reports to Congress. The first in 1790 included his plan to retire the government debt incurred to finance the Revolutionary War. Hamilton proposed that the federal government take on all of the states' debts, and then finance the entire amount owed with new government bonds paying roughly 4 percent interest. Hamilton hoped to establish a good credit rating for the United States. That would encourage investment and justify permanent public debt as "the powerful cement of our Union."[26]

For better or worse, we are still living in the financial world Hamilton built on banks and bonds. Certainly the United States has enjoyed an unprecedented history of prosperity. But, as we've seen, we've also allowed spending and public debt to spiral completely out of control. Thomas Jefferson opposed Hamilton, saying that his plan and its backers think that a perpetual debt "is a perpetual blessing and, therefore, wish to make it so large that we can never pay it off."[27]

Hamilton was a Federalist; Jefferson an Anti-Federalist (a Republican, sometimes called Democratic-Republican). Hamilton wanted a strong central government; Jefferson preferred strong state governments as checks on the federal government. Hamilton wanted a strong national bank to help finance trade, business, and industry; Jefferson felt a strong national bank would penalize and undervalue farmers and the working class.[28] Hamilton was favored, for the most part, in the industrial North, while Jefferson drew his support from the agrarian South.

Though they opposed each other, Jefferson was Hamilton's beneficiary. Not only did Hamilton tip the scales for Jefferson politically by supporting him over Aaron Burr in the presidential election of 1800, but the financial system he created allowed Jefferson to finance the Louisiana Purchase.

Jefferson was not opposed to borrowing, but he did recognize the danger of ballooning government deficits and increasing taxes. "Though much an enemy to the system of borrowing, yet I feel strongly [about] the necessity of preserving the power to borrow. Without this, we might be overwhelmed by another nation, merely by the force of its credit."[29] (Was Jefferson prophesying our roughly $1.5 trillion debt to China?) He elaborated to George Washington, "I am anxious about everything which may affect our credit. My wish would be, to possess it in the highest degree, but to use it little."[30]

It's unfortunate that more leaders didn't agree with Jefferson, or James Madison, who said at the time, "I go on the principle that a public debt is a public curse."[31] Jefferson's attitude toward debt was simple, and he gave the best advice one could get: "The conclusion then, is, that neither the representatives of a nation, nor the whole nation itself assembled, can validly engage debts beyond what they may pay in their own time."[32] They believed in the biblical precedent, "the wicked borrows and does not repay."[33]

THE FAULT LINES IN THE FEDERAL RESERVE

Part of the reason America is in its financial fiasco is because we've abandon the financial principles and vision of our Founders. Instead, we've created a central system revolving around the Federal Reserve. But I agree with Judge Andrew Napolitano, who said, "We know more about the CIA than we do about the Federal Reserve."[34]

The Federal Reserve is the Freemasonry of government agencies. It is a virtual secret society unto themselves—a group of unelected brokers who hold the value of our dollar in the palms of their hands. This one agency, with its power to raise and lower interest rates, has exercised more control over the economy than any other government body.

So with that type of single-handed power, why should we be surprised when the U.S. Senate blocked a bill this past year to audit the Federal Reserve? It's true! Congressman Ron Paul and more than half of the House cosponsored the Federal Reserve Transparency Act, HR1207.[35] On the Senate side Senators Jim DeMint, Mike Crapo, and David Vitter cosponsored S 604, companion legislation introduced by Bernie Sanders. But it was stopped cold before even being introduced on the floor on "procedural grounds."[36]

Could it really be a mere coincidence that the bill to audit the Federal Reserve was refused from even being introduced and that this agency remains the "quick convenience store-house of money" for the Obama administration's borrowing and bailout monies?

Again, as Judge Napolitano said, "The Obama administration not only doesn't want the Federal Reserve audited, it now wants to put the power to regulate all financial institutions—banks, insurance companies, brokerage houses—into the hands of this super-secret bank. What are they afraid we might see if we get a chance to look at their books?"[37]

As if there are not enough signs of the federal government's inadequacy, two expert economists[38] on the Federal Reserve specifically warned Congress not to expand the power of the federal government to oversee and monitor public financial structures. Allan H. Meltzer, professor of economics at Carnegie-Mellon University and one of the central bank's most prominent historians, having written a three-volume reference work on it, conveyed a series of U.S. financial collapses over the past three decades in which the federal government had either failed to take preventive action or made things worse.

And the White House and the majority on Capitol Hill want to give the Federal Reserve more power and autonomy?

So why does this federal agency need a complete auditing? It's very simple. Because America is in the worst economic situation since the Great Depression, the value of the dollar is tanking on the world market, and the Federal Reserve wields the greatest power to control it with virtually no accountability—let alone that the American people and even Congress have virtually no knowledge of what those inside are doing day to day.

On December 23, 1913, President Woodrow Wilson signed the Federal Reserve Act, creating a seven-member board of governors (appointed by the president and approved by Congress) and twelve regional banks. Thereafter, banks continued lending money to the public, but the federal government controlled the flow of money via fluctuating interest rates and the tides of credit and money supply and demand. (This was the gravest governmental mistake of 1913. A close second was the ratification of the 16th Amendment to the Constitution, which mandated income taxes as national law.)

The way I see it, there are two primary problems with the Federal Reserve. First, its very existence is a sheer contradiction of the 10th Amendment of the Constitution. As Ron Paul explained,

> Our Founding Fathers never intended for a single entity such as the Federal Reserve to have this much power. In fact, there is no authority in the Constitution for the federal government to create a central bank, to enact legal tender laws, or to print paper money. The Tenth Amendment is quite clear that "The powers not delegated to the United States by the Constitution, nor prohibited by it to the States, are reserved to the States respectively, or to the people."

The fact is, the Federal Reserve is one of the best examples of government control run amok and its oppression over its people.

It rules by dangling carrots, cheap rates, and loans, before the American public, which in turn oppresses people by their inability to resist further debt. The federal government is the dealer in greed and debt—and its drugs are easy money and credit. Under the Federal Reserve System, Americans and our economy have to return to the Federal Reserve for repeated fixes like a drug addict, otherwise everything goes into the tank.

Second, the Federal Reserve is flat out bad for the economy in the long run, because it creates false fronts or temporary escalations in the free market, which eventually cycle around and lead to downturns or more needs for other federal government fixes. Even if it creates several cycles of credit rushes (which they deem as "signs of prosperity"), sooner or later the false foundation crumbles, and we find ourselves in an economic hole that neither we nor the federal government can't bail us out of—which is exactly where we are now in this recession.

The fact is: if we can get the flow of the Federal Reserve under control, others drawing from its wells will become more manageable and accountable. Its open market operations and dealings with central banks and foreign powers at very least must have oversight!

But you can bet politicians like Nancy Pelosi and Harry Reid are going to fight to prevent the passing of any legislation that regulates the Federal Reserve, because they are in cahoots with the White House and also don't want the trade secrets of the Federal Reserve revealed or its' power restricted. Why? Because its power benefits them, plain and simple. It is right now being used by the Obama administration and the Democratic majority for political expedience and special interests.

Many of the Founders warned about America's potential fiscal woes under the power of a central bank. Thomas Jefferson was one of Hamilton's biggest opponents, almost prophesying as president in 1803 to Albert Gallatin,

> This institution is one of the most deadly hostility existing, against the principles and form of our Constitution. . . . I deem no government safe which is under the vassalage of any self-constituted authorities, or any other authority than that of the nation, or its regular functionaries. What an obstruction could not this Bank of the United States, with all its branch banks, be in time of war? It might dictate to us the peace we should accept, or withdraw its aids. Ought we then to give further growth to an institution so powerful, so hostile? . . . Now, while we are strong, it is the greatest debt we owe to the safety of our Constitution, to bring its powerful enemy to a perfect subordination under its authorities.

America is in the biggest financial fiasco since the Great Depression. And while we can put anesthetic on her financial injuries via temporary government bailouts, we're heading for another economic earthquake that will ultimately widen and deepen her wounds. But it's not too late, especially if we follow the sound fiscal advice of experts, which include our Founders.

What we need today are far more men and women in government with our Founders' financial forethought and cautiousness. But that is not what we have. That is why I've joined the voter revolution across this land to oust political and congressional corruption and stalemate. If you're ready to join millions of other Americans in that commitment, then here are three steps: 1. Make a pledge to bring about political and congressional change in future elections; 2. Recall unconstitutional congressional incumbents; 3. Raise up and elect above-reproach, nongreedy selfless representatives who aren't afraid to stand up to governmental status quo and corruption, will vote for constitutional restrictions of government, reduce big government (deficits, budgets, spending, and taxes), reform the tax code (by providing a Fair Tax or its equivalent), and fight for a constitutional amendment for a mandated balanced federal budget.

Private debt is a private matter. But it should not be encouraged or enticed, especially by the Federal government. That's why I believe the Federal Reserve needs to be abolished. The U.S. ran just fine without it—before its inception in 1913. We had financial crises before its existence and after it, but its intervention has been proven historically only to make things worse. Our Founders would have never tolerated its abusive power or methods of bribery. It is not only a detriment to the economy and the very existence of a representative form of government like ours, but to all Americans who want to experience true freedom.

Henry Ford was probably right when he said, "It is well enough that people of the nation do not understand our banking and monetary system, for if they did, I believe there would be a revolution before tomorrow morning."

RECALL THE PURPOSE OF GOVERNMENT

To get back to the wisdom of Washington, Jefferson, Madison, and the other Founders, we need to get back to their shared principles. However much they differed on some issues, they were agreed that the federal government existed to protect our liberty. None of them believed that the government should plan, provide for, and rule our lives as though we were wards of the state.

The only way to get our country back on track is by directing our finances in ways that are consistent with the Constitution. That means dramatically shrinking the size of the federal government, as per the Tenth Amendment to the Constitution: "The powers not delegated to the United States by the Constitution, nor prohibited to it by the states, are reserved to the states respectively, or to the people." It means divesting government of many of its responsibilities and recognizing that we need to be responsible for ourselves. It means electing politicians who not only pledge to uphold the strict government limitations of the Constitution, but who have the moral character to mean what they say and don't try to bribe voters to support them through government programs. To be a free citizen, you need to be an active and informed citizen, and you need to vote. Don't be Missing in Action on election day! Vote your conscience. And remember that freedom is not about what government can do for us, but about keeping government from doing things to us. Keeping government small is the best way to keep government manageable by we the people.

And if we reduced the size of Congress as I outlined earlier (pp. 33–34), financially speaking, that would save taxpayers approximately $200 million annually in salaries, if you consider all the staff, overhead, pension plans, etc. Just a thought.

RESTORING FISCAL SANITY

If we are ever to restore the fiscal and leadership sanity to our government and economy, we need not to reinvent the Great Depression wheel of Roosevelt's New Deal. Our economy can't add or handle another version of President Johnson's Great Society. We need to look to a time when Congress was more frugal in their spending and stabilized our government and economy.

In the past one hundred years, one of the best examples of that occurred when Newt Gingrich led the Congress in the mid-to-late '90s. I'm not justifying every financial move they made, but, despite losing a balanced budget amendment to the Constitution by only one Senate vote, they still committed to spending caps and balancing the budget, which they did for four consecutive years for the first time since the 1920s.

The Congress of the 1990s steadied and strengthened the economy by following four priorities and principles, which, fascinating to note, are being turned on their heads at this moment by the present administration. As Newt noted in his excellent book, *Real Change*, Congress made it their top priorities to:

1. cut taxes to increase economic growth and therefore increase revenues (unlike Obama's tax hikes, which will retard economic growth and depress revenues);

2. set priorities and increase spending in key areas while reducing it in non-essential areas (unlike Obama's fiscal priorities of "health care, energy and education,"[39] which are based not upon what is best for the economy, but what is reflective of typical partisan preferences and doing what is politically expedient);

3. eliminate pork barrel spending (unlike the 9,000 earmarks in the $410 billion omnibus spending bill, which is nothing short of absolute economic ludicrousness, mismanagement and waste within our present crisis);

4. shift from expensive, wasteful systems to smarter spending; don't merely look at more inexpensive ways but productive ones too (unlike Obama's theory to spend our way to prosperity, which is a sure way to sink America)

In an interview last year on TBN,[40] I explained that, if we are going to reawaken America, we also have to return to our Founders principles, which includes their fiscal prudence. We must follow the advice of those like Thomas Jefferson, who also warned us long ago, "To preserve [the] independence [of the people,] we must not let our rulers load us with perpetual debt." (Now read that again—then one more time!)

How do we do that? The same way we start with our personal lives: we cap our spending and allow the supply and demand levels to drop slightly lower to points commensurate with our incomes (not credit lines). We must learn to downsize and live within our means, not borrowing excessive amounts for even investment debt like a home or business. We must cut spending, reduce our budgets, pay down our debts, and stabilize our households and nation.

And, as far as our clueless Congress goes, we must demand that our representatives seek a balanced budget amendment to the Constitution, which will require the government to live within its means. We must return to a pay-as-you-go government and nation. It's our last resort for an out-of-control economy and people.

If our country is to survive, we must elect only those who show proof of fiscal discipline, refuse under all circumstances to increase our national deficit, and who commit to pass and live under a constitutional amendment for a balanced budget. And if our incumbents voted for the bailouts or bail on their fiscal frugalness, then vote them out of office the next chance you can.

Time is running out, but it's not too late to reverse Washington's fiscal frenzy. Don't just write but hound your representatives to live and legislate by the preceding four proven priorities and principles of governmental and monetary prudence.[41]

RETURN TO A PAY-AS-YOU-GO GOVERNMENT

There is simply no justification for allowing our politicians to increase our federal and state budgets to the degrees that they have in modern times. We must hold them accountable. We need to elect and demand politicians who will slash government spending and refuse to pay for programs that we cannot afford. Borrowing, bailing out, and offering more entitlements won't fix our economy. As George Washington said, "To contract new debts is not the way to pay for old ones."[42]

More than ever we need a balanced budget amendment for the federal government. That is the only way we are going to stop their reckless spending. I know that legally required balanced budgets work because Governor Mike Huckabee served his state of Arkansas under one and he led the state in balancing theirs for twelve years in a row.[43] It's time we required our federal representatives to do the same.

We need to make sure that our politicians make the case that every reduction in government spending is a positive step forward; it is taking power from government and returning it to the people; and it is also morally right: it is living within our means, not contracting debts we cannot ourselves pay, and taking responsibility for our own actions. Thomas Jefferson said that "the maxim of buying nothing but what we had money in our pockets to pay for . . . [is] a maxim which, of all others, lays the broadest foundation for happiness."[44]

In his farewell address, George Washington said that while the execution of good government belongs to the people's elected representatives, "it is necessary that public opinion should co-operate. To facilitate to them the performance of their duty, it is essential that you should practically bear in mind that towards the payment of debts there must be revenue; that to have revenue there must be taxes; that no taxes can be devised which are not more or less inconvenient and unpleasant. . . ." In other words, there is no free lunch. The only money government has to spend is money it takes from you in taxes, and there are no taxes that are not "inconvenient and unpleasant." What we need now more than ever is smaller government and lower taxes.

Thomas Jefferson was particularly eloquent on the problem of government debt and taxes:

> To preserve [the] independence [of the people,] we must not let our rulers load us with perpetual debt. We must make our election between economy and liberty, or profusion and servitude. If we run into such debts as that we must be taxed in our meat and in our drink, in our necessaries and our comforts, in our labors and our amusements, for our callings and our creeds, as the people of England are, our people, like them, must come to labor sixteen hours in the twenty-four, give the earnings of fifteen of these to the government for their debts and daily expenses, and the sixteenth being insufficient to afford us bread, we must live, as they now do, on oatmeal and potatoes,

have no time to think, no means of calling the mismanagers to account, but be glad to obtain subsistence by hiring ourselves to rivet their chains on the necks of our fellow-sufferers.[45] [Another prophetic statement?]

At the same time we cut spending, reduce our budgets, and pay down our debts, we must bring down our taxes. True fiscal conservatism incorporates both lower taxes and lower spending. Tax reductions are always good. Every one serves as a catalyst for economic growth. I love Ron Paul's simplistic approach here: "I apply a very simple test to any proposal to overhaul the tax code: Does it reduce or eliminate an existing tax? If not, then it amounts to nothing more than a political shell game that pits taxpayers against each other in a lobbying scramble to make sure the other guy pays."[46]

IMPLEMENT A FAIR TAX: THE ULTIMATE ECONOMIC STIMULUS PACKAGE

We need to return to a taxation system similar to that established by our Founders. They did not penalize productivity through taxes the way we do today. They had no Internal Revenue Service. They believed in minimal taxation.

- They did *not* pay income taxes, which were prohibited by the Constitution[47]
- They did *not* pay export taxes, which were also prohibited by the Constitution[48]
- But they did tax imports. The Founders believed in free trade within our own borders and a system of tariffs on imported goods[49]

If we followed these three taxation rules, we would not be in the predicament we are today in which free trade outside our borders has been responsible for the loss of more than three million manufacturing jobs from outsourcing or companies literally moving outside the U.S. We need to return to our Founders' system of taxing only imports—not exports—in order to prevent more jobs from leaving the U.S. while bringing others back into the country.

That's a system that makes sense to me. It is a system designed to preserve individual liberty and encourage productivity (through no income taxes and no discouragement of domestic production through export taxes), while choosing to keep taxes as painless as possible (as taxes on foreign imports). And it doesn't require an Internal Revenue Service to run it.

The Founders would have been horrified at the bloated federal bureaucracy we have now and the maze of taxes we have to navigate: income taxes, employment taxes, capital gains taxes, estate taxes, corporate taxes, property taxes, Social Security taxes, gas taxes—it was excessive taxation like this that drove the Founders to rebel in the first place. All of the Founders were opposed to domestic taxes. They regarded high taxes and aggressive tax collectors as tyrannical, and always to be guarded against. Patrick Henry warned: "Excisemen may come in multitudes; for the limitation of their numbers no man knows. They may, unless the general government be restrained by a bill of rights, or some similar restriction, go into your cellars and rooms, and search, ransack, and measure, everything you eat, drink, and wear."[50] [Mmmm . . . another prophetic statement?]

The Internal Revenue Service wasn't started until nearly a hundred years after the Revolutionary War in 1862[51] as the Bureau of Internal[52] Revenue. Its creation coincided with the creation of the income tax, which it was designed to collect. Both were the work of President Lincoln and Congress, which saw them as necessary to pay for Civil War expenses.[53] It is interesting to note, however, that the income tax law was revoked ten years later, revived in 1894, and then ruled by the Supreme Court as unconstitutional in 1895. Yet in 1913 it became law through the Sixteenth Amendment. Ever since then, the income tax has deprived families of their rightful earnings, restricted our liberties, and deprived our economy of money that could be invested in productive enterprises.

Today the IRS is the number one enemy of your pocketbook. Who doesn't fear an IRS audit? It's the only federal agency before which you are considered guilty until proven innocent. It can't be overhauled or even reformed (Congress's attempts have failed).

How do you overhaul a tax code that has 66,498 pages? Not even the best in the IRS can understand it all. It is no wonder tax evaders have so many opportunities to avoid paying taxes through a host of loopholes. Examples are easy to find. According to the Department of Justice, Walter C. Anderson, a Washington-based telecommunications entrepreneur made at least $450 million buying and selling telecom companies. And he paid NO taxes.[54] In 2005, more than six thousand taxpayers making over $250,000 a year paid NO income tax. Hedge fund and private equity managers cost taxpayers more than two billion annually because they too have found loopholes in the huge tax code. Even with the IRS's massive budget, there are not enough resources or personnel to pursue these big offenders or their high-powered tax attorneys.[55] Congress can go ahead and raise our taxes, but men like Anderson will continue to find loopholes in our present tax code and pay no taxes. Do the rest of us really want to carry their tax burden?

The best answer is to abolish the IRS, sweep away the present tax code, and implement a Fair Tax that lives up to its name. As Mike Huckabee says, "Wouldn't it be nice if April 15 were just another sunny spring day?"

The Fair Tax does away with all taxes and puts in their place a single consumptive (fair) tax, which is the closest, practical, modern proposal to the taxation system favored by the Founders.

Congressman Ron Paul and former Arkansas governor Mike Huckabee favor abolishing the IRS and replacing our current tax system with a Fair Tax. That was one big reason, among many, that I supported Huckabee when he ran for the Republican nomination for president. With the Fair Tax, the harder you work and the more money you make, the better off you and our economy will be. You pay taxes only when you buy something, which means you can control how much you're taxed, and you're never penalized for working hard.

It's time we had a system through which people didn't have to figure out ways to cheat in order to save their money. It's the biggest stimulation package there is. Again, as Huckabee says, "The Fair Tax is a completely transparent tax system. It doesn't increase taxes. It's revenue neutral. But here's what it will do. It will bring business back to the United States that is leaving our shores because our tax laws make it impossible for an American-based business to compete . . . the fair tax was designed by economists from Harvard and Stanford and some of the leading think tanks across the country. . . ."[56] There are also trillions of dollars hiding in offshore accounts. With the Fair Tax, these people can bring their money back to invest here, which would give a huge boost to our economy.

If the Founding Fathers were here today, I believe they would support the Fair Tax. As James Madison said, "Taxes on consumption are always least burdensome, because they are least felt, and are borne too by those who are both willing and able to pay them; that of all taxes on consumption, those on foreign commerce are most compatible with the genius and policy of free States."[57]

We don't need more tax reform. We need a tax revolution! And the Fair Tax will provide it. If we all get on the Fair Tax bandwagon and demand that our representatives implement such a taxation system, we can make the financially impossible become possible.

CULTIVATE A CULTURE OF PEACE TO CURB SPENDING

While the Fair Tax will reduce our tax burden, we'll still need to keep a tight lid on government spending and demand balanced budgets. As Thomas Jefferson said, "It is incumbent on every generation to pay its own debts as it goes. A principle which if acted on would save one-half the wars of the world."[58] It would save one-half of the world's wars because we would pause to consider the financial, as well as the human, cost before rushing into battle.

The Founders counted on times of peace to store up wealth that might need to be tapped in times of war. In his Farewell Address, George Washington said:

> As a very important source of strength and security, cherish public credit. One method of preserving it is to use it as sparingly as possible, *avoiding occasions of expense by cultivating peace*, but remembering also that timely disbursements to prepare for danger frequently prevent much greater disbursements to repel it, avoiding likewise the accumulation of debt, not only by shunning occasions of expense, but by vigorous exertion in time of peace to discharge the debts which unavoidable wars may have occasioned, not ungenerously throwing upon posterity the burden which we ourselves ought to bear. [Emphasis added.][59]

I believe those are timely words. They were echoed in part by Thomas Jefferson who said, "Our distance from the wars of Europe, and our disposition to take no part in them, will, we hope, enable us to keep clear of the debts which they occasion to other powers."[60] If seasons of peace serve as momentary respites to pay down debt, then we definitely need more seasons of peace.

Jefferson drove the point home: "I consider the fortunes of our republic as depending in an eminent degree on the extinguishment of the public debt before we engage in any war; because that done, we shall have revenue enough to improve our country in peace and defend it in war without recurring either to new taxes or loans. But if the debt should once more be swelled to a formidable size, its entire discharge will be despaired of, and we shall be committed to the English career of debt, corruption and rottenness, closing with revolution. The discharge of public debt, therefore, is vital to the destinies of our government."[61] It is to Jefferson's credit that during his administration the national deficit was cut by nearly a third, despite America's having to fight a war against the Barbary Pirates.[62]

DON'T MISS THE MIRACLE

Prudence is one of the four cardinal virtues and greed is one of the seven deadly sins. It's really as simple as that. And it would help if we, as individuals, and as a nation, reminded ourselves constantly that happiness and true prosperity does not come from things, from accumulating objects, or big government handouts. It comes first and foremost from trusting in God, our Creator, as the Founders did. "In God We Trust" is inscribed on our money for a reason—so that we might never forget our true source of security. There's a verse in the Bible that summarizes it for me, "Instruct those who are rich in this present world not to be conceited or to fix their hope on the uncertainty of riches, but on God, who richly supplies us with all things to enjoy."[63] That is why Thomas Jefferson could say, "I sincerely pray that all the members of the human family may, in the time prescribed by the Father of us all, find themselves securely established in the enjoyment of life, liberty and happiness."[64]

God is not a cosmic killjoy. He has given us everything to enjoy. All we are and possess is ultimately a gift from Him. To some degree we all have been blessed by His hand. But we're also called to be a blessing to others. God didn't just call us to gather but also to give away. It's something we all learned as children, but too many have forgotten as adults: sharing is another way of caring. I can still remember when neighbors used to make pies for neighbors and would come to one another's aid when they lacked anything. We need to get back to that type of America, and it starts not just by thinking about what we can get from this life, but what we can give back to it. Look around. There's someone, somewhere today, who needs your help.

I began this chapter by speaking about greed. I'm ending it by speaking about giving—greed's polar opposite. Because the only thing that can break a spirit of greed is a spirit of generosity. Financial counselor Ron Blue says, "Don't miss the miracle!"[65] The miracle of giving. No one has taught that principle better than my friend Randy Alcorn in his bestselling books, *The Treasure Principle* and *Money, Possessions, and Eternity*. Randy explains exactly why giving is so powerful:

> Another benefit of giving is freedom. It's a matter of basic physics. The greater the mass, the greater the hold that mass exerts. The more things we own—the greater their total mass the more they grip us, setting us in orbit around them. Finally, like a black hole, they suck us in. . . . Giving changes all that. It breaks us out of orbit around our possessions. We escape their gravity, entering a new orbit around our treasures in heaven.[66]

Giving might not be the path of popularity, but it is the way of wisdom. And, as the wisest man in the world, King Solomon once said in Proverbs, "He who walks with the wise will be wise . . . and will be rewarded with prosperity."[67]

CHAPTER FOUR

★ ★ ★

Secure and Protect Our Borders

SINCE SEPTEMBER 11, 2001, America has been fighting a renewed war on terror. Yes, renewed. Americans need to remember that Muslim extremists first attacked our country right after the Revolutionary War. Their jihad against America was conceived in the Barbary Powers Conflict,[1] a confrontation between Muslim extremists or pirates[2] from the five Barbary nations (Tripoli, Turkey, Tunis, Algiers, and Morocco) and what they considered the "Christian nations" (England, Denmark, France, Spain, and the new United States). I enjoy reading about America's heritage and believe this particular two-hundred-year-old lesson on extremist Muslim-American relations could be helpful to our country right about now.[3]

While the United States was cleaning up from the Revolutionary War, it was also squaring off against largely Muslim pirates in the Mediterranean.[4] These sea bandits cruised the coastlines stealing cargo, destroying villages, and enslaving millions of Africans and hundreds of thousands of Christian Europeans and Americans. Because America was a newborn nation, we had relatively little naval defense. Our rebellion against Britain severed our protection by the Royal Navy. And while France helped during the War, the United States was on its own as of about 1783. And so our merchant ships were exceptionally vulnerable to attack in and out of the Great Sea. As a result our cargo and seamen were captured and our country's leaders were forced to either go to war or negotiate with the Barbary Pirates. They decided to negotiate.

In 1784 envoys were dispatched to secure peace and passage from the Barbary Powers. Treaties were made. Tributes and ransoms were paid. Our cargo and captives were freed. And our ships traveled safely. Over the next decade and a half, millions of dollars were given to these radicals—estimated at 20 percent of America's federal budget in 1800. (Despite the fact men like Thomas Jefferson argued vehemently against paying ransoms and tribute—he believed the only road to resolution would be "through the medium of war.")[5]

America's first four presidents (Washington, Adams, Jefferson, and Madison) each dealt with this east-west conflict of powers to varying degrees. Though numerous negotiations and treaties were made,[6] including "the Treaty of Tripoli"[7] in 1796–1797, Tripoli (in present Libya) still declared war against the U.S. in 1801. It is sometimes called America's first official war as a new nation.

The Founders believed in a foreign policy of noninterventionism, but Jefferson realized that protecting America's borders also meant protecting American lives and property overseas. He confessed to Congress in 1801 that he was "unauthorized by the Constitution, without the sanction of Congress, to go beyond the line of defense," but he still ordered a small fleet of warships to the Mediterranean to ward off attacks by the Barbary Powers.

Marines and warships were deployed to the region, which eventually led to the surrender of Tripoli in 1805. It would take another decade, however, to completely defeat the Muslim pirates, or should I say cause them to temporarily retreat until a distant time when they would again attack our country. America's victory back then over those Muslim sea radicals is commemorated today in the Marine Hymn, with the words, "From the halls of Montezuma, to the shores of Tripoli, we fight our country's battles in the air, on land, and sea."

DIPLOMATIC LESSONS FROM LONG AGO

The voices of our forefathers cry out from the Barbary Powers Conflict in hope of imparting some wisdom to us. As the adage goes, we will either learn from history's mistakes or be doomed to repeat them.

1. Muslim extremists have always had a disdain for America. Before America was a new nation, Muslim extremists hated the West. When America was born, she was aligned with the Western ("Christian") countries, which to Muslim extremists automatically made America an enemy. What we witness today in our relations with extremists is essentially no different than back then, except the stakes are much higher and more costly. Nothing will ultimately satisfy their bitterness but our destruction or complete subservience. The fact is our enemies know what America stands for and they hate us because of it. Extreme Islamic belief will always oppose us because it is threatened by our values and way of life. From our freedom of religion to the liberties of women, America's inherent makeup is contrary to radical Islam's core value system.

2. Negotiations and treaties don't work with extremists and terrorists. Our primary problem today, as it was back then, is not our lack of international relations or communications. Seeking to clear perceptions about America might work with some, but not radicals and terrorists. Tribute and treaties are only temporary at

best; they didn't stop them from declaring war against us then and they won't stop them now. In the Barbary Conflict we caved into their demands and empowered them by doing so. Paying them only encouraged further attacks.

Pacifying extremists and those who harbor and support them is still bad international business or foreign policy. Who better to prove that in the twentieth century than President Jimmy Carter! While his heart might be right in wanting to win over our enemies, his unilateral goodwill trip to Palestine and hugging the leaders of Hamas, as far as I'm concerned, was a treasonous gesture. Quite frankly, he should have learned from his past presidential mistakes with Iran. President Carter is a major reason we are in our Middle Eastern dilemma with Iran today. Because, in the name of human rights, he set the stage for the rise of two of the worst human rights violators in history—the Ayatollah Khomeini and ultimately his modern successor, the current president of Iran, Mahmoud Ahmadinejad.

Jimmy Carter would not support the Shah of Iran while he was in power, which allowed the Ayatollah Khomeini to seize power. And, as a result, we are now reaping the harvest of the Ayatollah Khomeini anti-American fanaticism and extremism. The sadness of the story is that Carter abandoned an American friend. The tragedy is that the course of history has been changed by one man.[8] (Please read the Notes section!)

3. Once a religious war, always a religious war. Whether justified as vengeful sentiment for the Crusades or not, Islamo-fascism cannot see any argument or altercation

with the West outside the lens of religion. In his April 8,
1805 journal entry, even General William Eaton said of
Muslim radicals, "We find it almost impossible to
inspire these wild bigots with confidence in us or to per-
suade them that, being Christians, we can be otherwise
than enemies to [Muslims]. We have a difficult under-
taking!" To this day extremists still view America as
being packaged together with the other European countries and as a target for Muslim conquest. To them the
jihad never ends.

4. The best defense is a good offense. For thirty years, from
    roughly 1785 through 1815, America fought by sea and
    land Muslim extremists in the form of pirate slave trad-
    ers. Today that fight continues with Muslim pirates who
    capture our planes and use them as weapons.

    In a post-September 11 age of globalization, multi-
    ethnic societies, and possible suitcase nukes, contain-
    ment is impossible. Preemption is still our best solution.
    Our offense must be as strong as our defense. It took
    military might, leadership, ingenuity, fortitude, and
    national perseverance to win the day against those
    Muslim extremists two hundred years ago. And it will
    take the same today. If it took our forefathers thirty
    years to resolve the Muslim-American conflict then, do
    we think we can settle it now in just a few years? It's
    unfortunate that it seems America can no longer fight a
    war it can't win in a minimal amount of time. We don't
    have the patience we used to. God forbid we get into a
    war that requires our perseverance before our prefer-
    ence to finish. Is that not where we are today with the
    war on terror?[9]

Years before September 11 we tragically forgot the lesson of history, dropping our guard to a monumentally shocking end. When more than three thousand innocent American citizens were brutally murdered by terrorist counterparts to the Barbary Pirates, we were delivered a devastating wake-up call. We relearned the lessons of the Barbary Powers Conflict: that despite negotiations and even bribes, Muslim extremists are still engaged with America in a jihad or holy war.

Islamo-facism continues to rob us of our liberties, cripple us by fear, and destroy our country. Proof is found by simply asking how many of us will still not fly on September 11? They've stolen a day of liberty from our calendar. Let's not allow them to seize another. And they won't, as long as we stay resilient, learn from the lessons of history, and remember the God of 911, Psalm 91:1 that is, for "He who dwells in the shelter of the Most High will abide in the shadow of the Almighty." Above all, this truth still stands, "Blessed is the nation whose God is the Lord" (Ps. 33:12).

FROM NONINTERVENTION TO INTERVENTION

Protecting our borders means also protecting our boundaries. And some of those boundaries, in connection with commerce and especially the welfare of Americans abroad, sail far from the shores of America. As with Jefferson, I believe in defending American liberties wherever Americans reside.

Nevertheless, sometimes I think America has stretched her boundaries too far into other countries' business. I believe America overplays the role of world peace officer. I believe America sends too much money abroad. I believe we dole out too much foreign aid. I believe we need to invest more in our own commerce than we do in other countries. I believe we should direct our energies more on our economy and less on imperialism and nation building.

As George Washington said, "The great rule of conduct for us in regard to foreign nations is in extending our commercial relations, to have with them as little political connection as possible. . . .Why quit our own to stand upon foreign ground? Why, by interweaving our destiny with that of any part of Europe, entangle our peace and prosperity in the toils of European ambition, rivalship, interest, humor or caprice?"[10]

I completely agree with what Washington called "the great rule of conduct," and that our nation and its citizens should do our best to live by it. I just wonder if our Founders would have made "an exception to the rule of conduct" if they were here when the Twin Towers exploded as a result of Islamic terrorists hijacking our planes to use as missiles. We must remember the noninterventionist attitudes of our Founders were born not in Islamic terrorist onslaughts but through a bad divorce with Britain and an understandable sensitivity to the abuses of political connections. That sensitivity was still ringing in 1808, when Thomas Jefferson wrote near the end of his presidency, "We consider the interests of Cuba, Mexico and ours as the same, and that the object of both must be to exclude all European influence from this hemisphere."[11]

I don't believe our Founders would have sat back in response to September 11 and merely built up our borders for further protection. We must remember that at least twenty-nine of the fifty-five delegates to the Constitutional Convention served in the Continental forces, most in command positions, and they were men highly attuned to protect this country and her liberties.[12] I believe they lived by (and we should live by) a noninterventionist code of conduct, but that the line of intervention is crossed wherever Americans are threatened and killed. If Jefferson crossed that line and went to war for American commerce and hostages in the

Mediterranean, would he also not cross them for mass American killings in New York?

Fatal attacks on our soil from foreign powers and continued threats from Islamic terrorists not only warrant but mandate us to reconsider the precedent or "exception to Washington's rule." As with our Founders, I believe that to protect our borders and sovereignty we need at times to utilize some overt and covert action abroad, especially when warranted by national emergencies and threats. To sit back and wait here in a noninterventionist stance when our country is threatened by overseas thugs will lead only to further attacks on our country. We will either fight extremists overseas or we'll fight them here. Two hundred years of our history proves that.

OUR MIDDLE EASTERN WARS

As General Sherman once said, "War is at best barbarism. Its glory is all moonshine. . . . War is hell." I agree, but if our country is threatened as it was in the First and Second World Wars, and I believe we are in another World War, then it is necessary. I commend our freedom fighters, the men and women who have fought and are fighting, to secure our freedom. I am humbled by their service and grateful for their courage.

That is why in 2006 and 2007 I visited our troops in Iraq. I went to twenty-eight bases and shook hands with nearly forty thousand troops. It was an experience I will remember for the rest of my life.

Even in the gravity of war, I was pleased to see our troops could enjoy lighter moments, even using my name and face. I still smile as I see the Special Forces who named their vehicle after me. Other units not only adopted my image on their vehicles, but one even had the call sign of "Walker."

While I was there, one soldier said the only way he would reenlist is if the unit "got Chuck Norris out here." I was told about this while I was visiting the base where he was stationed.

Standing by him, the soldier asked me to "give him an arm bar" (twisting his arm) as he happily signed the reenlistment paperwork. I'm a patriot, so what else could I do but oblige? When I first arrived in Iraq, the troops held up a huge sign that said, "Chuck Norris is here, we can go home now!" I wish that were true.

Of course we all know there is nothing funny about war.

Here's where I stand. Whatever the reasons we went in, we're there now. And our troops are fighting for the freedom and democracy of more than twelve million Iraqis, who courageously went to the polls a few years ago to establish a new constitution and government, under the threat of death by the insurgents. And just two countries away, our service men and women in Afghanistan are simultaneously fighting against the Taliban's control over that country and al-Qaida's reign of terror over ours. All of our troops in the Middle East are fighting for our security and freedom here in America, just as all our other veterans have done. They are attracting our enemies into foreign territory and fighting them there, instead of within our own borders. Is that not a form of border patrol and protection?

I'll be honest with you. I understand why people are against the war and even our present government. But I simply don't understand how anyone could neglect to support these fine service men and women. It is not only unpatriotic, it is unjust.

The military is very close to me, because it turned my life around. Joining the military helped me get on the right path. I still believe it can help others too. That is why I stand with the majority of Americans who say to all our service members, their families, and indeed all the veterans who have served this great country and the cause of freedom, we salute you. We support you. And we will continue to pray for you.

Each time I returned to America from Iraq, I received hundreds of letters and e-mails from troops in Iraq and their families. This letter from a Marine's mom summarizes well why I went to Iraq and why we all need to continue to support our troops:

I just received an email from my son who is a Marine serving in Iraq. In it he tells me that he got to meet Chuck Norris and that he has pictures that he will be sending soon. He sounded so excited. Thank you for making my Marine's day a little brighter in a very, very dark place and time and by doing so you have also touched this Mother's heart. With sincere appreciation, Thank you. [Name withheld][13]

I do understand their pain, every time I think about my brother, Wieland, who paid the ultimate price in Vietnam. I'll never forget when I received the news.

At the height of the Vietnam War, both of my brothers, Wieland and Aaron, enlisted in the U.S. Army. As a veteran myself, I understood their desire to serve and I concurred with their decision to enlist. If the Air Force helped me get on the right path, maybe the Army would do the same for my brothers. Aaron was stationed in Korea, and Wieland was sent to Vietnam. As Wieland headed off to Nam, I hugged and kissed him and said, "I'm going to miss you. Be careful."

On June 3, 1970, I was informed that my brother Wieland was killed in action. I simply sat in shock, thinking about my little brother; my best friend whom I would never see again in this life. Then I began to weep uncontrollably.

I tried to help mom the best I could, but hers was a pain particular to parents of war. I still miss my brother terribly—we all do. I think of Wieland often and am comforted only by the certainty that one day our family will all be together in heaven.

MEXICO, CARTELS, AND BAGGY BORDERS

Do you ever wonder how we can conquer the Middle East but we can't close our own borders from illegal immigration and contraband?

In just one week of news this past year, I clipped this small sampling of headlines:

- "Locals, Feds Prepare for Any Escalation of Mexican Border Violence"[14]
- "N[ew] M[exico] delegation asks for border task force"[15]
- "Texas lawmakers angered by border security money being spent in other regions"[16]
- "U.S. Sues Railroad Over Smugglers"[17]
- "Border drain open for hours before 8 entered it"[18]

More than ten thousand lives have been lost in Mexico's drug wars since just January 2007.[19] Border towns are experiencing outrageous escalations in crime, including more than three hundred drug-related kidnappings in Phoenix alone in 2008 (most involved Mexican immigrants with ties to drug cartels).[20]

What's amazing is that in 2009 we sent $214 million to aid Mexico in their drug fight,[21] but the biggest aid would come from simply stopping the flow of drug traffic (commerce) through our own borders and ports. Do we really think Mexico's move to decriminalize small portions of possession and personal use of marijuana, cocaine, heroin, methamphetamine and LSD will lessen the problem of illegal traffic for the U.S.A?[22]

Isn't it finally time we built a wall that works?[23] Isn't it time we quit restricting our border agents by granting illegals more rights than our citizens?[24] Isn't it time we post military personnel at particularly hot illegal crossings?

We don't need another government study on Mexican border safety led by Homeland Security Secretary Janet Napolitano.[25] We don't need any more visits or negotiations by Secretary of State Hillary Clinton.[26] We don't need any more "wait-and-see" mentalities or moves from the White House.[27] We need action, yesterday![28]

Rather than the Obama administration sending hundreds of millions of dollars to aid Mexico in the drug fight or shifting tens of millions of dollars from investigating U.S. employers guilty of hiring illegal immigrants to fighting Mexican drug cartels,[29] they should leave those monies alone and hunt down the hundreds of millions that corporate executives robbed from taxpayers in their bailouts and use that instead. It sickens me that we have enough money to satisfy all of Washington's pet projects, but there never seems to be enough to stop illegal immigration.

We've got to quit playing political games with the border and allow our border agents more protection and liberty to get their job done. When bureaucracy bullies border agents, we've already lost the battle.

An example came this past year when a ten-year U.S. Border Patrol veteran shot and wounded a man in the left buttocks who assaulted agents at a violent stretch of the U.S.-Mexico border. Despite that the man was among a group trying to illegally enter the United States and were throwing rocks and concrete chunks at agents, officials at the Mexican consulate in San Diego criticized the agent and demanded the U.S. conduct a full investigation.[30]

The incident occurred after one agent witnessed and called for backup because three to four illegals were trying to scale the border fence. So four to six more agents responded by using a gate in the fence to get to its south side—still within the U.S. The agents fired pepper balls and tear gas to disperse a group of about seven to fifteen people, and most fled. Two of the suspects, however, stayed and threw rocks and concrete chunks at the Border Patrol agents. Fearing for his safety, one agent fired two rounds from his rifle from about fifty feet away, striking twenty-two-year-old Edgar Israel Ortega Chavez, who then was standing on Mexican soil.

Consul General Remedios Gómez Arnau responded, "Any kind of shooting toward Mexican territory is rejected by the Mexican government.[31] They should have waited for response of the Mexican authorities."

Are you kidding me? Do I smell another Compean & Ramos[32] case in the making? Do illegals think border crossing is nothing more than a game of cat and mouse? Do Mexican officials think we're only playing "rocks, scissors, and paper" at the borders? When will we finally draw a line in the sand and stop this insanity at our nation's boundaries? When will we back our agents and their Bill of Rights? When will we give them the complete resources, permissions, and support they need to fully carry out their duties?

When Supervisory Border Patrol Agent Daryl Reed reports[33] that there were 330 assaults on agents in 2008, compared with 254 reported incidents in 2007, it's time for our government to ante up and better protect and secure our borders and agents.

Congress authorized a border fence in 2005—that was five long years ago (as of this writing) for anyone bad at basic math. They approved $2.6 billion for border enhancement, but we still have illegals and contraband crossing our borders like gnats through a screen, though stricter enforcement, fed-up Americans, and the recession have slightly lowered the influx.[34]

And the question that keeps coming back to my mind is: how is it we can militarily overthrow a tyrant like Saddam Hussein in Iraq, yet we can't keep illegals from crossing our borders?

NO BORDERS—NO NATION

A few years ago I had the opportunity to fly along America's borders with my good friend John Hensley, who was the assistant commissioner of U.S. Customs. We flew on a Black Hawk helicopter and checked out locations along the California border where there was heavy traffic of drug dealers and illegal aliens coming into the United States from Mexico.

As we were flying over the desert, we landed in the middle of nowhere. We stepped out of the helicopter and John asked me, "What do you see?" I replied, "Absolutely nothing but desert." As soon as I said that, up popped U.S. border agents, who were hiding in holes covered by beige tarps that blended in with the terrain. They were waiting for illegal traffic trying to sneak into our country. I thought, what dedication this takes to hide out here in this intense heat for hours at a time—just waiting.

There's no doubt Americans possess the resources and passion to close off our borders and ports from illegal immigration and contraband. If we can overthrow another country, we ought to be able to protect our own. Yet to this day, our national borders and ports of entry are like lattice work with plenty of holes through which illegals now come in.

I don't lay the blame on our dedicated border agents. But I do blame an overly bureaucratic government that still has not given agents the proper resources and permissions they need to get their job done. I also blame government for undermining national security by being more concerned with global commerce than national sovereignty. They would rather please the international masses than enforce our own laws.

Let's ask ourselves, why is Congress not securing our borders? Could it be they have greater global goals that will ultimately dissolve this Union? Whether intentionally or not, government has failed for decades to secure the borders. It is up to us to make sure it gets done by taking several points of action I'll be outlining in this chapter. The time is now. And if we don't do our part, America as we know it will dissolve like a sugar cube in coffee. From the coastland to the heartland, we will lose our distinctions and no longer even recognize our country. As President Ronald Reagan said, "A nation without borders is not a nation."[35]

BUILDING UP OUR BORDERS

As with others, I opposed the amnesty bill proposed by the Senate in 2007. And I support Congress' $3 billion directed to build up border security—monies used to train and deploy twenty-three thousand more agents, build seven hundred miles of fence and three hundred miles of vehicle barriers, add four drone airplanes, and erect one hundred and five radar and camera towers.

Border patrols and homeland security have made some headway in securing our borders. But our nation's boundaries, ports, and airports remain largely open runways for illegal and terrorist transport. U.S. Senator Jeff Bingaman from New Mexico reminded his constituents of that very fact when he described another type of illegal crossing, those *from the United States to Mexico*. It appears drug cartels are again using revenue derived from their "free trade" to illegally purchase weapons in the United States and smuggle them back into Mexico, with the result that murder rates have shot up 100 percent in certain towns.[36]

One of the aspects of illegal immigration often overlooked is the affect upon the thirty thousand street gangs with up to one million members in the United States. The gang considered the most dangerous is the MS-13, which has ties to the Mexican Mafia. It is estimated at ten thousand members, many of whom are illegals. Seven hundred MS-13 members were arrested by law enforcement in 2005. According to the *Washington Times*, MS-13 is believed to have a major smuggling operation, which transports drugs, firearms, and people.[37] What's even more alarming is that in 2005 the Honduran Security Minister and the president of El Salvador warned that MS-13 was in dialogue with al Qaeda to transport terrorists into our country! With MS-13 currently in forty-four states, we must secure the borders now. (Seventy percent of the kids in our martial arts program, KickStartKids (www.KickStartKids.org), are Latinos and gangs are constantly trying to recruit them. But we will not allow anyone to participate in the program if they are a part of any gang. KickStartKids has provided an alternative and safe haven for young people from gangs and that is one more reason I believe the KickStartKids program should be in every state across the nation.)

Exacerbating the border crisis is the fact that there continues to be a shortage of both border patrol and other government security officials. The Homeland Security Department is still trying to fill 2007's 138 vacancies in high-level jobs—an employment crisis it calls "a critical homeland security issue that demands immediate attention."[38] And that crisis will continue until we increase the pay and benefits for border agents. I believe this so strongly I have done public service announcements encouraging their enlistment.

I was reminded of their need for a salary increase when I was on the campaign trail with Mike Huckabee. We stopped in Laredo, Texas, and met with the Border Patrol. They gave us a tour of the area and explained to us what their operations were there. One of the Border Patrol agents and I struck up a conversation. As we were talking, I asked him if his pay as a Border Patrol Agent was adequate. He said in certain states he gets by, but while stationed in California, he had to split rent with two other agents in order to afford the cost of living. I didn't ask how much their salary was, but I've always felt law enforcement from every branch was underpaid for the responsibility they have in protecting us. If we expect to attract and maintain quality personnel, then state and federal governments need to work together to make the position of border agents more financially appealing.

Now more than ever, we must protect our borders and sovereignty. So far, our government has failed to produce suitable solutions to the illegal immigrant crisis. Amnesty is not the answer. And immigration laws aren't effective if we continue to allow them to be dodged or ignored. Furthermore, globalization efforts have only confused security matters, further endangering our borders as well as our national identity—our sovereignty. Washington doesn't stop illegal immigrants or have a clue where they all are. That is why Mike Huckabee says, "If the government can't track illegals, then let's outsource the job to UPS or FedEx."[39] If they can track a lost package anywhere in the world within minutes, they can track down illegals.

MY SOLUTIONS TO ILLEGAL IMMIGRATION

From America's birth, our Founders struggled with national enemies and border troubles, from the sea of Tripoli to the western
frontier. While welcoming the poor, downtrodden, and persecuted
from every country, they also had to protect the sacred soil they
called home from unwanted intruders. According to the Declaration of Independence, "obstructing the Laws for the Naturalization[40] of Foreigners" was one of the objections leveled against
Britain that warranted the American colonists' secession. Yet even
the Founders believed a total open-door policy for immigrants
would only lead to complete chaos. Under the Articles of Confederation (our "first constitution"), each state possessed authority
over naturalization. Such diversity, however, led the Founders at
the Constitutional Convention to shift the power of naturalization to the federal government. The Constitution therefore reads
in Article I, Section 8, that the Congress shall have the authority
to "establish a uniform rule of naturalization."

While we discuss and debate new ways to resolve the social
crisis we call illegal immigration, our Founders again pointed the
way over two hundred years ago. They considered and promoted
American citizenship as a high honor and so they set up a system
that only allowed immigrants who could contribute to the building up of America. There were four basic requirements for
"enrollment and acceptance" that we still utilize to this day:

> Key criteria for citizenship of the Naturalization Act of 1795
> remain part of American law. These include (1) five years of
> (lawful) residence within the United States; (2) a "good moral
> character, attached to the principles of the Constitution of the
> United States, and well disposed to the good order and happi-
> ness of the United States"; (3) the taking of a formal oath to
> support the Constitution and to renounce any foreign alle-
> giance; and (4) the renunciation of any hereditary titles."[41]

In order for us to regain control of the chaotic mess of illegal immigration and press on to achieve the success our forefathers had in immigration, we must apply those four criteria to our naturalization process in a more practical way. Here are my streamlined recommendations to attain those goals.

First, Congress must redirect the streams of immigration. No farmer irrigates his land by merely opening the floodgates of water. Rather water flow is restricted and guided for optimum productivity. That is how our forefathers used to handle immigration. Congress needs to re-evaluate and change our virtual open-door policy toward worldwide immigration. We need a new system that is selective but fair. We need to treat all people without prejudice, but we shouldn't fear restricting the immigration streams into our country, or ultimately we will hand our sovereignty over to other nations.

I agree with Newt Gingrich, who has prepared an outline list of ten or so excellent suggestions for curbing the flow of illegal immigration, like stopping their government aid and closing safe harbors in sanctuary cities.[42] However, I respectfully disagree with Newt at the end of this one point: "Workers who came here illegally but have a good work relationship and community ties (including family), should have first opportunity to get the new temporary worker visas, but instead of paying penalties, they should be required to go home and get the visa at home."[43]

We can argue the need for illegals to go home, but we all know that it will never happen. The technicalities and costs for more than twelve million illegal aliens (and their families) to be tracked down, rounded up, and deported is so staggering and impractical that its mere mentioning as a necessity borders on absurd. Right or wrong, can we even imagine what would happen to our economy if we were to require all illegal aliens out of the country immediately?

We must provide a better practical solution that doesn't cost our country billions in deportation costs and economic losses. I believe our Founders provided us with a better process to make citizens out of immigrants and not lose the economic flow they are providing to our country. Let me explain.

In 1790 our Founders required immigrants to live in the United States for two years before they could become citizens, in order to prove they could remain employed, obey our laws, and be good members of the community. The Naturalization Act of 1795 extended the residency requirement for citizenship from two years to five years.[44] I believe a combination of our Founders' 1790 and 1795 naturalization recommendations would work to solve our illegal alien problem and serve as a proper protocol for citizenship.

All illegal immigrants would be given an immediate three-month grace period to apply for a temporary worker's visa. (If they failed to apply within that time, they would be considered fugitives, and when found they would be deported.) Once they applied and qualified for a temporary worker's visa, immigrants would be placed on a two-year (the original 1790 requirement of residency) probationary period. At the completion of that time, and if they remained in good standing, they would be issued a permanent worker's visa. After an additional three years, they would qualify to apply for U.S. citizenship.

During the two-year probationary time, it would be their responsibility to report in with assigned government officials and prove their productivity and progress in becoming Americans. Specific criteria would of course be established by Congress and enforced by probationary personnel from the departments of naturalization. During that two-year probationary period, if immigrants didn't report in, and didn't have a good reason, they would be deported. If they didn't demonstrate a good moral standing and satisfactory contributions in their community, they would be deported.

This is how America was built, and it is how it can be rebuilt again today. We should secure our borders, establish selective legal immigration criteria, and offer a responsible path to citizenship for immigrants who are working here and want to become Americans.

★ ★ ★

CHAPTER FIVE

From Here to Eternity

A WHILE BACK I was watching a PBS science special on television. It endeavored to detail the creation of the universe chronologically. As the host of the show spiraled up a stairway inside a tower, he encountered many windows with closed wood shutters. Each window in the tower represented a particular point of creation, regressing to the very birth of the universe. As he moved up the stairway, he would open the wooden shutters on each window. Each revealed a porthole picture of creation at a specific time of its fifteen billion year or so history. I was curious to see the last window (at the top of the tower) and what the host would say about it. The farther he moved up the tower the more my anticipation grew (like a mystery movie reaching its climax).

When only a few windows away from the top, he commented on what would have been micro-fragments of a second after the Big Bang. All of creation would have been compressed to a size smaller than the head of a pin (or so he said). When the host reached the top of the tower stairway, there was a window with a brilliant light behind it, emitting rays through the cracks in the wooden shutters. The host tried to open the shutters but couldn't.

He shook his head, stared into the camera, and said, "And what's behind these shudders we may never know."

The next scene was of the inside of a cathedral. The host said that many believe a Creator is behind the last window. To my surprise he didn't disparage such belief. He left the origin of the Big Bang as a mystery.

While many atheists like to think science has disproven the idea of a Creator God, the fact is it hasn't. Scientists can't rule out God, and certainly most people don't. Polls show that roughly 92 percent of Americans still believe in a Creator.[1]

But what they mean by a Creator has changed over the years. America used to be a very religious country. We still are, compared to other countries in the Western World. But our religious beliefs are in flux. A recent poll showed that one in four Americans has left the denominational faith in which they were raised. One in five claims no particular faith. And one in four young adults, between the ages of eighteen and twenty-nine, is an avowed atheist or agnostic.[2]

This is a far different picture from early America, where Christianity and our republic were intricately intertwined. Alexis de Tocqueville wrote in his landmark work *Democracy in America* (1834):

> I do not know whether all Americans have a sincere faith in their religion; for who can read the human heart? But I am certain that they hold it to be indispensable to the maintenance of republican institutions. This opinion is not peculiar to a class of citizens or to a party, but it belongs to the whole nation and to every rank of society.[3]

Many today may not realize that there was an active clergyman (Presbyterian minister John Witherspoon) among the signers of the Declaration of Independence. Two others had previously been ministers. Others were sons of clergy or had studied theology. Of the thirty-nine signers of the Constitution, thirty-seven were professed Protestant Christians (though at least one of those, Benjamin Franklin, was probably a deist), and two, Daniel Carroll and Thomas Fitzsimons, were Roman Catholics. They were a diverse group of men in some respects, but they were united by their belief in a Creator God.

As Professor David Holmes from the College of William and Mary wrote in his landmark book, *The Faith of the Founding Fathers*, "The founding fathers of the United States were remarkable, even noble men. Like most people, they understood their religion in the terms of their background and of their day. Those trained in parsons' academies had studied the Bible more thoroughly than all but a small percentage of Christians today. In the spirits of their times, they appeared less devout than they were—which seems a reversal from modern politics."[4]

THE BASIS FOR FREEDOM AND GOVERNMENT

I didn't write this chapter to prove God's existence.[5] This chapter has priority because our Founders gave the Creator priority. It is no coincidence the Declaration of Independence begins with a spiritual emphasis:

> When, in the course of human events, it becomes necessary for one people to dissolve the political bands which have connected them with another, and to assume, among the powers of the earth, the separate and equal station to which the laws of nature[6] and of nature's God entitle them, a decent respect to the opinions of mankind requires that they should declare the causes which impel them to the Separation.
>
> We hold these truths to be self-evident, that all men are created equal, that they are endowed by their Creator with certain unalienable rights, that among these are life, liberty, and the pursuit of happiness—that to secure these rights, governments are instituted among men. . . .

For the Founders, God and government were intricately linked. As Thomas Paine echoed one year earlier, "Spiritual freedom is the root of political freedom. . . . As the union between spiritual freedom and political liberty seems nearly inseparable, it is our duty to defend both."[7]

Atheism was virtually nonexistent in those days. As Ben Franklin's 1787 pamphlet for those in Europe thinking of relocating to America highlighted:

> To this may be truly added, that serious religion, under its various denominations, is not only tolerated, but respected and practiced. Atheism is unknown there; Infidelity rare and secret; so that persons may live to a great age in that country without having their piety shocked by meeting with either an Atheist or an Infidel. And the Divine Being seems to have manifested his approbation of the mutual forbearance and kindness with which the different sects treat each other; by the remarkable prosperity with which he has been pleased to favor the whole country.[8]

Some might retort that Paine and Franklin were deists rather than Christians. But what is unmistakable is that they wrote and spoke for a Christian country, that they believed in a personal Creator, and that the Founders' ideas of government were firmly rooted in the notion of God-given rights.

James Wilson, a signer of the Constitution who was appointed to the Supreme Court by George Washington, explained the relationship between religion and law:

> Human law must rest its authority ultimately upon the authority of that law which is divine. . . . Far from being rivals or enemies, religion and law are twin sisters, friends, and mutual assistants. Indeed, these two sciences run into each other. The divine law as discovered by reason and moral sense forms an essential part of both. The moral precepts delivered in the

sacred oracles form part of the law of nature, are of the same origin and of the same obligation, operating universally and perpetually.[9]

Article VI of the Constitution guarantees that "no religious tests shall ever be required as a qualification to any office or public trust under the United States."[10] But, as a matter of free speech, it is perfectly acceptable for government officials to advocate the election of Christians. As John Jay, the first Chief Justice of the United States, appointed by George Washington, wrote, "Providence has given to our people the choice of their rulers. And it is the duty, as well as the privilege and interest, of a Christian nation to select and prefer Christians for their rulers."[11]

So is America a Christian nation? Those who say no often point to Amendment XI in the 1797 Treaty of Tripoli. It says: "The government of the United States of America is not in any sense founded on the Christian religion . . . ." But those words were there for a specific reason: to convince state-sponsored Muslim pirates to release kidnapped American seamen, ships, and cargo and avert further Muslim attacks on American shipping. Those words were meant to reassure the Muslims of Tripoli, who believed that any "Christian" state was inherently anti-Muslim, that America was not their enemy. This is clear if we look at the full context of Article XI, which states:

As the government of the United States of America is not in any sense founded on the Christian religion *as it has in itself no character of enmity against the laws, religion or tranquility of Musselmen [Muslims] and as the said [United] States have never entered into any war or act of hostility against any Mahometan [Islamic] nation,* it is declared by the parties that no pretext arising from religious opinions shall ever produce an interruption of the harmony existing between the two countries.[12]

It is typical of the underhanded tactics that opponents of America's Christian history will pull that quote out of context, misrepresent its true meaning, and simultaneously ignore the wealth of evidence—the plain facts—that confirm the Christian history and principles that defined our founding. The Founders themselves never denied this. It was President John Adams, the very same president who signed the Treaty of Tripoli, who said, "Our Constitution was made only for a moral and religious people. It is wholly inadequate to the government of any other."

And to what religion was Adams referring? He gave us an answer when he wrote, "The general principles on which the Fathers achieved independence were the only Principles in which that beautiful Assembly of young Gentlemen could Unite. . . . And what were these general Principles? I answer, the general Principles of Christianity, in which all these Sects were united."[13]

America was founded as a Christian nation, open to all faiths, and removed from the sectarian squabbles of Europe, but a Christian nation nonetheless. The Founders saw themselves as putting into practice Christian ideas of human rights and government. Our children and grandchildren must understand this history, and if they don't get it in school, they need to get it from their parents and grandparents.

We, the people, must acknowledge America's rich religious history. We must devote ourselves as our forefathers did (even in denominational diversity) to a Creator because He, in the words of the Founders, is the source of our human rights, which put limits on government power. Most of all, we must call on Him for the healing of our land. He is the ultimate agent for national renewal.

Ben Franklin told the Constitutional Convention that:

> In the beginning of the contest with Britain, when we were sensible of danger, we had daily prayers in this room for the divine protection! Our prayers, Sir, were heard; and they were graciously answered. All of us, who were engaged in the struggle,

must have observed frequent instances of a superintending Providence in our favor. To that kind Providence we owe this happy opportunity of consulting in peace on the means of establishing our future national felicity. And have we now forgotten that powerful friend? Or do we imagine we no longer need its assistance? I have lived, Sir, a long time; and the longer I live, the more convincing proofs I see of this truth, That God governs in the affairs of men! And if a sparrow cannot fall to the ground without his notice, is it probable that an empire can rise without his aid?[14]

If Franklin, a presumed deist, could believe that "God governs in the affairs of men," it is certain that all or nearly all of the Founding Fathers did as well. That belief shaped our country, it is part of our heritage, and I do not believe we can neglect or repudiate that belief—that we are responsible to God—without endangering our future.

ETHICS AND LEADERSHIP

One of the reasons America's Founders thought God was the most critical constituent of the American experiment was because he equipped and enforced civility and morality. Moral absolutes (like the Ten Commandments) affect morals absolutely. Immanuel ("God with Us") is at the heart of ethics. And when He is ignored or avoided, character is compromised and culture is corrupted.

Ethics (the practice of morality) is the foundation of a healthy character, family, and country. If ethics wane, so goes the people and eventually the nation. As Founding Father Elias Boudinot once said: "If the moral character of a people once degenerate, their political character must soon follow."[15]

Case in point.

President Obama promised during his campaign to "clean up both ends of Pennsylvania Avenue" with "the most sweeping ethics reform in history."[16] He   repeatedly declared that "an Obama administration is going to have the toughest ethics laws of any administration in history."[17] I would assume administration means the whole group of leaders.

But in just its first year, this administration has already been plagued with a series of personnel problems, from past infidelity to tax evasion and abuses of political power and use of Chicago-style politics.

First, there was New Mexico Governor Bill Richardson, who withdrew his name from consideration as Commerce Secretary because of a grand jury investigation into whether donations to his political committees were mingled with state contracts.

Second, there was William J. Lynn III, a lobbyist for a major military contractor, slated to become the number 2 at the Defense Department.[18]

Third, there was Treasury Secretary Timothy Geithner's nomination, which somehow squeezed through Congress, despite his failing to pay more than $34,000 in self-employment taxes.

Fourth, there was former Treasury official Nancy Killefer who withdrew her name as the government's first chief performance officer because of not paying her taxes.

Fifth, there was Senate majority leader Thomas A. Daschle, who withdrew his name to lead the Department of Health and Human Services, but only after a barrage of confrontation over his failure to pay $146,000 in taxes.

Sixth, there was Representative Hilda Solis, Obama's nominee to be Labor Secretary,[19] whose husband had to pay $6,400 in tax liens against his business—some outstanding for sixteen years. (But she claims innocence and even press secretary Robert Gibbs said, "We're not going to penalize her for her husband's business mistakes." Is her husband's business and money not also hers? Have you ever noticed how nothing is anyone's fault anymore?)

And then there was lucky number seven:[20] Obama nominated David Ogden to be the Deputy Attorney General—the second person in command in the U.S. office of the Attorney General. According to the American Family Association, as an attorney in private practice, Ogden has filed briefs opposing parental notification before a minor's abortion as well as the Children's Internet Protection Act and the Child Protection and Obscenity Enforcement Act. He has also litigated numerous obscenity and pornography cases on behalf of clients like Playboy, Penthouse, the ACLU and the largest distributor of hard-core pornographic movies.

Is Ogden's nomination a part of "the most sweeping ethics reform in history" too?

With more than ninety thousand names of registered sex offenders turned over from MySpace alone,[21] do we really want one more high-ranking politician who is soft on sexual crime and immoralities?[22]

Am I missing something? Remember when tax evasion was a crime? Remember when porn was bad? Remember when lying came in other colors but white? Remember when ethics actually mattered in our choices for politicians? Remember when there were expected moral standards for leaders? Remember when politicians were role models?

Personnel problems didn't just plague the opening months of the Obama administration. In the fall of 2009, White House green jobs adviser Van Jones resigned after evidence of him was exposed that he wondered if the (Bush) government caused 9/11, used a vulgar expression to describe Republicans, and, in 2005, was quoted in a California Bay Area publication describing the impact of the acquittals in the police beating case of Rodney King in 1992: "By August, I was a Communist."[23]

Van Jones joined a long line of about two dozen special advisers or "czars" appointed by the Obama administration but unauthorized by Congress and against whom bi-partisan opposition by politicians and the public had been mounting. Senator Lamar Alexander, the third-ranking Republican in the Senate, called the czars "an affront to the Constitution" since they were not approved by Congress.[24]

Have we grown so calloused of political indiscretions and corruption that we don't care about any leader's ethical and moral standings anymore? Do we really want controversial cabinet members running our country? Are we supposing they will help usher in the "most sweeping ethics reform in history"?

I heard leadership guru John Maxwell once say, "We replicate that which we are." He also described the "law of the cap,"[25] a leadership growth truth that an organization cannot grow any greater (higher or deeper) than the personal health of its leadership. That has troubled me as I watched President Obama appoint his administrative leadership team and advisers.

Of course, illegalities, immoralities, and other ethic violations have existed in every age, including our Founders, but they weren't as readily accepted and tolerated as they are today. Most led good, moral, and decent lives. And most fought to elect those who would do the same, and so should and can we.

After more than a half-dozen failed appointees, I know Obama told multiple network news stations in a dozen different ways, "I screwed up" and "Nobody is perfect."[26] I have made my share of mistakes too, but I'm not the president and I didn't promise all Americans to make historic ethic reforms in Washington. I'm all for *mea culpas* but what about my country?

The fact is Obama has at his disposal more resources than any corporation on the planet to do a battery of background and psychological tests before even nominating anyone, but is he using them? Does he really have so few moral candidates from whom to choose that the only qualified ones are those who have straddled and gone over the ethical edge? All the vetting in the world won't matter if one ignores the Almighty.

Call me Pollyannaish, but I believe leadership should be exemplary. I believe leadership should be above reproach. And if Obama can't find an ethical criteria for choosing other politicians, then let me pass along some advice from our Founding Fathers.

THE BASIS FOR MORALITY AND CIVILITY

Whatever happened to decency, respect, and fair play? Remember when a handshake was the only contract needed in negotiations? Whatever happened to the days when fourteen-year-olds (like the young George Washington) set themselves to learn and write out freehand by their own volition the *110 Rules of Civility & Decent Behavior in Company and Conversation*[27] (a book written by Jesuits for the instruction of young gentlemen)?

Most of the people reading this book are probably, like I am, advocates of strong law and order. But we also know that morality comes before law and that bad laws can actually create more immorality. The worse things get, the greater the temptation to write endless, often counterproductive, laws. I believe it is more effective not to add a new statute book of law—we already have plenty of laws—but to return to the statute book of morality that makes fewer laws necessary. As Samuel Adams said, "Nothing is more essential to the establishment of manners in a State than that all persons employed in places of power and trust must be men of [exceptional] characters."[28] If we elected exceptional characters into every office, we wouldn't have half the problems we do now in governing positions.

Good morals precede good laws, which is why government isn't much help. Unless the people and their legislators are grounded in morality, the best of laws will be broken and the worst of laws will be made, legalizing immorality. We can't look to government to improve decency, civility, and morality. For that we need to look to another source.

John Adams put it well when he said:

> We have no government armed with power capable of contending with human passions unbridled by morality and religion. Avarice, ambition, revenge, or gallantry, would break the strongest cords of our Constitution as a whale goes through a net.

Our Constitution was made only for a moral and religious people. It is wholly inadequate to the government of any other.

Government isn't the answer. And neither is education, at least without religion. As Benjamin Rush, also a signer of the Declaration of Independence, explained, "Without religion, I believe that learning does real mischief to the morals and principles of mankind."[29]

Our Founders had a better answer than government or even education. God is the answer. God is the moral compass of America. Or He should be, if we ever want to restore morality in our homes and civility to our land. Our Founders believed morals flowed from one's accountability to God, and that, without God, immoral anarchy would result. John Quincy Adams believed there were "three points of doctrine, the belief of which forms the foundation of all morality." He explained them:

The first is the existence of a God; the second is the immortality of the human soul; and the third is a future state of rewards and punishments. Suppose it possible for a man to disbelieve either of these articles of faith and that man will have no conscience, he will have no other law than that of the tiger or the shark; the laws of man may bind him in chains or may put him to death, but they never can make him wise, virtuous, or happy.[30]

To the Founders, religion was an essential buttress of free government. That is why Patrick Henry wrote, "The greatest pillars of all government and of social life: I mean virtue, morality, and religion. This is the armor, my friend, and this alone, that renders us invincible."[31]

Charles Carroll of Carollton, a Catholic who signed the Declaration of Independence on behalf of Maryland, wrote, "Without morals a republic cannot subsist any length of time; they therefore who are decrying the Christian religion whose morality is so sublime and pure . . . are undermining the solid foundation of morals, the best security for the duration of free governments."[32]

George Washington put it best in his Farewell Address:

> Of all the dispositions and habits which lead to political prosperity, religion and morality are indispensable supports. In vain would that man claim the tribute of patriotism, who should labor to subvert these great pillars of human happiness, these firmest props of the duties of men and citizens. The mere politician, equally with the pious man, ought to respect and to cherish them. A volume could not trace all their connections with private and public felicity. Let it simply be asked: Where is the security for property, for reputation, for life, if the sense of religious obligation deserts the oaths which are the instruments of investigation in courts of justice? And let us with caution indulge the supposition that morality can be maintained without religion. Whatever may be conceded to the influence of refined education on minds of peculiar structure, reason and experience both forbid us to expect that national morality can prevail in exclusion of religious principle.[33]

The Founders were men of the Bible and in that book of books it says, "Blessed is the nation whose God is the Lord."[34] It is unlikely, to say the least, that they would have been optimistic for an America that decided to abandon God and repudiate His moral commandments. And it is ironic that, in our own time, the public display of the Ten Commandments, which the Founders regarded as a fundamental basis of American law, has become controversial. John Quincy Adams, who bore arms during the Revolution and served under four presidents before he became one, believed that "the Law given from Sinai [the Ten Commandments] was a civil and municipal as well as a moral and religious code."[35] Noah Webster, who helped draft the Constitution, explained two centuries ago: "The duties of men are summarily comprised in the Ten Commandments, consisting of two tables; one comprehending the duties which we owe immediately to God—the other, the duties we owe to our fellow men. . . ." John Witherspoon, president of Princeton and signer of the Declaration (and one who served on over one hundred committees while in Congress) declared: "The Ten Commandments . . . are the sum of the moral law."[36]

Given the emphasis the Founders placed on the religious foundation of our republic, they would surely be shocked to see that prayer has been abolished from taxpayer-supported schools, that such schools are prohibited from teaching the Bible, and that such schools assume and teach that religion is not essential to life and learning (because religion, unlike everything else, is kept out of the classroom).

They would be astounded that the Ten Commandments have been removed from public buildings. They would be dumbfounded that acknowledging the Creator God that they acknowledged is regarded as impermissible at school commencement exercises. They would be mortified that a coach praying with his student athletes at taxpayer-supported schools could be prosecuted for allegedly violating the Constitution that guarantees that Congress shall make no law abridging the free expression of religion. They would be filled with dread at our too easy acceptance of such government intrusion—call it judicial tyranny—on our natural (God-given) rights and liberties.

Friends, I am a patriot and an optimist at heart. I, as with many of you, believe that we can become a great nation again, known more for who we are than what we have. But that's not going to happen by traveling down the same road we've been on. If America has lost its moral compass, the answer is to return to the old path, the path followed by our Founders who put God first, trusting in Him—not big government—to be our salvation. The most important action you and I can take is to do that in our own lives: to put God first and raise up a new generation of decent, law-abiding, people-loving, and God-fearing citizens.

And there is hope! A recent poll taken over nine countries (the United States, Britain, France, Germany, the Netherlands, Italy,

Spain, Russia, and Poland) concluded that America was "the world's most 'Bible-literate' people." Seventy-five percent of Americans had at least cracked open a Bible over the last year. In the other nine countries surveyed, only 20 to 38 percent could affirm that.[37] If Americans put God first, in the Judeo-Christian tradition of this nation, then they will put the golden rule first, and they will at least strive to be good fathers, good mothers, good neighbors, good friends, and good citizens.

Want to help America? That is the decision before us: to be a part of the solution or a part of the problem. John Witherspoon said, "He is the best friend to American liberty, who is most sincere and active in promoting true and undefiled religion, and who sets himself with the greatest firmness to bear down on profanity and immorality of every kind. Whoever is an avowed enemy of God, I scruple not to call him an enemy to his country."[38]

To make America a better, more decent, more civil place, to become a nation that once again puts its faith not in laws and man, not in the big government solutions, but in the freedom and responsibility of liberty safeguarded by morality, we need to make God first in our lives. To be faithful to the Founders we need to be faithful to the Creator—the Creator they believed was the providential guide of our destiny.

MY RETURN TO THE CREATOR

I guess this would be the best time to tell you why I'm so passionate about writing this book and this particular chapter.

It goes all the way back to when I was being raised by my mom. My dad was an alcoholic and philanderer and was hardly ever around. We had to live on welfare for years, but Mom was always optimistic and would reassure me and my brothers that God will never abandon us. Mom was a strong Christian woman who kept us boys in church. I accepted Jesus Christ as my savior at the age of twelve and was baptized. Mom constantly reminded us that without God, you will have empty lives, no matter how much money you make. I never knew how true those words would be until later in life.

After earning my black belt in the Martial Arts in Korea, I went on to a successful career as a fighter and instructor, leading me into the world of entertainment. I have done twenty-three movies and 203 episodes of *Walker, Texas Ranger*. During my twenty-five years as an actor, my faith would be tested and I would succumb to the sweetness of fame and fortune. It cost me my first marriage and, despite my driven and optimistic attitude, I drifted farther and farther from my faith. I'm not saying I didn't still believe in God, but I moved Him from my heart to my head. I kept Him there so He wouldn't interfere with my decadent lifestyle.

God would periodically send messengers into my life to remind me, "He still loved me." One messenger was a young man named Lee Atwater, who was George H. W. Bush's campaign manager. We became very close friends.

When Lee was diagnosed with a malignant brain tumor and was lying in bed near death, I was allowed to see him and tell him good-bye. As I was standing at the foot of his hospital bed, Lee motioned for me to come closer. I went up to Lee and bent down to hear what he was trying to say to me. He whispered in my ear, "Trust in the Lord, Chuck, I love you." As he said that, the hairs stood up on the back of my neck and I felt an incredible ache in my heart.

I kissed him on the forehead and walked out of the room. I was so full of emotion I burst out crying.

While I was filming the *Walker* series, I invited one of my best friends, Larry Morales, to Dallas to do a part on the show. While we were sitting out in the back yard of my house after filming all day, I was having drink after drink. Larry knew I was miserable, but trying hard to cover it up. Out of the blue, Larry said, "I have someone I want you to meet. She is a special lady and I think you would really like her. Can I invite her to Dallas?" I said, "Sure," only half listening. Gena came to Dallas and I was (to use a passionate term) smitten with her from the start. Little did I know she would become my beloved wife, best friend, and the instrument to renewing my spiritual life.

After Gena and I were married, she, being a very strong Christian, would read the Bible every morning. I would see her reading the Bible and she would ask me if I would like to sit down and join her, but I would always find something else to do. Finally one morning I did sit down, thinking I would just placate her, but for some reason I kept doing it. As time went on God's Word was beginning to penetrate my heart. One morning I took the Bible from Gena and began reading to her. As I'm reading, I look up and see this big smile on her face. As time went on I heard the Holy Spirit say to me, "It's time to come back home, you've been gone too long." Then the most amazing thing happened: the hole in my heart was filled. That was nine years ago (at this writing) and I'm not about to leave home again.

You see, even though I thought I had everything: money, fame, etc., I had nothing but a huge hole in my heart. I finally understood what Mom told me over fifty years ago and our Founders told us more than two hundred years ago: "Without God, we will have empty lives."

CHAPTER SIX

★ ★ ★

Reclaim the Value of Human Life

TWELVE DAYS into my wife Gena's pregnancy with our twins, she developed a severe case of Ovarian Hyperstimulation Syndrome, a complication from fertility medications. Her abdomen swelled up with fluid called Ascites, making her look like she was already nine months pregnant. Her ovaries were the size of footballs. The fluid caused so much pressure on her internal organs that she needed oxygen to breathe.

Gena's condition was critical and the doctor stated she had just two options. Because there was no immediate remedy, she could choose to try and ride out the long, painful, and unpredictable road to recovery, realizing she and the twins' lives were hanging in the balance. Or she could abort the pregnancy. Gena and I felt vulnerable and helpless.

Many of our well-meaning friends and family advised us to abort the pregnancy. Gena and I talked and prayed together about what we should do.

Then Gena shared with me the story of what happened to her during the embryo transfer. Our babies were just two days old. Gena was lying on the hospital bed in the small procedure room, nervously waiting for the embryos to be transferred into her womb.

The nurse asked the doctor to show my wife something. Agreeably the doctor shook her head yes and the nurse elevated the head of Gena's bed. What she saw had the appearance of a window encased in solid steel. Fascinated and curious, Gena thought whatever is behind that secured window must be of great value.

As the doctor opened the steel plated door exposing the window, a bright light illuminated out. What followed the light is what changed Gena's view of conception forever. She was listening to the most beautiful classical music she had ever heard, being quietly played to our two-day-old unborn children. At that very moment she realized these doctors knew embryos responded well and had a better chance at survival when provided with a life-enriching environment such as this. Gena was forever changed at that moment. She realized that human life truly begins at conception.

After Gena conveyed her experience, she asked me, "Why would God be so gracious to bless us with these two miracles of life if He was not going to see us through this pregnancy? We need to trust Him!" I agreed with her. We should follow what our hearts were telling us was the right thing to do. I then looked at her and said, "Honey, this has changed me too, for I also questioned when life truly began."

This was just the beginning of a long journey, and God's lessons along the way, to the birth of our twins, Dakota and Danilee, who are now eight years old.

HUMAN LIFE IN EARLY AMERICA

Our Founders shared the same view of human life and conception—that humanity was special, unique, and set apart from the rest of creation. And it affected how they treated people, from the political arenas to their personal life. In fact, in early America there were two basic beliefs that shaped most people's view of humanity: that God created us and that we were created equal. Most early Americans believed humans were the highest creation of God. Their views were based in the Bible and expressed in the Declaration of Independence.

> Then God said, "Let Us make man in Our image, according to Our likeness." And God created man in His own image, in the image of God He created him; male and female He created them.[1]
>
> We hold these truths to be self-evident, that all men are created equal, that they are endowed by their Creator with certain unalienable Rights, that among these are Life, Liberty and the pursuit of Happiness.

The Founders believed equality would give legs to freedom. As John Adams said, "We should begin by setting conscience free. When all men of all religions . . . shall enjoy equal liberty, property, and an equal chance for honors and power . . . we may expect that improvements will be made in the human character and the state of society."[2]

The Founders knew America was not perfect. Slavery, in particular, troubled the consciences of many of them. And the Founders themselves, of course, were imperfect. They were human. As George Washington wrote, "We must take human nature as we find it. Perfection falls not to the share of mortals."[3]

Nevertheless, our Founders believed there was something inherent in humanity that called it to a higher purpose. For all the shortcomings of early American society, the remedy was always there—expressed in the founding documents of our nation.

The Declaration of Independence set America's course. Though we have sometimes drifted from its highest principles, all Americans have ever had to do was steer by its compass to acknowledge or rediscover the inherent equality of slaves, women,[4] the poor, Indians, and the unborn. All were—and are—

children of God, endowed by their creator with "certain unalienable rights." As John Adams wrote:

> The dons, the bashaws, the grandees, the patricians, the sachems, the nabobs, call them by what names you please, sigh and groan and fret, and sometimes stamp and foam and curse, but all in vain. The decree is gone forth, and it cannot be recalled, that a more equal liberty than has prevailed in other parts of the earth must be established in America.[5]

The Declaration of Independence announced to the whole world that America was established upon the biblical belief that "all men are created equal." When it came to slavery, George Washington said, "There is not a man living who wishes more sincerely than I do, to see a plan adopted for the abolition of it."[6] John Adams said: "Every measure of prudence, therefore, ought to be assumed for the eventual total extirpation of slavery from the United States. . . . I have, through my whole life, held the practice of slavery in . . . abhorrence."

According to Benjamin Franklin: "Slavery is . . . an atrocious debasement of human nature." Alexander Hamilton noted: "The laws of certain states . . . give an ownership in the service of Negroes as personal property. . . . But being men, by the laws of God and nature, they were capable of acquiring liberty—and when the captor in war [the British army] . . . thought fit to give them liberty, the gift was not only valid, but irrevocable." And James Madison confessed: "We have seen the mere distinction of color made in the most enlightened period of time, a ground of the most oppressive dominion ever exercised by man over man."[7]

The Founders could not immediately abolish slavery. It was too entrenched in the economy of the South, but the Declaration eroded its foundations in a way that made its end inevitable. That "all men are created equal, that they are endowed by their Creator with certain unalienable rights" is one of the most powerful principles ever enunciated in the history of politics.

THE DESCENT OF MAN

But treating others with respect, dignity, and value is not exactly an American trait or forte today. How often do you see offenses to the dignity of others? How often do you see rudeness, lack of consideration, flagrant disrespect of other people? Every day on television? Nightly on the news? At home, school, or work? Every time you read postings on the Internet? In all those forums, you've probably never heard anyone say, "You can't treat people like that. All of us are made in the image of God." But America and the rest of the world would be better places if we did.

Today the Declaration of Independence is a historical document encased under bulletproof glass in Washington, D.C. It's something tourists go to see, like all the relics of the past. It reminds us of a valiant time when men fought to gain our independence from Britain. But it should be more than that. It should be a living document. It should be a constant reminder and challenge to us to live up to its ideals, to remember that all men are created equal, to treat one another fairly.

Do we still need the Declaration of Independence? More than ever. We are in dire need of reminding that all men are, indeed, created equal. If we held those words to heart, we would be reminded of what some of us were once taught as the golden rule: to do unto others as we would have done unto us.

But how often do we see that simple truth put into practice today? On the contrary, we see it violated every day. And when common civility is no longer common, what do people do (besides behave in rude, vulgar, nasty, disloyal, disrespectful, violent, and even criminal ways)? They turn to the courts, and we become a nation of lawsuits; they turn to government—big government—to take care of our needs and legislate away our freedoms.

We got this way by abandoning the past, by debunking tradition, by trading the Good Book for the pocketbook. We've redefined life in a more selfish way: it's all about me. The way we treat one another proves it.

The problem comes down to our basic view of the world and one another. Many of us no longer think that man is the pinnacle of creation, with obligations both to God and to our fellow man. Instead, too many of us think we are the product of random chance and selection, ultimately no different than cockroaches; and in such circumstances selfishness is a virtue, or at least no vice.

My nephew Andrew Cox, is a strong young Christian man, was in the fifth grade when his teacher, a young lady who graduated from the University of Berkeley, told the class to write a report about evolution. Andrew said he couldn't do that because he didn't believe in evolution. He went on to say he believed God was our Creator and creator of the heavens and the earth. The teacher gave him an "F" instead of allowing him to write about what he believed in based on his own convictions. Throughout the year, the teacher would ask Andrew in the midst of any subject being taught, "What would your Jesus say about that?"

When Andrew went into the sixth grade, he ended up with the same teacher and she harassed him again all year about his Christian beliefs. Andrew's parents complained many times about the teacher harassing him, but it did no good. She kept on harassing him.

His parents said if she followed him again to junior high that they would file a lawsuit. Thankfully she didn't, but this young boy had to endure two years of ridicule for having the moral courage to stand up for what he believed in from an extremely liberal young lady. But he did and rather than believe he was a glorified ape, he believed he was a child of God made in His image. He is in Army Intelligence now, serving our country in Iraq.

Thank God my nephew believed better about himself. And shame on that teacher for trying to usurp his family's views and values of humanity. And replace them with what? In her view, humanity has no inherent value. People are disposable. Abortion is the quintessential example of this. It is the killing of an "inconvenient" human life. Abortion is not about a woman's "right to choose"; it is about a more fundamental "right to life," which is one of three specifically identified unalienable rights in the Declaration (and the Constitution through Article VII and the Bill of Rights). And it is a violation of government's primary purpose: to protect innocent life.

Under our Constitution, the federal government should protect that right to life. But besides affirming that foundational human right, the details of the laws governing abortion should be left to the states. Despite the Supreme Court's unconstitutional striking down of abortion laws nationwide in 1973 and instituting a completely unconstitutional federal right to abortion, there is still much we can do at the state level to protect human life by promoting pro-life legislation and education.

Some people think after thirty-five years of ceaseless controversy since the Supreme Court's ruling in *Roe v. Wade* that abortion is an "old" issue better dropped. But as my friend and prolific author Randy Alcorn wrote, "Abortion has set us on a dangerous course. We may come to our senses and back away from the slippery slope. Or we may follow it to its inescapable conclusion—a society in which the powerful, for their self-interest, determine which human beings will live and which will die."[8]

Thomas Jefferson wrote in 1809, "The care of human life and happiness, and not their destruction, is the first and only legitimate object of good government."[9] He was not, of course, writing about the America of today, with state-sanctioned and subsidized abortion, and a movement to promote the killing of the elderly through euthanasia. But he could have been. And his belief in what should be "the first and only legitimate object of government" should still stand.

FIRST PRINCIPLES

But Thomas Jefferson's views of government and human life are far from that of the present administration. I must confess I am shocked that President Obama, who claims to be a valiant warrior for minorities, is such a crusader for extending abortion rights and terminating human life in the womb. Nevertheless, I forget that he too is a product of his culture, being raised in the context of human devaluation that I just outlined.

Therefore, it should not come as a surprise that Obama emphatically promised during his presidential campaign that "The first thing I'd do as president is sign the Freedom of Choice Act. That's the first thing that I'd do."[10] Whether or not he would immediately live up to that pledge, it still states his priority and value for life in the womb.

For those who might not know, The Freedom of Choice Act (FOCA)[11] is a sweeping bill that would abolish all pro-life regulations across the nation, from parental notification laws to bans on federal funding of abortion.[12] The Office of the General Counsel for the U.S. Conference of Catholic Bishops has identified thirteen categories of pro-life laws that would be stampeded and nullified by FOCA.[13] As far reaching as the decision of *Roe v. Wade* is into the States' jurisdictions and our lives, even it, for example, showed certain respects for state laws and limits on infringing regulations in the medical fields. FOCA shows no such restraints, but nails shut the coffin on pro-life choices and safeguards.

And why has Obama pledged his allegiance to pass FOCA? Not only because he has the most passionately liberal pro-choice record of nearly any president to date,[14] but, as he told a meeting of Planned Parenthood during his campaign, "it is time to turn the page"[15] to a new day when pro-life views, laws, and debate on abortion are passé.

And if he and the Democratic majority have their way, America will have that new day, one in which hundreds of thousands more abortions will be performed annually.

The fight to pass FOCA is being waged despite a nationwide survey revealing that four out of five U.S. adults (82 percent) would limit abortion's legality.[16] One out of three (38 percent) would limit abortion to rape, incest, or to save the mother's life.

One out of three (33 percent) would also limit abortion to either the first three or first six months. Only nine percent said abortion should be legal for any reason at any time during pregnancy. These statistics are in stark contrast to the goals and objectives of FOCA, which would close the culture debate on abortion in an unprecedented way for any piece of legislation.[17]

The truth is, when our country elected Obama as president, we placed a man in the highest office in the land who has the most liberal views and voting record on abortion of any president in American history.[18] As a state senator in Illinois, he led opposition three years in a row (2001–2003) to a bill similar to the Born-Alive Infants Protection Act, which prevents the killing of babies unintentionally left alive by abortion. He also opposed the ban on partial-birth abortion, and strongly disapproved of the Supreme Court decision upholding the partial-birth ban. He does not support the Hyde Amendment, which prohibits taxpayer funding of abortion through Medicaid. He also voted to block a bill that would have required a doctor to notify at least one parent before performing an abortion on a minor girl from another state. Strangely, Obama even once said he would not want his daughters to be "punished with a baby" due to an unwanted pregnancy.[19]

Since assuming the presidency, Obama has pushed pro-choice platforms and practices in ways America hasn't seen since the original 1973 *Roe v. Wade* ruling. Obama overturned the "Mexico City Policy," now allowing federal funds to support international family planning groups who provide abortions.[20] Restrictions for federal funding for embryonic stem cell research have been lifted. And FOCA is closing fast on the political horizon.[21]

America doesn't need to "turn the page" on culture wars like abortion; it needs to reopen the pages of its history to our Founders heightened views and rights of all human beings as documented in the Declaration of Independence and our Constitution.

And we need to revive and re-instill that value of humanity back into society, our children, and our children's children.

But to get back to Jefferson's view, we need to get back to a view of humanity that emphasizes the immortal worth of every human being. Without that, we can never believe all men are created equal, that they have inherent, unalienable rights, and that the protection of those rights is "the first and only legitimate object of good government."

I believe in a Creator. I believe people are made in the image of God. I try to treat people that way. And I firmly believe that if we want to restore civility, responsibility, and the first principles of free government, we need to allow God not only into our private lives, but into our public life as well. God should not be banned from the classroom. Excluding God while requiring Darwin in taxpayer-supported schools is *not* a requirement of the First Amendment; in fact it is a violation of it—abridging the free expression of religion and giving a state-sponsored monopoly to a secularist, evolutionist view of the world.

EDUCATIONAL FREEDOM

Others more qualified than I can debate evolution,[22] but I do know that most of our Founders were enthusiastic advocates for teaching religion and the Bible in public schools. Benjamin Rush wrote, "Let the children who are sent to those schools be taught to read and write and above all, let both sexes be carefully instructed in the principles and obligations of the Christian religion. This is the most essential part of education."[23]

George Washington once addressed some Delaware chiefs among the Lenape Indians, who desired to train their young people in American schools, saying, "You do well to wish to learn our arts and ways of life, and above all, the religion of Jesus Christ. These will make you a greater and happier people than you are. Congress will do everything they can to assist you in this wise intention."

Gouverneur Morris, who represented Pennsylvania at the Constitutional Convention in Philadelphia in 1787 and subsequently signed the U.S. Constitution, said: "Religion is the only solid basis of good morals; therefore education should teach the precepts of religion and the duties of man towards God."

If America's Founding Fathers had no problem with the Bible being taught in taxpayer-supported schools, why do we? The Bible is the most influential book in Western civilization. It is the most important book undergirding American law and literature. To prohibit it from our nation's classrooms is a blatant and biased withholding of proper public instruction.

It's time for every parent, teacher, and school district to answer in the affirmative the question of Fisher Ames, who assisted in the creation of the First Amendment and was also chosen but declined (for health reasons) the presidency of Harvard University in 1805: "Should not the Bible regain the place it once held as a school book?"

Our Founding Fathers would respond with a resounding yes.

That is also why my wife Gena and I are on the board of "The National Council of Bible Curriculum in Public Schools," which is helping our schools implement an elective course on the Bible as history and literature. Roughly 443 public school districts in thirty-seven states are offering a course on it, and 210,000 students have already been taught from it. You too can learn more about the curriculum, why its teaching is constitutional, and how it can be implemented in your public school by contacting:

National Council On Bible Curriculum In Public Schools Post Office Box 9743, Greensboro, North Carolina 27429, (877) OnBible (336) 272-3799, (336) 272-7199 (fax), www.bibleinschools.net

THE FOUNDING CREATIONISTS

Evolution has been around a lot longer than Darwin. The Founding Fathers were familiar with the arguments for and against theism and naturalism. These arguments date back millennia.[24] And the Founders' views on the subject are as relevant today as they were in their own time.

Thomas Paine was probably the most outspoken against religion among the Founders, yet even he stood up for the idea of a Creator God:

> It has been the error of schools to teach astronomy, and all the other sciences and subjects of natural philosophy, as accomplishments only; whereas they should be taught theologically, or with reference to the Being who is the Author of them: for all the principles of science are of divine origin. Man cannot make, or invent, or contrive principles; he can only discover them, and he ought to look through the discovery to the Author.[25]

Benjamin Franklin echoed his affirmation of a Creator:

> For, if weak and foolish creatures as we are, but knowing the nature of a few things, can produce such wonderful effects . . . what power must He possess, Who not only knows the nature of everything in the universe but can make things of new natures with the greatest ease and at His pleasure! Agreeing, then, that the world was first made by a Being of infinite wisdom, goodness, and power, which Being we call God.[26]

John Adams put an interesting twist on describing those who pretend to understand the ins and outs of everything in the universe:

It has been long—very long—a settled opinion in my mind that there is not now, never will be, and never was but one Being who can understand the universe, and that it is not only vain but wicked for insects [like us] to pretend to comprehend it.

John Quincy Adams wrote:

It is so obvious to every reasonable being, that [God] did not make himself; and the world which he inhabits could as little make itself that the moment we begin to exercise the power of reflection, it seems impossible to escape the conviction that there is a Creator.[27] . . . [T]he first words of the Bible are, "In the beginning God created the heavens and the earth."[28]

While the Founders differed in their denominations and detailed theological beliefs and religious practices, they were united in acknowledging a Creator God and in understanding that such belief was essential to education and the free republic they envisioned and created.

RECLAIMING THE "WOW" FACTOR

Several years ago, Gena and I went on a safari vacation to Africa. During our trip, we got to do all the exciting things, such as visiting the Finch Diamond Mine, going down to a depth of more than one thousand feet watching them dig for diamonds. Then we visited the Kimberly Diamond House where thousands of diamonds were being separated and displayed right in front of us. We saw Bushmen doing their annual rain dance. Of course we saw lions, hippos, rhinos, and more.

But of all we saw, the most rewarding part of our trip was visiting an African elementary school. These youngsters had a glow in their eyes that could only come from happy little beings. These children monetarily had nothing, but in their hearts they have everything. There was a constant smile on their faces. They didn't know who I was, but they all hugged me and Gena to show their love and joy in us visiting them. I would love to see that same glow in the eyes of our children here in the states. The real diamonds of Africa don't come from mines but from the children. Our Founders' wisdom works in Africa as well as America.

Of course, we can't just mandate the beliefs of the Founders. If we are going to restore a theistic view of man as an essential underpinning of good behavior and good government, we need to start where we live. My friend Gary Smalley, a prolific author, speaker, and counselor on marriage and family, encourages people to do what he did while raising his children. He would randomly exclaim as he looked at his kids, "Wow! Look at that! The greatest creation of God!" His children were sometimes embarrassed when he did this in front of their friends, but later in life they thanked him for instilling in them a sense of value and wonder for God's creation. We need to value one another the way Gary values his kids.

We need to let our light—the light of civility, respect, and fairness—shine before the world. And it starts by brightening the corner where we are, even in the face of adversity and dark times.

Let's be honest. It won't be easy. It's not easy. It gets discouraging just seeing how darkness has prevailed over our land. Everything seems to tell us we can't win—we're not good enough, strong enough, valiant enough, good looking enough, worth enough, rich enough, or tenacious enough to overcome. I used to hear those voices all the time when I was trying to break into the movie business at thirty-four years of age. But, as the old adage goes, we'll never know until we try, and especially unless we believe there is something within us that can still make a difference.

That mentality is exactly the one that brought the heroes and heroines victory in the fourth book of the classic Chronicles of Narnia series by C. S. Lewis, *Prince Caspian*. In it four young people, Lucy, Edmund, Susan, and Peter, return to an old, war-torn, fictitious island of Narnia through a porthole that opened while the children were waiting for a train in an English station. It is a time much removed from when they first entered Narnia through the English closet in *The Lion, the Witch, and the Wardrobe*. Now, in the face of adversity, without the physical presence of their fearless leader Aslan (the lion who represents God and Jesus), the children must assist Prince Caspian to overthrow the evil King Mirax and restore Narnia to its glory days. But the odds are clearly against them, at least from their perspective. For Prince Caspian, who is the king's nephew and son of the murdered rightful king, and the children, this is a daunting task that easily prompts them to feel doubt and fear. It will take faith to overcome. It will take courage. It will take them being united. It will take time. But first it will take them all remembering who they are, or were, and what they still have the potential of doing. And it is from that vantage point that Aslan reminded their hearts (and, might I add, ours as well): "'You come of the Lord Adam and the Lady Eve. And that is both honour enough to erect the head of the poorest beggar, and shame enough to bow the shoulders of the greatest emperor in earth.'"

★ ★ ★

CHAPTER SEVEN

Calling All Millennials!

THERE ARE SOME GREAT stories about the influence of teenagers in the Revolutionary War. C. Brian Kelly's enjoyable work, *Best Little Stories from the American Revolution*, includes at least a few of them. One in particular is about the Marquis de Lafayette, who was only sixteen years old when he joined the Black Musketeers, an elite unit of royal troops who rode black horses. After the Black Musketeers were disbanded in 1776, Lafayette volunteered to fight in the Revolutionary War. Congress granted the nineteen-year-old Frenchman the temporary rank of major general.

Lafayette became a favorite of George Washington because he was never discouraged, always brave, and a true battlefield commander, unfazed by wounds or setbacks. Two months after the British surrender at Yorktown, Lafayette returned home as a "hero of two worlds."[1]

It's amazing for us today to think about how much this young Lafayette sacrificed and accomplished for our country and his own back then. We are still inspired by that type of youthful courage and heroism. However, quite frankly, most adults would say it rarely exists anymore. But, as I meet and hear from young

Americans here and around the world, I beg to differ. While our society often denigrates the teen years and values very little from them, I believe there exists a latent power in this particular generation of young people (called the Millennials) that waits to be awakened and reveal its full potential. We clearly see it when it's called upon. It's easily observable in action, as our young service men and women have demonstrated in Iraq and Afghanistan. Despite how we feel about the war, there's no mistaking our troops' resiliency and fortitude. While we debate the success of surges, they are overseas accomplishing them. And just as Lafayette returned home to a hero's welcome, so should each of them, who bravely serve in harm's way. They deserve nothing less than a hero's welcome when they return home as well.

THE DISCONNECT

There is no doubt the America of today is not the America for which Lafayette and Washington fought. They associated freedom with virtue. Today, virtue is forgotten and freedom is an excuse. We know the statistics about drug use and drinking among teens. We know that sexually transmitted diseases are an epidemic among young people.[2] But what would Washington and Lafayette make of taxpayer-supported schools teaching and supporting homosexuality, bisexuality, and "transgender sexuality" as alternative lifestyles? What would they think of the pornography that floods our electronic media? What would they think about young people who, on average, spend seventy hours a week plugged into electronic media, which is often saturated in violence, sex, abusive language, and behavior? I think they'd be appalled.

Sin is not new, and the time of our Founding Fathers was not perfect, but immorality among people was shunned, and certainly not catered to, in those days. It was assumed young people would abide by the Judeo-Christian morality of the Bible, which they were taught (often at public expense). Young people were to be prepared to work, to serve apprenticeships, to be educated to be leaders, to live moral lives, and to carry on the American legacy. Their lives then had purpose, which too many teens today—who are taught that there is no higher goal than self-indulgence—lack, with devastating effects.

THE RECONNECT

We can picture the generations of Americans running a relay race, as one generation passes the baton to the next. Unfortunately we dropped the baton several laps ago. We've left a Baby-Boomer generation who see no point to life beyond gathering up as much stuff and money as they can as quickly as they can. Beyond them are the Generation Xers, or Baby-Buster generation, who grew up with Kurt Cobain and Starbucks, and who were disillusioned by materialism and prosperity and so went back to simpler times. However, they didn't go back far enough. But now there are the Millennials—forty-seven million young adults between the ages of eighteen and twenty-nine.[3] These are young people who have grown up with technology. They use it for everything from listening to music, to getting jobs, to ordering everything they need, to dating and communicating with everyone they know and want to know. Though Millennials are not necessarily savvy to marketing ploys of the past, they are experts on the Internet and can use it almost single-handedly to do whatever they want, including raising up armies of collective consciousness and winning future elections. They are tired of wars, rumors of wars, and America's mentality that it must save the world. They prefer to feed the poor and encourage the downtrodden. They believe charity begins at home. (The Lord knows we have millions of people in America who need our assistance.) Their primary fight is socially conscious service. To them, government is some gargantuan gargoyle spiraling out of control. And they are willing to fight to get it under control but are not sure how. One thing they know for sure is that something different is needed in

Washington, and they are willing to do whatever is necessary to get the job done.

Millennials are the future of America but are not connected to its past. Due to our distortions and revisions of history and oversights in education, the Founders are simply folklore but not a legacy to follow. Young Americans are willing to move America forward, but don't see any other way ahead beyond the creation of a more socially conscious, domestically strong, globally peaceful nation. But we must help them to hear the voices of the distant past and that they share commonalities with early Americans.

But herein lies their potential soft spot: Millennials can too easily be swayed by slick sellers of tolerance and compassion, because jumping off the bandwagon of bigotry is their allegiance and generational calling card. From Popsicles to politics, truth can be too easily obscured, obliterated, and even abandoned, in their pursuit of domestic welfare, unity, and acceptance. That is why I don't (and we must not) shy away from encouraging and challenging Millennials' quest to broaden their thinking even to consider the potential benefits of and truths in those things their peers might generally refuse or oppose (like conservative beliefs, dogmatism, national security, government, etc.). It's good to have a healthy skepticism before you are sold on a decision, but we also want to caution throwing the baby out with the bathwater. As it says in Proverbs, "The wise in heart will be called discerning."[4]

If we're going to win the culture war, we need the Millennials to do it. There is no way around it. We need to reengage with our young people and plug them into America's glorious past so they can build a brighter future. I'm not trying to sell them on a patriotic platform (like Republicanism) but a patriot one (like our Founders had). I'm convinced that this is why Ron Paul's candidacy for president grew into a mighty grassroots swell—it tapped into the technologically and socially based Millenials, who possess a strong anti-imperialism, lets-take-care-of-home mentality and passion. That is a great message. But it might not be the total message.

THE MILLENNIAL MODELS

I believe my young friends, the twin brothers Brett and Alex Harris, are two model Millennials. I consider them cultural heroes or generational warriors, who are willing to bear the baton of early American values and beliefs and march forward with a battle cry to raise the expectations and contributions of following generations. They are on the front lines of battle for the Millennials. They possess the heart and gusto to reawaken their generation to the real American dream. At just sixteen, they were interns at the Alabama Supreme Court house. And at nineteen they wrote their first book, published in mid-2008—one I encourage everyone to read and give to a teenager or Millennial they know. The book is called *Do Hard Things: A Teenage Rebellion against Low Expectations*.[5]

Alex recently described the goal of the book and their conferences in an interview: "We're calling our peers to rethink the teen years and rebel against the low expectations society has for young people. The book is really the outgrowth of our conviction that God is doing something huge in our generation. We believe there is so much to the teen years and to life, and it starts with understanding the way God has created us to grow and thrive: by doing hard things."

There are five hard things they discuss in their book. The first is "hard things that take you outside your comfort zone." The second is "hard things that go beyond what is expected or required." The third is "hard things that are too big for you to do alone." The fourth is "hard things that don't pay off immediately." The fifth is "hard things that go against the crowd." Sounds like a book even adults can benefit from! I was so impressed by reading their book that I gladly wrote the foreword.

I believe the Harris brothers are absolutely correct when they say what our society needs most is not a revolution but a *rebelution*: a rebelling movement against the low expectations of young people today—a rising up of Millennials to take their rightful position as baton bearers of this great country. They explain, "We're not rebelling against institutions or even against people. Our uprising is against a cultural mindset that twists the purpose and potential of the teen years and threatens to cripple our generation. Our uprising won't be marked by mass riots and violence, but by millions of individual teens quietly choosing to turn the low expectations of our culture upside down."[6]

If you look at early American history (or biblical history), you'll see that great things were expected from young people—as workers, as leaders, as warriors, as young mothers and fathers. Doing chores and getting good grades, treating adolescence as a semi-restricted recreational vacation that can be extended into your twenties, is a pale and unworthy imitation of what life was like for young people in past eras. Alex and Brett are trying to help us raise the bar on youth potential. I say we do all we can to support them and others like them, especially by buying their books and encouraging others to attend their conferences.[7]

MY BATTLE PLAN TO FLANK THEIR ENEMIES

While Alex and Brett, and others like them, are battling on the front lines for their generation, I have a battle plan for the rest of us to flank the enemies of the youth and provide them safer arenas through which to march to success. We personally might not be able to relate to Millennials, but I guarantee you we can recognize their enemies and focus our energies on warding them off. In other words, we need to let them know: "We got your backs!"

My battle plan to do so can be summarized in four words: assist, protect, reconnect, and provide. You don't need to be a parent or grandparent to do these things. You just have to care— and we should all care about our future and about the precious lives entrusted to us here. No one's life is anything short of invaluable. We need to see the value in our teenagers, protect that value, and build them up. If we are going to see them succeed as successors to the present leaders of our nation, it is going to take a collective effort in which we all must take part.

Assist Youth

Last year several people asked me if I rescued a group of sailors off the coast of England. I hadn't. But someone with the nickname of "Chuck Norris" did.

On Thursday, January 18, 2007, the British container ship MSC Napoli was damaged and taking in water in a severe storm off Lizard Point—the southern-most tip of Great Britain and an area notorious for its shipping hazards. The command was given to abandon ship and load the lifeboats.

Just after 10:00 a.m., the Coast Guard alerted 771 Search and Rescue Squadron at the Royal Naval Air Station Culdrose in Cornwall. Two Sea King search and rescue helicopters were dispatched immediately to the sight.

Lieutenant Guy "Chuck" Norris, forty-two, had served in the Royal Navy for eighteen years and flown more than two hundred search and rescue missions. This father of two described the tempestuous oceanic surroundings that day as the worst ever: "It was one of the most challenging missions I have been involved with. The weather on the Napoli job was very extreme. The sea state was high and, at times, you would look out the cockpit window and see waves coming towards you at helicopter height. There were also a lot of people to be rescued."[8]

The helicopter crews found the seamen being tossed about in their lifeboats by forty to fifty feet high swells. Petty Officer Air Crewman Jay O'Donnell, a thirty-three-year-old father of two, was lowered on a rope and "trawled" through the waves to the lifeboats. "It was the worst conditions I have encountered. The seas were mountainous. When you are there, you are very focused about what has to be done. But looking back at some of the footage which was taken, you think, 'Oh my God, I didn't realize it was that bad.'"[9]

As a result of their valiant courage, twenty-six seamen were snatched from the jaws of the perilous waves and airlifted to dry land. Petty Officer Jay O'Donnell received the Queen's Gallantry Medal, and Sea King pilots Lieutenant Norris and Lieutenant Commander Martin "Oz" Rhodes were awarded the Queen's Commendation for Bravery in the Air.[10] Also commended by the men themselves were the ground crew, the engineers, and the Coast Guard. Petty Officer O'Donnell said, "There are a lot of people in the background who you don't see but who are just as important as the people who go out."

What these men of the Royal Navy did to rescue drowning sailors from the sea, we—you and I—need to do to help young people from the waves of a violent, degraded, popular culture.

Look around you today. If you are a parent or a grandparent, you need to start with the children closest to you. Nothing is more valuable than building their character and working for their future. There are many young people who need our help. They need to find their way home—to God, to the Founding Fathers, to love of country and of the opportunity America offers. We need to reach out and help them from the dire situations so many find themselves in. We need to spend more time with them and understand the worlds they are in, and help lead them to the world of the patriots of yesteryear, and show them how their concerns parallel those of our Founders. We need to assist them in their battles against the waves of enemies in this life, and provide emergency rescue help to spare them from the onslaught of often overwhelming, dark conditions.

Protect Youth

President Ronald Reagan once said, "Freedom is never more than one generation away from extinction. We didn't pass it to our children in the bloodstream. It must be fought for, protected, and handed on for them to do the same, or one day we will spend our sunset years telling our children and our children's children what it was once like in the United States when men were free."[11] Those words could not be more applicable than they are today. That is why we must do all we can to assure the protection of freedom, particularly as it is handed down through the younger generations.

It's high time we quit feeding America's children to the lions of our culture. Under the guise of trust, many parents or guardians send their children onto the Internet or off on spring break. We put no boundaries around their dating or living relationships. We say nothing about their drinking, smoking, or hanging out with those who do. We place few if any restrictions on them. Unfortunately as we limit our protection of them, we simultaneously allow for the intrusion of all types of negative influences and immoralities. We submit them to the laws of the jungle and they find its jaws behind almost every tree.

If we are expecting our children to live more disciplined moral lives, then we need to raise the bar on their boundaries and our protection of them. From day care to dating, we need to re-evaluate potential negative influences and help protect them from those influences.

If we really care about their future and the future of this country, then we need to think about exposing our children not to what's worst, but to what's best; not to those who want to tear down, but to those who want to build up; not to the grossest temptations but to the finest virtues. We need to armor them for life.

In the book of the Song of Solomon in the Bible, the author admonishes that we not awaken love before its time. Protection was not just encouraged in the Bible, but also by our Founders.

Benjamin Rush, a professor of medicine and a signer of the Declaration, wrote about the importance of not exposing young people, or anyone, to corruption before they can handle it. He noted: "In order to preserve the vigor of the moral faculty, it is of the utmost consequence to keep young people as ignorant as possible of the crimes that are generally thought most disgraceful to human nature. Suicide, I believe, is often propagated by [what's in the] newspapers. For this reason, I should be glad to see the proceedings of our courts kept from the public eye when they expose or punish monstrous vices."[12] We should be protecting our children's rights, not just our own. As Thomas Paine once wrote, "The rights of minors are as sacred as the rights of the aged."[13]

One particular threat we didn't face when we were children is the Internet. According to the Canadian Broadcasting Corporation, more than twenty-nine thousand registered sex offenders have been found on the popular Internet site MySpace.[14] MySpace is "extremely popular with young people, and while you're supposed to be fourteen before you can register with the giant networking site, a significant number of registrants, according to Consumer Reports, are underage."[15]

We all know the Internet has become the sexual predators' playground. Yet too few of us, as parents, take that threat seriously. Putting anti-pornography defenses on our computers is not nearly enough, nor is simply monitoring our children's computer activity. Today Internet access is provided through cell phones, Blackberries, iPods, and game devices, so the threats to our children are continually growing through all this technology.

Arnold Bell, special agent from the FBI's Cyber Division, says "six out of ten kids online have gotten an e-mail or instant message from a perfect stranger . . . and more than half have written back. One in three kids has been aggressively solicited to meet their 'cyber friend' in person. One in four kids, ages ten to seventeen, has been exposed to unwanted sexual material online.[16]

America's FBI is fighting to lead the way in exposing and capturing cyber-sexual criminals. While the U.S. Department of Justice still needs to prosecute more of its sixty-seven thousand complaints of obscenity on the Internet,[17] the FBI boasts an impressive 350 percent increase in federal prosecutions over ten years. It even trains law enforcement officials from other countries to track down online marauders. [18]

So what can you do? The first step is to realize criminals out there are targeting all of our children through the Internet. We all have to be aware of the dangers. The FBI has given us "signs your child is at risk:"

- Your child spends large amounts of time online, especially at night.
- Your child turns the computer monitor off or quickly changes the screen on the monitor when you come into the room.
- Your child becomes withdrawn from the family.
- You find pornography on your child's computer.
- Your child is using an online account belonging to someone else.
- Your child receives phone calls from men you don't know or is making calls, sometimes long distance, to numbers you don't recognize.
- Your child receives postal mail, gifts, or packages from someone you don't know.[19]

Though the risks are great, we're not helpless against them. Here are some practical steps you can take to protect your children:

1. Read "A Parent's Guide to Internet Safety,"[20] a primer put together by the FBI and available on its Web site.
2. Review what is on your child's computer and other electronic devices. If you don't know how, ask a friend, coworker, relative, or other knowledgeable person.
3. Be sure you have access to your child's e-mails.
4. Teach your children about online dangers: how to spot them and how to avoid them.

5. If your computers are not protected by anti-porn software, you need to do that now.[21] The best of these software programs can filter peer-to-peer communications, e-mails, instant messages, and chat room exchanges.

6. Introduce your children to Web Wise Kids,[22] which seeks to empower young people to make wise online choices.

7. Put the family computer in the room where you spend most of your at-home time. If your child uses a laptop, make it a rule they flip it on only with your permission and in an open space, like your living room.

8. Use Caller ID to track who is calling your child. Your phone company can also protect your privacy by blocking your number from appearing on other people's Caller ID.

9. Report all online obscene criminal activity. Information submitted to Obscenity Crimes[23] is forwarded to U.S. attorneys in the fifty states and to the Justice Department's Child Exploitation and Obscenity Section in Washington, D.C.

10. If you suspect your child has received pornography, been sexually solicited, or is in communication with a child predator, talk to your child. If your suspicions prove true, contact your local FBI office[24] or make an online report to the Cyber Tipline[25] or call by phone at 1-800-843-5678.

11. You can also check the National Sex Offender public Web site[26] or your individual state's Sex Offender Registry Web sites[27] to see the names and locations of cyber-pedophiles in your area and beyond.

12. If you suspect pornographic or sexually addictive behavior in your household or with your children, you

need to check out the "Help & Hope Resources" on Michael Leahy's Web site at www.bravehearts.net.

The truth is the Internet is a huge blessing and a huge curse. It's a great source for disseminating news, reading commentary, keeping up with family and friends, and shopping for books and other products. But as FBI agent Arnold Bell put it, the "Internet is a great place . . . [but] there are certain parts of town you don't want to be."

And computers are not the only culprit, because there are a host of other electronic media devices that can share similar potential abuses and dangers, from iPhones and iPods to Black-Berries and various game devices and regular ol' cell phones.

One example is the popular and fast growing trend among youth sending nude photos and videos via cell phones (called "sexting"). Sexting is not new, but it is on the rise. Cases are bubbling up all over the country. This past year in Virginia at least two Spotsylvania County students were facing child pornography charges in a sexting case. The naked images of three juvenile females (including an elementary student) were discovered on seven phones, traced back to the accused two students. In Greensburg, Pennsylvania, high school girls were also charged with child pornography after sending seminude photos of themselves to male classmates.

Other similar incidents have resulted in charges in Ohio, Kentucky, Wisconsin, Georgia, and Florida.[28] Law enforcement has recently been called out to investigate sexting-related crimes by dozens of teens involving many states across the nation.[29]

And sexting is not just a male-dominant problem. One Pennsylvania county reported that 20 percent of teenage girls admitted to sexting, and 18 percent of boys admitted it.[30] A new national survey[31] concurs that at least one-fifth of all youth have sent via cell or posted online, nude or explicit photos or videos of themselves.

Most astonishing, sexting is becoming a normative part of the dating scene and protocol among youngsters. Marian Merrit, Symantec's Internet Safety Advocate, who writes and speaks about issues impacting the online security and safety of kids and families, explains:

> Teens believe taking and sharing the sexy photo of themselves is a natural progression point in a romantic relationship. It's not just "step 1, hold hands; step 2, kiss." Now it's "step 1, Friend on social network; step 2, Chat on IM or text; step 3, Send sexy photos." Crazy![32]

So who's responsible?

That's easy. There's the juvenile committing the crime. But there are other culprits as well—accomplices to these acts. Who's providing the electronic devices? Who pays the phone bills? Whose name is on the plan? What messages and models are these guardians setting as those who frown upon pornography? Then there's a culture that is moving away from moral absolutes,[33] and that includes calling pornography wrong—even a sin.

So are your kids or grandkids involved in or at risk of sexting? Are they practicing safe cell-phoning? Ask them these five questions from Symantec's Marian Merrit's advice for helping parents and guardians protect their children from this latest strain of cyberporn.

1. Give me a tour of your cell phone. Any cool features or tricks you can do with your cell phone?
2. Show me how you take a photo with the phone. How do you send it to another e-mail or phone?
3. Where do you save the photos? Show me what you've got saved.

4. Has anyone ever sent or shown you a sexy photo of themselves or someone else?
5. Anyone ever asked for your photo? If yes, how did you handle it? If no, what would you do and why?[34]

How can we stop a sexting proliferation?

First, parents can no longer pass out cell phones like pancakes to their family and not monitor how they are used. Guardians need to reconsider the purposes of communication and security, especially when children are using cell phones for seduction and porn. Teens need to be educated about sexual illegalities, moralities, and reminded that, if convicted of child pornography crimes, they could face felony consequences and see the words "sex offender" on their juvenile records.

We might live in a technological wonderland, but that doesn't mean it's good to eat from all of its fruits. Most especially, we can never throw up our hands in surrender to marketing and peer (or parental) pressure in order to give our kids everything the Joneses' have, especially when those things expose them to others exposing themselves! As a wise man said many centuries ago (well sort of), "If your cell phone causes you to stumble, cut it off from your family's communication plan."

It's time not just to answer the question: Do you know where your kids are tonight? But also, do you know what they're doing with their cell phones?

Unfortunately electronic mediums are not the only problem areas; so are our schools. Over the last eleven years, juvenile violent crime has increased 48 percent.[35] I've counted at least fourteen different murderous gun sprees at academic settings across our nation since 2000, resulting in at least sixty fatalities and dozens more wounded. Dr. Marisa Randazzo, a psychologist who contributed to an extensive study of school shootings for the Secret Service, confirmed what we all feel, that "the intensity and frequency of the attacks [within our schools] have increased since the events at Columbine."[36] If our government won't secure our schools as safe havens, then we the people must.[37]

Edmund Burke's famous phrase that evil flourishes when good men do nothing is as true now as it ever was. Good men need to step up by mentoring kids who need help and by volunteering to keep our schools safe. That can be as simple as offering your services as a playground or hall monitor, participating in a neighborhood watch program if you live near a school, or joining the PTA and attending school board meetings.[38]

A decade ago my friend Mike Huckabee wrote a book titled *Kids Who Kill* about school shootings and how to prevent them. He identified several cultural factors that have turned our schools into danger zones in ways they weren't when we were growing up. We can put our finger on many of these factors ourselves. But the bottom line is that if we teach our children they are nothing more than glorified apes, then we shouldn't be surprised if they behave like animals. If we place our value in things, we shouldn't expect our children to value people. If we disrespect one another, we can't expect our children to be respectful. If we terminate children in the womb, we shouldn't be surprised that our own children think they can terminate others. If we teach our children there is no God and there are no moral absolutes, then we shouldn't be surprised if they turn down immoral alleys to find meaning, purpose, and identity in their lives. The point of freedom is to be liberated from unjust laws—to have the opportunity to do what is right. But if we choose injustice, if we choose immorality, we endanger the very basis of our freedom. As James Madison once wrote, "Liberty may be endangered by the abuses of liberty, as well as the abuses of power."[39] This is why the Founders believed our liberty was ordained by God—and for that liberty we were responsible to God.

The Reverend Rob Schenck, speaking after two recent horrible school shootings, said: "When kids kill kids, there's something desperately wrong in the culture. No amount of laws, police officers, courts, or prisons can stop a murder from happening. Only a conscience built on the fear of God can do that. Whether it's teaching the sanctity of life or God's commandment against murder, Christian leaders must tell young people that accountability for doing wrong doesn't stop with death. We will ultimately face God as a righteous judge. People who contemplate committing this kind of act need to know that."[40]

Like our Founders, I respect people of all religions.[41] I wholeheartedly agree with Benjamin Rush, a signer of the Declaration and a member of the presidential administrations of Adams, Jefferson, and Madison who wrote: "Such is my veneration for every religion that reveals the attributes of the Deity, or a future state of rewards and punishments, that I had rather see the opinions of Confucius or Mohamed inculcated upon our youth than see them grow up wholly devoid of a system of religious principles. But the religion I mean to recommend in this place is that of the New Testament. . . . [A]ll its doctrines and precepts are calculated to promote the happiness of society and the safety and well being of civil government."[42]

In 2006, there was a terrible murder of Amish schoolchildren. The parents responded not with threats or demands for new laws, but by offering their forgiveness for the horrible offense done to them and by praying. The journalist Rod Dreher wrote about how the parents' faith brought them freedom. He noted that "sometimes faith helps ordinary men and women do the humanly impossible: to forgive, to love, to heal, and to redeem. . . . The Amish have turned this occasion of spectacular evil into a bright witness to hope. Despite everything, a light shines in the darkness, and the darkness did not overcome it."[43]

Other great models of mercy and forgiveness are Darrell and Craig Scott, the father and brother of the first victim of the Columbine High School massacre, Rachel Scott. Shortly before her death, she wrote in a school essay, "I have this theory that if one person can go out of their way to show compassion then it will start a chain reaction of the same."

I agree with Rachel, and so does her family. They carry on her compassion and benevolent dare through Rachel's Challenge,[44] a nationwide school outreach program for the prevention of teen violence. I was so moved by her life and faith that I dedicated my autobiography, *Against All Odds*, to her. It was reported after the shootings that one of the murderers asked Rachel, who had already been wounded by the gunmen, if she still believed in God. She said, "You know I do." And then the teen murderer shot her in the head. Rachel refused to compromise her faith in God, even in the face of death.

This poem, written by her father, Darrell Scott, aptly describes the problems we face, and provides the answer, for those courageous enough to believe. He actually wrote and spoke these words as he addressed the U.S. Congress:

> Your laws ignore our deepest needs
> Your words are empty air
> You've stripped our heritage,
> You've outlawed simple prayer
> Now gunshots fill our classrooms,
> And precious children die.
> You seek for answers everywhere,
> And ask the question, "Why?"
> You regulate restrictive laws,
> Through legislative creed,
> And you fail to understand
> That God is what we need!

Reconnect Youth

I realize that for many kids, history is not their favorite subject. I used to hate it, too. But I have gained a great appreciation for it, especially since I've learned to see it as an unfolding drama.

In my opinion, if you want to learn (or teach) history, it needs to be treated as a story. Everyone loves a story, and the best historians, from a reader's perspective, are those who take just this tack. I wonder if more kids would be more interested in history if it were treated as an adventure story. Publishers used to do this for kids with series like the old Landmark Books. I've recently seen history-based, educational comic books that give good descriptions of Civil War and World War II battles. Big name authors used to relish writing historical adventures for kids. And if you poke around, you can still find some great historical fiction for kids, including some with Christian content.[45]

There are many classic children's or teen-appropriate stories that deal with the American Revolution or other periods of American history—books like *Johnny Tremain* by Esther Hoskins Forbes, or *Drums* by James Boyd, or *Daniel Boone* by James Daugherty.

If we took the time to learn more about America's heritage, we might find a good story for bedtime or for table talk. And, of course, there are great, classic movies that have adapted American history, not always accurately, but often in ways that will inspire kids to want to learn more about it (like John Wayne's *The Alamo*).

As parents, we need to take responsibility for our children's connection to the past. We can't leave that—or anything else that matters—to the public schools. Our children are our responsibility and no one else's. The best schools can help us, but the worst schools can actually poison kids with ignorance or politically correct propaganda. In almost all public schools, the most inspiring history book of all time is banned from classrooms. I'm talking, needless to say, about the Bible.

In terms of drama, the Bible is a wonderfully adaptable book. In terms of Western civilization, there is no more important book. In terms of cultural literacy, all of us should know—and make sure our children know—the biblical accounts of the creation of the world, Noah's flood, Moses and the Ten Commandments,

David and Goliath, and the life of Jesus. The Bible of course is more than a history book. It teaches us where we came from, why we're here, and where we're going, as well as how to live, how to honor God, and how to respect and love one another.

Often one needs Bible knowledge to even understand America's stories. Take for instance the seal of the United States. Thomas Jefferson first recommended one reflecting the "children of Israel in the Wilderness, led by a Cloud by Day, and a Pillar of Fire by night," but later accepted Benjamin Franklin's suggestion to adapt the Old Testament account of God's parting of the Red Sea.[46] Their ideas were rejected but the final design includes, on one side, the Eye of Providence—a representation of the Creator who endowed us with our unalienable rights. How could one understand the full meaning of these proposed seals without knowledge of Scripture?

The Founders took biblical literacy for granted and supported teaching the Bible in our schools. Samuel Adams said, "As piety, religion and morality have a happy influence on the minds of men, in their public as well as private transactions, you will not think it unseasonable, although I have frequently done it, to bring to your remembrance the great importance of encouraging our University, town schools, and other seminaries of education, that our children and youth while they are engaged in the pursuit of useful science, may have their minds impressed with a strong sense of the duties they owe to their God," through regular reading of the Bible.[47]

The government was so in favor of Bible reading that in 1777, one year after the creation of the Declaration of Independence, Congress voted to import twenty thousand copies of the Bible for the people of this new nation (though they actually didn't need to order them, most likely because Bibles began to be produced in the U.S. about the same time). The Committee of Commerce recommended Congress order these copies because "the use of the Bible is so universal, and its importance so great."[48]

We must assure that our children learn more than merely about the secular workings of the executive, legislative, and judicial branches of government. They must learn about the widespread passion early American governments (both federal and state) possessed for instilling Judeo-Christian belief in their citizens.

If we expect to reconnect our children to the past, then we must teach them in our churches and homes about America's complete history and about the Bible. Combined, these two studies, biblical history, and American history will teach our young people to place themselves within the context of our country's great story, and thereby help to build a better America tomorrow.

Providing for Youth

We must do more than just protect our children. We must provide them with the love and attention that bring out and cultivate their best potential. In decades past, providing for our children included raising them in an environment with a loving home, safe community, and good school. Nowadays, with broken homes a dime a dozen, a pervasive fear of crime in many neighborhoods, and secular liberalism reigning in schools, the challenge to provide a warm environment is much more difficult. But it is still doable.

You can't legislate love and good parenting, but what we can do is realize, as parents, that we have no more important job than raising our children in loving homes and communities.

We must be socially active with our children and the young people in our communities, if we are going to help them believe we care for others. We need to challenge them also to be involved with politics in ways that make a difference in our country and this world in a practical way. We need to be involved politically to fight against laws that seek to legislate immorality and undermine the family. And we need to be deeply involved in our children's education—both as concerned parents and concerned citizens.

But there's something the U.S. government doesn't want you to know. It came out again in 2009 with the Heritage Foundation report on education.[49] It conveyed that the general public is increasingly dissatisfied with public schools, with a rising number opting for private education.

The report explains that during the 2007 and 2008 legislative sessions, forty-four states introduced school-choice legislation. And in 2008 choices for private school were enacted into law or expanded in Arizona, Utah, Georgia, Florida, Louisiana, and Pennsylvania. And as of 2009, fourteen states and Washington, D.C., offer voucher or education tax-credit programs that aid parents sending their children to private schools. But that may be short lived.

Despite the growing public preference for private education, Congress cancelled Washington D.C.'s Opportunity Scholarship Program[50] created in 2004 to offer students from low-income families in the nation's capital an opportunity to join the voucher educational community. The law provided $14 million in scholarships to help pay tuition at a private school of their choosing. But no longer.

Why did they nix the program, especially when recent studies showed that students receiving vouchers since the program's inception were academically 18.9 months ahead of their peers?[51] (I read recently that 100 percent of Thurgood Marshall Academy's charter graduates are accepted to colleges.)[52] And why would Congress phase out a program that costs $7,500 per student annually, compared to the $15,000 it cost in Washington's public schools to educate a child?

So the cancellation is not a result of costing too much, since it's half the price of public school. And it's not because of inferior quality, since the kids enrolled in the program were scoring higher than students in regular schools. There's only one reason Congress cancelled it: federal control and educational indoctrination.

What's amazing too is how hypocritical it is for Congress to make this decision. The Heritage Foundation report also conveyed that 44 percent of current United States senators and 36 percent of current members of the U.S. House of Representatives "had at one time sent their children to private schools." While the Foundation discovered that 11 percent of American students attend private schools, twice that rate (20 percent) of the members of 111th Congress attended private high schools. And they want to remove the voucher option for private school education?

Phasing out a federal program might seem appealing, since so many of us are crying for less not more government. But when phasing out leads to bigger government and less personal choices, they're again revealing one more sign of a system gone awry. That's pure and simple lip service to educational reform. The federal government seems fine with options to education, as long as they are controlled by them or their puppet-union organizations. Their educational tyranny is now clearly seen from the nation's Capitol to the "left-coast."

While Obama's administration professes to have education as a top priority, they did nothing last March when Congress chose to discontinue the Opportunity Scholarship Program. Why? Because they all are in cahoots together not only to choose our medical care for us, own the mortgage insurance and finance businesses, and place caps on corporate earnings, but now they are aspiring to control our educational choices for our children. A tragic case in point this past year was Amanda Kurowski, a ten-year-old homeschooled girl, who performed well academically and was socially well-adjusted, but her strong Christian beliefs were sufficient reason for a New Hampshire court to order her out of homeschooling by her mother and into a public school![53]

More proof of an academic system run awry came to my ears when I was speaking to a friend in California who has taught in public schools there for thirty years. She told me the school no longer begins their day with the Pledge of Allegiance, but a "patriotic observance." During the presidential election, teachers were lined up in the library to take a photo with a stand-up cut out of Barack Obama (no other candidate offered). Without any prior consent or vote, the school union allocated $1 million to fight pro-Prop 8 (anti-gay marriage amendment). At the beginning of a faculty meeting, a teacher spoke up to remind everyone to vote against Prop 8, to which no rebuttal was welcome. My friend told me that at this point conservatism in any form is completely ostracized in her school—something that has radically changed over the past three decades. But aren't we supposed to be offering education rather than merely left-indoctrination?

Parents deserve educational choices—choice is what this country was founded upon. Government control and monopoly of education or anything else is just another avenue for usurping power and control on the slippery slope to socialism. And it's unbecoming for a republic like ours when our Founders created a system of freedom, choice, and minimal government intervention.

I was certainly grieved earlier this year when a California state appeals court ruled that parents without teaching credentials do not have a Constitutional right to homeschool their children. Besides statewide consequences, this decision could set a legal precedent for other states as well.[54] (This hits particularly close to home because my wife Gena and I personally homeschool our seven-year-old twins.)

At the core of these types of ludicrous rulings is the assault on the parent-child relationship by judges who refuse to support or even acknowledge parental rights. This California appellate judgment is likely to be and should be overturned—but it and other similar rulings are warnings to us all of how liberal judges are seeking to infringe upon the freedoms and rights we have as parents and to subvert the Constitution. Rather than say that government has no powers except those explicitly given it by the Constitution, these judges reverse that logic so that parents and individuals have no rights except those explicitly stated in the Constitution.

And it gets worse. Increasingly, in the eyes of liberal judges, international law is more important than domestic law and the traditional rights and liberties of American citizens, including parents. That is why gatherings like the United Nations Convention on the Rights of the Child, which sounds so nice in theory, is so dangerous in practice. Do we want international bureaucrats telling us how we must raise our kids?[55]

The reason government courts are cracking down on private instruction has more to do with suppressing alternative education than assuring educational standards. The rationale is quite simple, though rarely if ever stated: control future generations and you control the future. So rather than letting parents be the primary educators of their children—either directly or by educating their children in the private schools of their choice—liberal social engineers want to deny parental rights, establish an educational monopoly run by the state, and limit private education options. It is so simple any socialist can understand it. As Joseph Stalin once stated, "Education is a weapon whose effects depend on who holds it in his hands and at whom it is aimed."[56]

Is it merely coincidental that homeschooling was outlawed by the Soviet State in 1919, by Hitler and Nazi Germany in 1938, and by Communist China in 1949? If California is next, and if other states follow, it will be presented to us not as a blatant usurpation of our rights, but as for the good of the children. They will say it is necessary to establish common educational standards. They will say we need to leave education to the experts and not to parents. And I fear that too many of us will simply give into the whims of state and federal governments. God has entrusted us with a gift—our precious children—not the government or the United Nations.

If you want to join me in stopping this road to educational, judicial, and legislative tyranny, then consider doing any of the following:

1. Get involved in local, state, and national politics and make your voice heard. We cannot be passive in the face of such threats. As Thomas Jefferson once said,

"All tyranny needs to gain a foothold is for people of good conscience to remain silent."[57]

2. Learn your state's laws on education[58] and understand your parental and educational rights,[59] and teach them to others. To quote Thomas Jefferson again, "Educate and inform the whole mass of the people. . . . They are the only sure reliance for the preservation of our liberty."

3. Whether you homeschool or not, support an organization like the Home School Legal Defense Association,[60] which protects families who do.

4. Petition your representatives to support a constitutional amendment protecting the child-parent relationship from unreasonable government intrusion.

Our right to liberty includes our right to educate our children as we, not the government, prefer. Indeed, our Founders would be appalled if we surrendered this right, which they took for granted in their own time.

If you think homeschooling and private education are safe in your state, think again. Liberal judges in other states will be emboldened if liberal judges in California get their way.

My warning to judicial tyranny is this: best not to test Texas. If you thought we fought hard for the Alamo, wait until you see what we can do for the right to educate our children. You can hide behind your number 2 pencils, but our branding irons will find your tail sides.

If you have a good public school, congratulations. Stay active in the PTA and attend school board meetings to keep it that way. But for many parents the only responsible choice is to send their children to a Christian, parochial, or private school or to homeschool. It's a travesty we have even come to this point that we have to protect our children from the public school systems by looking to alternative methods.

On December 27, 1820, Thomas Jefferson wrote about his vision for the University of Virginia (chartered in 1819), "This institution will be based on the illimitable freedom of the human mind. For here we are not afraid to follow the truth wherever it may lead, nor to tolerate any error as long as reason is left free to combat it."[61]

That seems to me the charter of a true American system of education. But as we know, our nation's public schools, and especially our nation's colleges and universities, are the seedbeds of politically correct and liberal indoctrination. It shouldn't be that way, but it is.

Dr. Jim Nelson Black, founder and senior policy analyst of Sentinel Research Associates in Washington, D.C., wrote an excellent book titled *Freefall of the American University*. In it he documents the lopsided left-wing prejudices of our nation's universities. Dr. Black notes that the 57 percent of faculty members represented in our most esteemed universities are Democrats (only 3 percent are Republicans) and 64 percent identify themselves as liberal (only 6 percent say they are conservative). Moreover, 71 percent of them disagree that "news coverage of political and social issues reflects a liberal bias in the news media." And the number 1 answer they gave to the question, "Who has been the best president in the past forty years?" was Bill Clinton (only 4 percent said Ronald Reagan).

Too many parents blindly assume that any college—or any college with a big name—will do for their sons and daughters. Don't believe it. Before you send your child to the local college or university, take a close look at it. You might be appalled at the sort of radicalism you quickly discover. If the school is a taxpayer-supported college or university—and almost every college or university is, directly, as a state-supported school, or indirectly, through federal research dollars—you have every right to take your concerns to the administration and to your state and federal representative. If you get no proper answers, then go public and expose university wrongdoing by blogging and e-mailing about it and warning other parents. If our government is not going to hold our taxpayer-supported academic institutions accountable, then we must.

Whether you attend school or not, there's more you can do. Ask your local college or university to accept The Academic Bill of Rights[62] and The Student's Bill of Rights.[63] Most of all, have your children consider attending a private, conservative, or Christian college or university, such as Liberty University, Biola University, Bethany University, Hillsdale College, Christendom College, Wheaton College, Grove City College, etc.[64] If your sons or daughters dream of becoming professors, encourage them. The only way we'll truly change academic bias is by correcting academic imbalances.

I believe so strongly in the power of private or Christian education that in June 2008 I accepted an invitation to give a commencement speech at Liberty University's graduation in Lynchburg, Virginia. I don't accept many offers to speak. I don't consider myself very adept at it. But if it is something I feel God wants me to do, then I will accept and try to do my very best. That is how I felt when Jerry Falwell Jr., the chancellor of Liberty University, called and asked me to speak to the graduating class of 2008. I told Jerry I had never done anything like that and asked him why he picked me. Jerry said, "I didn't. The students did. They voted on who they wanted and you got the most votes." I replied, "Well, I guess if the students would go to that much trouble to get me to come there, then how can I not say yes? How many people will I be addressing?" He said, "Around fifteen thousand people." "Wow!" I exclaimed.

My wife Gena and I flew to Lynchburg on a Friday evening to give the commencement speech early that Saturday morning. As I waited that morning to give my speech, to my surprise Jerry Falwell Jr. called me up to the podium and I was presented with an Honorary Doctorate in Humanities. What a humbling experience

From left to right: my brother Wieland, my mom, my brother Aaron, and me. This picture was taken in early 1970 just before my brothers enlisted in the U.S. Army.

Right: Here I am fighting Joe Lewis for the International Karate Grand Championship in Long Beach, California, in August 1967.

Left: My first tournament win: the Los Angeles Open in 1964.

Combat training with the Delta Force team for the movie *Delta Force II*.

Here I am sparring with one of my Black Belts, Richard Tirschel.

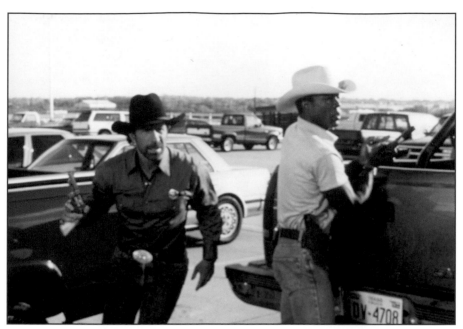

A shoot-out scene from *Walker, Texas Ranger* with my partner Trivette (Clarence Gilyard).

Giving commencement speech at Liberty University after receiving my Honorary Doctorate in Humanities.

My wife and I admiring our miracle babies, Danilee (left) and Dakota (right).

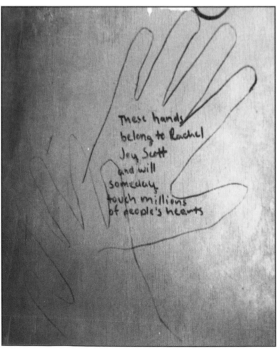

These hands belong to Rachel Joy Scott and will someday touch millions of people's hearts

The hand drawing of Rachel Scott, the first victim of the Columbine High School shooting, who prophetically declared at a young age the impact her life would have upon the world.

A **KICK**START city-wide demo team.

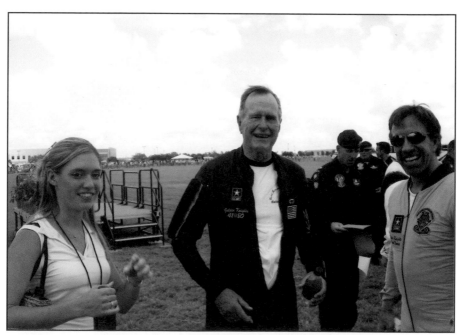

Just after a successful skydiving jump with President Bush on his 80th birthday. My daughter, Kelley, is still smiling after a kiss on the cheek from the president.

Here I am with the real Texas Rangers after they made me an honorary member.

In Iraq (on my first tour in 2006) shooting an M-14. If you look closely, you can see where the scope nailed me between the eyes!

Signing my name on the barrel of a tank.

These are the troops who welcomed me and my friend, actor Marshall Teague, when we first arrived in Iraq in 2006.

Standing with some troops on a task with a *Walker* drawing on the protective shield.

I am encouraging a soldier to re-enlist.

With my wife Gena.

for a guy who almost quit high school to go into the military. But, by the grace of God and strong encouragement from my mom, I did finish high school before entering the military. As I put on the black robe and Jerry fastened the doctoral sash around my neck, all I could think was, "Never in my wildest dreams could I believe something like this would happen to me."

I was so overwhelmed I had a hard time trying to refocus on what I wanted to say to the students. And the wind was blowing so hard that I could not even use my notes. So I prayed, "OK Lord, I have to talk from my heart now, so please help me with the words." I told the crowd of more than twenty thousand people there (the largest turnout in the University's history) that I have a difficult time with public speaking and this was my first commencement speech at a university. I shared with them my struggles growing up and my drifting from God, but how He also never left me. I explained that when I finally did get right with the Lord and began reading the Bible, I came upon Proverbs 19:21, "Many are the plans in a man's heart, but the Lord directs his steps." I realized that even though I had drifted from my faith, the Lord still had plans for me. That's why He allowed me to become successful in the martial arts and successful as an actor. His ultimate plan for me, I believe, was to start my KickStartKids Foundation, helping at-risk children. I could not have started this program if I did not have the martial arts ability and my celebrity status to initiate it. I finished my speech by simply saying, "The Lord directed my steps and still does; let Him direct your steps as well. You can't go wrong if you do." I wonder if I would have been allowed to say those things at a secular university today.

Government needs less of a role in running our children's education and more of a role in supporting parents' educational decisions for their children. Children belong to their parents, not the government. And the parents ought to have the right, and government support, to personalize their child's education as they so wish. And where the Department of Education, teachers' unions, or any other organizations impede their decisions, they must be stopped.

And what if public schools don't change? The minds and hearts of our children are on the line. And if the curriculum doesn't match the values in our homes, then we must seek other alternatives. If enough of us remove our children from the public schools, they'll get the message, and the good people who run Christian, parochial, and private schools will get our support.

Our children deserve the best education we can give them. We can't be satisfied by failed government-run schools that don't provide the level of education we want. But there are alternatives—and I encourage you to look into them. Private schools for one. And home schooling for another. My wife Gena and I are very committed to homeschooling. Once upon a time it was a movement; now it's a bona fide solution to the liberal assault in our schools. And the quality of those students graduating from homeschooling are ranking among the top in every field of society. They are making a difference, even politically and socially. Just like Alex and Brett Harris, and also young men like Tim Tebow, who made NCAA history as the first sophomore to win the Heisman Trophy as the best football player in the nation in 2007. These young men are just a few examples of the fact that parents have always raised children better than government.

A FINAL KICKSTART

It's easy to criticize the inadequacies of young people. It's far more difficult to invest in kids—but much more rewarding. It's even harder to tell them, "We need you to help us reawaken America and rebuild what our Founding Fathers started." But that's exactly what we, the Builder and Baby-Boomer generations, need to say to them. If you're a Millennial, consider this an invitation. We need your help. I need your help to join me and millions of others in a revolution (or, if you will, a rebelution), not to abandon the principles of the past but combine them with social action in the present to build a better tomorrow. In other words, it's time to make some noise!

It all starts by being willing to make a difference, and finding a way to help, whether it's socially, politically, financially, or by volunteering in your community, church, school, or government. You might have a calling to be a county supervisor, state congressman, or U.S. Representative. Don't reject any option as impossible. Your help might be planned or it might be spontaneous. But you need to be ready, in season or out of season, for whatever your calling might be.

It sounds kind of canned, but I truly believe that there is a hero in all of us. We all were designed by God to be a blessing to others—a champion to someone. And our kids today need champions. They need heroes. And don't think you can't be that hero. You might not be called upon to save someone's life. But all of us can make a difference for the better in someone's life. You might teach them a skill that will enrich their lives. You might remind them of who they are (a child of God) and what they can offer (love and understanding). Each one of them needs to know someone loves them, someone cares for them, God has a plan and purpose for their life, and their life is the most priceless thing on this planet.

Continuing to contribute to society is one of the reasons I created KickStartKids,[65] which is a martial arts program for at-risk students taught in public middle schools in lieu of physical education. President George H. W. Bush helped me start it in 1992. To date we have graduated sixty thousand children in Texas. My wife Gena and I consider KickStartKids our life's mission.

It is a character-building, life-skills program, the fundamental purpose of which is to give our nation's students the tools to strengthen their self image. When children develop a strong sense of self-awareness and inner strength, they are able to resist negative peer pressure that might involve taking drugs, drinking alcohol, or joining gangs. In addition, martial arts training provides them with the core values and philosophies associated with leading a productive and healthy life: things like discipline, hard work, and respect for other people. That is what we are all about: to give every child a chance for a productive life in which they can make healthy decisions and achieve their goals and dreams. Someday, it is our vision to have this program in every middle school in America. Our goal is to see the seventy-three hundred students we have in forty-one schools in Texas multiply into millions of students throughout our country.

I am often given recognition for the way KickStartKids helps young people. But the real heroes of the program and these younger people's lives are the instructors. They are my heroes too, because they are the ones dedicating their time and energy to the lives of young people every day. The kids they are teaching in the KickStartKids program score higher academically and almost 100 percent of them graduate.

I'm still amazed when God uses my life to influence someone else in a special way. I've made plenty of mistakes in my life, and I sure don't claim to know all the answers. I am convinced, however, of the force of one. As Edward Everett Hale put it, "I am only one, but I am one. I can't do everything, but I can do something. The something I ought to do, I can do. And by the grace of God, I will."[66]

★ ★ ★

CHAPTER EIGHT

Honor and Care for the Family

I BET BENJAMIN FRANKLIN struggled as a husband and father. In fact, I know he did. He must have been an overachiever, a type-A if you will. He probably spent way too much time in the office and not enough time at home. How else could he have accomplished what he did? I know his wife must have complained a time or two that he couldn't get his eyes out of his books and onto her, if you know what I mean. I'm certain too that his children wondered at least once in a while why Dad had to spend so much time with all those other politicians.

Then there was that estranged relationship with his older illegitimate son, William (Billy) Franklin. At one point in Ben's life, William partnered with his father in his scientific experiments. He was eventually granted a doctorate from Oxford University because of it. Of course some allege Dad's extended influence and English connections made that possible. Still, no one can discredit William's service in the French and Indian War, and how he led the small regiment into the Ohio Territory. It's debated whether or not William was a premarital product from Ben's relations with his common-law wife, Deborah Read, or some other mistress. Nevertheless, Ben never denied that William was his eldest son.

In 1763 William was appointed as royal governor of New Jersey. During the colonial outrage over the Stamp Act in 1765, William lashed out over the "outrageous conduct" of the mobs in Boston. When father Ben returned from London in 1775, daughter Sarah met him with the salutation, "Billy is a Tory!" Ben's hopes of Billy resigning his British post were dashed to the royal wind. While Ben's pro-independence ushered in his inclusion as a representative to the Continental Congress, Billy swayed in further support of the crown, followed by several rebellious acts against the Patriots. His own New Jersey political disarray escalated to the point of his termination when the Patriots adopted a new state constitution. Billy was charged with treason and arrested, was a prisoner of war for two years, fled to New York, where he led a militia group who maimed and murdered Patriots—crimes for which he was wanted.

With the peace Treaty of Paris (1783), Billy moved back to England, where he saw his father for the first time in a decade. Reports say their reconciliation was amicable but strained at best. Ben returned to America in 1785, where he died five years later. Billy stayed in England, living out his remaining years until his death in 1813.[1]

Our Founders were not faultless politicians, patriots, fathers, or husbands. They were fallible human beings. Still, as you will discover, most were passionately concerned and committed to honor and care for their families.[2] I'm glad to know that these gigantic figures of the Revolution like Franklin struggled with family relations. Because I have too. And sometimes I still do.

Perfect families didn't exist then and they certainly don't exist now. You know the statistics. Family members are more distracted, more divided, more disloyal than ever before. Divorce and dead-beat dads are humdrum parts of almost every family landscape. Living together has become the cultural norm[3] and is even fought for as superior to marriage on some Web sites.[4]

Today the nuclear family has become one option among many. The homosexual community wants to replace their civil union with marital union.[5] Kids are being expected to call two people father or mother. Teenagers are given green lights to live in a land of licentiousness.

The American family is dissolving. Even more, it's being redefined. As family psychologist and President of the Family Institute at Northwestern University William Pinsof concludes, "At the core of this process is a basic redefinition of family from a unit defined exclusively by blood and procreation, to a unit increasingly defined by intentionality—what the participants intend."[6]

THE MISSING LINK

Times were not always this complicated for families. Though the Founders weathered their own particular family storms, they treasured traditional marriage and family as institutions created by God. Benjamin Rush wrote to his wife Julia about the superiority of his commitment to God and his family, when he said, "I shall be better satisfied if the same can be said of me as was said of the prophet of old, 'That I walked in the fear of the Lord, and begat sons and daughters' (Gen. 5:22), than if it were inscribed upon my tombstone that I governed the councils or commanded the arms of the whole continent of America."[7]

In 1799 Thomas Jefferson wrote to his wife Mary about the comparison between his governmental work and his family: "Environed here in scenes of constant torment, malice, and obloquy, worn down in a station where no effort to render service can avail anything, I feel not that existence is a blessing, but when something recalls my mind to my family or farm."[8]

Truth be known, I believe a significant reason for the breakdown of the American family and society lies in the growing population of male neglect and lack of passion for the home and family. Except for the role as providers, too many males have largely relinquished (and at times abandoned) other major responsibilities they once had in society, from being the educators in the home to the servant leaders in society.

When I say men need to pick up the ball and run with it, I'm not saying women don't or can't. I am glad for the freedoms women have experienced over the past couple centuries and praise their accomplishments. Remember, I believe in the words "that all men are created equal," which includes all women.

Of course women bear an equally critical role and responsibility in family and marriage. I just believe that most of them have a built in marriage-and-family manual inside them, and they are, by and large, living by those instructions.

Today we see women incredibly active in every arena of society. They are often wearing multiple hats, as mother, homemaker, professional, spiritual leader, and community leader. Many serve God, family, and country with the same fervor as those valiant female patriots of yesteryear. Women like Abigail Adams, Margaret Corbin, Molly Pitcher, Catherine Ferguson, Dolly Madison, Mercy Warren, Martha Washington, and Betsy Ross.

If there is any necessary challenge before some women today, it is that they continue to challenge and encourage men to reassume a few of those critical places of influence in marriage and family— those areas women often have to fill by default because of male absence. I particularly feel compassion for those women who have been left with the lion share of household responsibilities and I commend their tenacity and commitment to their children. It would be great if this chapter helps to remedy those types of domestic imbalances.

In fact, I don't believe one can truly experience life, liberty, and happiness as the Declaration of Independence states without a proper lineup of priorities for God, family, and country. These are the priorities our Founders lived by. Again, as Thomas Jefferson clearly revealed when he wrote his daughter the year before his presidency, "My attachments to the world, and whatever it can offer, are daily wearing off; but you are one of the links which hold to my existence, and can only break off with that."[9] He espoused the same sentiment eight years later at the end of his presidency to the renowned explorer William Clarke (of Lewis and Clarke), "By a law of our nature, we cannot be happy without the endearing connections of a family."[10]

I don't want to focus here upon what men haven't done, but what we can do. For I truly believe and have discovered personally, that God has appointed us to a position that can "rock our worlds" and transform our society. But we first have to recognize and admit to our shortcomings, before we can press on and convert them into our accomplishments.

I am not a perfect father or husband. Truth be known, I've learned far more from my failures than from my successes. However, I won't allow them to stop me from pressing on. And I don't believe you should allow yours to stop you either. What I want to say to you will probably not be totally new, but I know it will be practical and useful, like Benjamin Franklin's words, "Keep your eyes wide open before marriage, and half shut afterwards."[11]

I'm specifically addressing men in this chapter because I believe they hold the power to build up and unify family relationships. They hold three specific keys that can draw them, their spouses, and their children nearer to one another. Those keys are modeling, mentoring, and motivating. If we do these things, we will not only give our family members what they need, but I believe we will also receive what we need in return.

Before I get into the details of those three keys, I need to tell you where I learned everything I know about them—from a dearly departed saint and personal model, mentor, and motivator—Dr. Edwin Louis Cole.

Ed Cole is called "The Father of the Christian Men's Movement," because he influenced millions of men including today's Christian leaders. His mission statement was simple and powerful: "I have been called to speak with a prophetic voice to the men of this generation and commissioned with a ministry majoring in men to declare a standard for manhood, and that standard is that 'Manhood and Christlikeness are synonymous.'"[12]

His story is amazing. Ed was born in Dallas, Texas, but moved with his mother, Florence, to Los Angeles at just four years old, when a doctor told her that Ed would not survive without the sea air and sun to heal a severe case of scarlet fever. As a result, Ed grew up in the famous church, Angelus Temple, founded by Aimee Semple McPherson, in which he and his mother played a part in the ministry. Until her death at age ninety-six, Florence was a prayer warrior and evangelist, and she founded churches and preached in missions on Skid Row for more than fifty years, where Ed also played trumpet with street corner witnessing teams.[13]

Ed fell away from the church and later served in World War II, where he met and married a fellow member of the Coast Guard, Nancy Corbett from Massachusetts. Meanwhile, Florence continued to pray for Ed and his new wife, until he and Nancy confessed belief in the Lord. Within two years, Ed became a pastor of a church in the mountains of Northern California. About ten years later Ed became the men's minister for a major denomination. From there he spent the following decades particularly touching men's lives all around the world. He evangelized, discipled, ministered to, and influenced some of the biggest names in Christendom today around the world: Coach Bill McCartney (starter of Promise Keepers), Pat Robertson (president of the 700 Club), John Maxwell (President of Injoy Ministries), Sunday Adelaja (Ukraine), Kong Hee (Singapore), Eddy Leo (Indonesia), Robert Barriger (Peru), Alex Mitala (Uganda), Alexey Ledyaev (Latvia), Suliasi Kurulo (Fiji), Leon Fontaine (Canada), Kenneth Copeland, Oliver North, and me.

We first met Ed and Nancy in 1998 at a banquet honoring *Walker, Texas Ranger*. We also attended many of his seminars, where we got to know them more personally. One night Dr. Cole drove across Dallas through a thunderstorm to deliver a message God had laid on his heart for me—to encourage me to get grounded in the Bible in order to discern between the genuine and the counterfeit in life. What a great lesson. What a great man!

As I tell in my autobiography, *Against All Odds*, Ed called me in Los Angeles shortly before he died to pray for him. I told him, "I will do better than that. I will fly to Dallas to pray with you." So Gena and I flew out to be with him right before he passed to his heavenly home. I know Ed was happy to be reunited with Nancy in heaven, but I was sad that I no longer had my mentor to guide me.

I will never forget or take for granted Ed's influence upon my life as a Christian, husband, or father. He influenced me to increase my trust in God, to be a faithful husband and father and, even though I was a "TV tough guy," Ed challenged me to be a real man. God loved me through Ed Cole, and I thank God for him. And I look forward to thanking Ed again when I see him one day in heaven.

What I know, I owe to him. What I pass on here, I learned from him and am honored to share with you in his memory. If you'd like to learn more about the Ed Cole ministry, you can check out his Web site at the Ed Cole Library online.[14]

A MODEL FOR THE FAMILY

I believe God wants to reveal Himself to His creation and that some of His greatest relational avenues come through the family. God is spirit, so, when He created us, He could not physically care for us. Rather, He decided that procreation would be packaged with the nurture of a mother and a father. Parents are called to be children's primary caregivers. But I also believe they have another equally important duty. They are called to reflect God's image and nature until one day a child physically and emotionally leaves a parent and cleaves to his or her Creator. Austin L. Sorensen[15] was correct when he said, "A child is not likely to find a father in God unless he finds something of God in his father."

Parenting is largely about reflecting God's nature to children. That is particularly the case in fathering, since it is as a heavenly father that God has primarily revealed Himself. At its heart marriage is also all about sharing and experiencing God's love and nature as well. If God indwells us and gives us power to do what we are incapable of doing, then loving unconditionally and revealing Himself through our conduct in marriage must have a very significant purpose. That's why I believe a father's greatest role is reflecting his heavenly Father's image to his children. And a husband's greatest goal is reflecting Christ's love to his wife. In this sense men are heads of their homes: that they are called to be the greatest servant leaders. Fathers were designed to show their children what God is like. In that sense fathers are children's first Sunday school. That is likely why George Herbert said, "One father is more than a hundred schoolmasters."

With this honorable type of power in our original design, it is no wonder there is today a war on fatherhood and masculinity.[16] With men on the cultural butchering block, it is high time men arose not only to protect our national borders but the boundaries of the family.

Therefore, modeling God's character should be a father's greatest family goal. From this goal alone, a father's children will reciprocate with respect and adoration. And a wife will reciprocate with love and attention. Of course we will fail. That's God's assurance plan that neither our wife nor our children will replace us for Him who is perfect in all ways and to whom we all must ultimately look as the author of life, liberty, and happiness.

Of course, modeling God's nature and love cannot be done alone. It requires the help of others—the encouragement of others. That's why I encourage men to be continually influenced by outside sources, extended families, spiritual families, and spiritual mentors, like Ed Cole did for me and others still do for me.

There's a possibility that you might be hearing this fatherly advice for the first time. I remember when I first heard it from Ed. Even when I had children, though I loved them dearly, I was still too focused on me. I didn't reflect God as much as I should have. I'm glad He's not expecting perfection. But He's asking us for honesty with him and our family members.

Maybe you're in the same boat. I'm here to tell you it's never too late to change. As long as your children are alive, even at an older age, you can still have a positive, godly influence in their lives. Maybe like me you didn't have a positive role model in an earthly father. But I'm here to tell you that you can find one in our Heavenly Father. Seek to understand Him through prayer, reading the Scriptures, and learning from others. He'll show you what a true father is, a true husband is, and then you can reflect that type of love to your family.

We must practice what we preach. Parental hypocrites only have adverse effects upon their children's perpetuity of faith. As William Penn, the founder of Pennsylvania, once said, "A husband and wife that love and value one another, show their children and servants, that they should do so too. Others visibly lose their authority in their families, by their contempt of one another; and teach their children to be unnatural by their own examples."

We must show our children, grandchildren, and the youth of America that our conduct conforms with our beliefs in the Bible, the Declaration of Independence, the Constitution, and the Bill of Rights. Our family needs to see us reading our Bible. We need to read it with them. We need to post in some room in our house copies of the founding documents of the U.S., as well as the Ten Commandments. We need to stand by them as creeds that our households adhere to and live by. As Richard Stockton, lawyer and signer of the Declaration of Independence, said about his children's future reflection on their father's contributions and relation to this founding document:

> And as my children will have frequent occasion of perusing this instrument and may probably be particularly impressed with the last words of their father, I think it proper here not only

to subscribe to the entire belief of the great and leading doctrines of the Christian religion, . . . but also, in the bowels of a father's affection, to exhort and charge them that the fear of God is the beginning of wisdom, that the way of life held up in the Christian system is calculated for the most complete happiness that can be enjoyed in this mortal state.[17]

Men, it's time to move beyond the guilt and mistakes of the past and press on to be the fathers and husbands God has created us to be. We need continually to show our children and wives through our time and attention that they take priority over anything we do. As was conveyed by Douglas MacArthur, who bore the legacy of passion for his family equal to our Founders:

By profession I am a soldier and take pride in that fact. But I am prouder—infinitely prouder—to be a father. A soldier destroys in order to build; the father only builds, never destroys. The one has the potentiality of death; the other embodies creation and life. And while the hordes of death are mighty, the battalions of life are mightier still. It is my hope that my son, when I am gone, will remember me not from the battle field but in the home repeating with him our simple daily prayer, "Our Father who art in Heaven."

A MENTOR FOR THE FAMILY

I do not believe it is the primary responsibility of a school or church to instill religious conviction, morality, or patriotism in our children. I believe it is primarily the parent's responsibility. Both school and church are there to complement the parent's duty to God, country, and others.

Webster's Dictionary defines a mentor as "a trusted counselor or guide." For example, a model might reflect goodness. A mentor takes an active role in helping another to be good. A mentor is a leader—he knows the way, goes the way, and shows the way. Again, as Ed Cole taught me, every father and husband should be a mentor to his children and wife.

Of course no one starts off as a mentor. He or she must be mentored first. Maybe you're not the spiritual leader in your family yet. Maybe you look at your wife or even children as being far more spiritual than yourself. I understand. When I was young, my mother raised me and my brothers as Christians. When fame and fortune came, I drifted away from God. Though I never rejected Him, for years I was not spiritually growing as I should. When I met my wife, Gena, she brought me back to God. She was years ahead of me spiritually speaking. But then she reminded me that we were not in a competition but a co-op. She encouraged and challenged me to read the Bible daily. Now we spiritually encourage one another. I don't know if I will ever feel like the spiritual mentor I want to be to my wife and children, but it is a goal of mine.

Mentors come in many shapes and sizes. Some you know. Some you don't know. Some are authors. Others are pastors. Here again, in my opinion, Jesus was the greatest mentor who ever lived. He didn't have a wife or children, but He had His followers, His disciples. He spent three years investing His life in them, helping them to live out the life God calls us to live. There are no greater leadership lessons than those Jesus taught us. In fact, a score of mentoring and leadership books have been written on his life. One of my favorites is Bob Briner's, *The Leadership Lessons of Jesus*.

Being a mentor means we are willing to speak the truth in love, even when that is tough love. As Elias Boudinot, the president of Continental Congress, wrote to his daughter, Susan:

> You have been instructed from your childhood in the knowledge of your lost state by nature—the absolute necessity of a change of heart, and an entire renovation of soul to the image of Jesus Christ—of salvation thro' His meritorious righteousness

only—and the indispensable necessity of personal holiness without which no man shall see the Lord.[18]

One way Gena and I mentor our youngest children is through homeschooling. This is how we take an active role in their education, Christian enrichment, as well as train them in the tactics of America's culture wars while they're at home. We pattern our mentoring after parents like Gregg and Sono Harris, who homeschooled and built a legacy of leadership in their children. They are the parents of Alex and Brett Harris, whom I mentioned in the previous chapter. As successful parents and mentors, they have also created the Noble Institute for Leadership Development, where we all can find some incredible resources to build up our children as well as others around us.[19]

Another amazing couple we highly esteem as mentors are Bob and Pam Tebow. They have raised and empowered an amazing son, Tim Tebow, who made NCAA history as the first sophomore to win the Heisman Trophy as the best football player in the nation in 2007. Now they travel around the country sharing about their family and how Tim's life lessons began at home, on the family's forty-four-acre farm on the outskirts of Jacksonville, Florida where all five of the Tebow children were raised and homeschooled.[20] Bob states the goal for all men, when he says, "If I could get my kids to the age of twenty-five and they know God and serve God and have character qualities that please God, then I know God would be happy and I would be happy too."

We all need mentors, and most of all our children. No doubt parents serve as children's greatest model, mentor, and motivator. But others can serve in powerful ways too, especially when either of the parents are absent by death or neglect. Other mentors include youth workers (like those at churches), as well as the power of positive peers. Bottom line, it takes many mentors to raise children successfully in our age. That was true even in the time of our Founders. In the Revolutionary Era it was a collective effort that assured the positive rearing of children. As David

Ramsay, physician and member of the Continental Congress (1782–86) explained:

> Had I a voice that could be heard from New Hampshire to Georgia, it should be exerted in urging the necessity of disseminating virtue and knowledge among our citizens. On this subject, the policy of the eastern States is well worthy of imitation. The wise people of that extremity of the union never form a new township without making arrangements that secure to its inhabitants the instruction of youth and the public preaching of the gospel. Hence their children are early taught to know their rights and to respect themselves. They grow up good members of society and staunch defenders of their country's cause.[21]

Even as they aged, children remained respectful to their parents. And parents often reminded their young adult children of the principles on which they were raised. Before John Rush, the firstborn of Dr. Rush's thirteen children, departed for an overseas trip in 1796, Dr. Rush reminded his twenty-one-year-old son:

1. Be punctual in committing your soul and body to the protection of your Creator every morning and evening. Implore, at the same time, His mercy in the name of His Son, our Lord and Savior Jesus Christ.
2. Read in your Bible frequently, more especially on Sundays.
3. Avoid swearing and even an irreverent use of your Creator's name. Flee youthful lusts.
4. Be courteous and gentle in your behavior to your fellow passengers, and respectful and obedient to the captain of the vessel.

5. Attend public worship regularly every Sunday when you arrive at Calcutta.[22]

If the traditional family is to survive in our country, we need to focus more on giving our children a spiritual inheritance than a monetary or material one. And if the former is all we can leave them, then we've left them the best indeed. As the great orator and patriot Patrick Henry wrote in his last will and testament: "This is all the inheritance I can give my dear family. The religion of Christ can give them one which will make them rich indeed."

A MOTIVATOR FOR THE FAMILY

It is often said that the most powerful position in the world is the president of the United States. But I believe it hits much closer to home than the White House. I believe it is being a father or husband.

Calvin Coolidge, America's thirtieth president, once confessed, "I suppose I am the most powerful man in the world, but great power doesn't mean much except great limitations." Similarly, Thomas Jefferson once pleaded, "I hope our wisdom will grow with our power, and teach us, that the less we use our power the greater it will be." Their point is that power wasn't granted by God to be wielded like a sword, but to be used to empower and better others through wise decisions and actions. Unfortunately, we've forgotten that.

We equate power with dominance, rule, and self-glorification— that is unfortunate too. I believe when God created us in his image, he gave us the authority and autonomy to rule the earth, not one another. Power was given to serve, not enslave. As I've taught a myriad of martial arts students, the greatest form of power is still restraint and harnessing that potential to help others.

Great leaders have always understood this power principle, including Jesus, who demonstrated the original intent for our autonomy. He said, "Whoever wants to be first must be your servant—just as the Son of Man did not come to be served, but to serve, and to give his life as a ransom for many."[23] And so should we do the same.

When we don't properly utilize the power God has granted us, we naturally abuse it. An example of this can be found in my now deceased but once alcoholic father. Dad was generally a good man when he was sober, but sobriety was not his area of expertise or even practice. When he was drunk, the littlest things sent him into a rage. Even if he heard the water running while suffering from a hangover, he would explode in an abusive tirade, roaring threats and expletives against everyone in the house. The devil might be in the details, but he's also in the bottle—I've seen his spirits at work.

Growing up, my most difficult and confusing relationship was with my father. My father abandoned his role as a servant-leader, model, and mentor, dodging his duties and authority by drinking himself into a constant stupor. As a result, he failed to reflect a shadow of the Almighty's image to his children, something I believe is the highest calling of every father. He failed to see that what gives fathers a unique power is that they bear the same title and reflection of our Heavenly Father. He also was a poor reflection of a husband to my mother, which means I had to learn that role as well.

I genuinely believe it doesn't take as much as we think to be good husbands or fathers. I've learned it takes one primary thing: regular acts of love with kindness that consistently demonstrate that my family is my most valued treasure after God. As Tim Russert said in his excellent book, *Wisdom of our Fathers: Lessons and Letters from Daughters and Sons*, much of the adoration echoed from children for their fathers originates from simply taking time to be with them and making a big deal out of the simple things. As Bill Cosby put it, "Fatherhood is pretending the present you love most is soap-on-a-rope."

The Bible calls us to "encourage one another daily."[24] Who more would that apply to than husbands with wives and children? We must fight the urge to come home from a difficult day's work and take it out on our family. They don't deserve our energy to be harnessed into negative bickering or giving them our leftovers. We must reserve our best for them and empower them for living. Encourage them daily to live for God, country, and others.

Speaking of not giving our family the leftovers, my friend and well-known author and Christian family motivator, Gary Smalley, and coauthor John Trent, give a great illustration in their insightful book *The Language of Love*. In the book, a high school teacher named Jim came home too tired to talk to his wife. His wife, Susan, was left frustrated and angry. Susan then told Jim a story about a man who went to breakfast with his buddies. The man ate his favorite omelette, then afterward gathered up some crumbs in a bag. For lunch he ate a turkey-tenderloin pie and a huge salad, from which he gathered a few crumbs after and put in another leftover bag. When he came home that night, he handed his wife and two boys the little bags of leftovers. Susan said, "That's the way we feel when you come home with nothing left to give. All we get is leftovers. I'm waiting to enjoy a meal with you. Hoping for time to talk, laugh, and get to know you, longing to communicate with you the way you do every day with the guys, but all we get are doggy bags. Honey, don't you see? We don't need leftovers. We need you."

That's a powerful illustration that still touches my heart. Now I'm committed to my dying breath not to bring my wife and kids my leftovers. I hope you commit to that too. It has always been the commitment of great men, like Ed Cole and our Founders. Until their dying breaths, they praised their wives and children, and encouraged them to be everything they could be.

I want to finish by giving one last amazing proof of that from Dr. Benjamin Rush, who wrote this touching poem for his wife Julia the year before he died. I pray we all might be as passionate and communicative as he was. After thirty-six years of marriage, he still expressed how he was so grateful for her unwavering love and devotion to him:

When tossed upon the bed of pain,
And every healing art was vain,
Whose prayers brought back my life again?
My Julia's.
When shafts of scandal round me flew,
And ancient friends no longer knew
My humble name, whose heart was true?
My Julia's.
When falsehood aimed its poisoned dart,
And treachery pierced my bleeding heart,
Whose friendship did a cure impart?
My Julia's.
When hope was weak and faith was dead,
And every earthly joy was fled,
Whose hand sustained my drooping head?
My Julia's.
When worn by age and sunk in years,
My shadow at full length appears,
Who shall participate my cares?
My Julia.
When life's low wick shall feebly blaze,
And weeping children on me gaze,
Who shall assist my prayers and praise?
My Julia.
And when my mortal part shall lay,
Waiting in hope the final day,
Who shall mourn o'er my sleeping clay?

My Julia.
And when the stream of time shall end,
And the last trump the grave shall rend,
Who shall with me to heaven ascend?
My Julia.[25]

★ ★ ★

CHAPTER NINE

Be Fit
for the Fight

THIS CHAPTER IS a lot easier for me to write because it is about how I have lived for almost fifty years. Health and fitness is very important to me and I will give you guidelines I live by and advice by experts that I know are reputable and I respect.

I am going to tell you a little secret and you have to promise not to tell anyone. My wife Gena would like to celebrate a Golden wedding anniversary. That will only make me 108 years old. Do I need to say that I'm under a little pressure?

Okay, enough of that. Let's get to it. First of all, I want you to live as optimally as you can, with all the gusto your life can experience and offer. I haven't included this chapter merely to inspire you to eat better and exercise more, but to help set you free from the tyranny of the food industries processed foods and other cholesterol-clogging eatables.

The fast-food culture is mastering the bodies and minds of the masses. As a result, most Americans are overweight, undernourished, dehydrated, sick, and lacking the zip in their drive to even complete their to-do lists, let alone discover their dreams.

OBAMA'S FOODORAMA AND OUR OBSESSION WITH OTHERS' DIETS

Men's Fitness magazine deemed President Obama twice (in 2005 and 2008) among the "25 fittest men in America."[1]

Many present Obama's diet as one more reason why he should be our nation's supreme leader, for, they say, even it points to his rags to regal road to the White House. (In *Dreams from My Father*, Obama tells the story how he ate grasshopper, dog, and snake while living in Indonesia as a child).

Those who doubt Obama's pro-organic positions are referred to an array of nutritional news stories, blogs, photos, and video streams of him eating, golfing, playing basketball, working out at the gym, and so forth.[2] (You may recall last year how one of the largest Internet searches was sneaking a peak at the hearty and shirtless president-elect on the beach of his $9 million Hawaiian holiday getaway.) There's even a Web site committed to every possible link between food, drinks, and Obama—Obamafoodorama,[3] including the president's favorite trail mix and his hopeful beer of choice, the "audacity of hops."

While many admire Obama's physique and others commend his athletic ability, critics lambast some of his nutritional actions and habits are hypocritical. They say proof is in his personal consumption practices, which include periodic binges of fast and fatty foods[4] and occasional cigarette binges.[5]

Some say, however, graver for the nation's health is his choice for agriculture secretary, former Iowa Governor Tom Vilsack,[6] who many frown upon for his support of big agribusiness, genetically modified crops, and ethanol subsidies.[7] Also, many accuse Dr. Regina M. Benjamin, Obama's pick for surgeon general, as a bad model for being overweight in a nation where 34 percent of all Americans aged twenty and over are obese.[8]

"Americans were promised 'change,' not just another shill for Monsanto and corporate agribusiness," wrote Ronnie Cummins of the Organic Consumers Association.[9] He's not alone, as many nutritionists have giant concerns that the FDA will be last on Obama's governmental list of reform.[10]

To be honest, I'm not sure if Obama is fit enough to be America's next nutritional guru—and I don't think many Americans elected him for that reason. But I would remind him (especially as a relatively young president) that his health disciplines can help shape our country's youth like few others in the past, especially in a processed and fast-food nation, where there are more food additives than grains of sand at the beach, not to mention obesity now affects one-third of all youth.[11]

Here's something else of which I am quite certain: we should not be as fixated upon Obama's nutritional plan as we should be on our own. Whether Obama sneaks a few puffs or Oprah splurges on bagels and cream cheese,[12] we should be more self-reflective than judgmental and examine our own eating and exercise habits, not just those our culture admires. In an age where organic foods are making mainstream news,[13] gaining an upper hand on dinner tables and restaurant menus, we all need to fight to be fit and provide better models of well-being, instead of waiting for another "government bailout" in the form of universal health care to rescue us from our declining health.

THE CONSUMPTION WAR

At the heart of the culture wars is the most easily overlooked battle of all, because it's literally right before our eyes (about three times a day)—I call it the consumption war. Its ultimate goal is to control you as much as any other facet of the culture war—to win you over to its ways. And it appears to be working in most American homes and restaurants.

According to the World Health Organization[14] and the Centers for Disease Control and Prevention,[15] childhood and teen obesity in the U.S. has tripled over the last thirty years. Twenty-five percent of kids are overweight or obese and most parents don't even know it.[16] They also report one-third of adults are also obese, with another one-third being overweight.[17] And food isn't our only consumptive threat. An estimated one in five adults also smokes cigarettes in the United States. And more than 50 percent of American adults don't exercise enough to provide them any health benefits and 25 percent of adults are not active at all in their leisure time.[18]

That is not good! Why are we doing this to ourselves? Partly because our culture is entrenched in hedonism. We are all about pleasure. We go where we feel like going. We do what we feel like doing. We watch what we feel like watching. And we eat what we feel like eating. And God help those who tell us to do otherwise.

The problem is that we are literally killing ourselves in the pleasure process. I hear lots of people say that they want to retire early, but I never hear anyone say they want to die early. But that is exactly what we are doing. As my friend Mike Huckabee says, "We're digging our graves with our knife and fork."[19]

We've confused liberty for licentiousness. We think doing what we feel like doing is power and freedom, when really it's just carrying out what our flesh craves. True freedom is being able to look straight in the eye of what you feel like doing and possessing the power to say NO. Eating what we want isn't liberty—that's tyranny. Eating what is right is freedom—that's victory over oppression. And triumph over your body is exactly what I would like to help you obtain in this chapter.

Being overweight and obese go far beyond looks. It affects us physically, mentally and psychologically. Here are some of the things that can happen if you don't follow a healthy way of living. According to the Centers for Disease Control and Prevention, those include:

- Hypertension (high blood pressure)
- Osteoarthritis (a degeneration of cartilage and its underlying bone within a joint)

- Dyslipidemia (for example, high total cholesterol or high levels of triglycerides)
- Type 2 Diabetes
- Coronary heart disease
- Stroke
- Gallbladder disease
- Sleep Apnea and respiratory problems
- Depression
- Some cancers such as breast and colon.[20]

Some experts have referred to the health implosion as "diseases of comfort" and predict they will become the primary cause of death in this century and the following.

My friend, Dr. Tedd Mitchell, who is the medical director of the renowned Cooper Aerobics Center[21] in Dallas Texas, has a book out called, *Move Yourself*, and I would encourage you to buy it. It is the most comprehensive and practical book I have read explaining how being more active doesn't have to be difficult, time consuming, or expensive; and I might add, once you get started, it can be fun. You will get a clear understanding of how physical activity promotes health and protects you from disease and explains in detail how to get there.

Dr. Mitchell gives many lectures about health. During them he will half jokingly refer to the proliferating new order of inactive *Homo sapiens* as *Homo sedentarius*. He has told me that while he gets a big laugh from audiences when he says that statement, he realizes there is nothing funny about the alarming trend of inactivity and the mass scale of sickness, obesity, shortened longevity, and the financial costs to society that result from them. He says that, if you want a disturbing glimpse of how bad the situation has become in the last few years and an idea of the horrendous direction we're headed in, get on the Internet and go to the Web site for Centers for Disease Control and Prevention.[22] Check out the trends for obesity and diabetes. They will show you how we are collectively headed for the graveyard.

It's true that genetics, environment, socioeconomic status, metabolism, and behavior can be contributors to these ailments. But the fact is most Americans are overweight and obese because they eat poorly and don't exercise. Most of our foods are super high in fats, sugars, and salt. And, compared to other countries, we eat much larger portions.

Is it any wonder most Americans feel apathetic and lethargic, lacking the energy to move their lives and this country forward? How can we expect to fight a culture war when we can't win a consumption war?

AMERICA'S BIGGEST THREAT

While the CIA and FBI track terrorist intelligence and activity, our military seeks to calm international unrest abroad, border patrol and minutemen try to guard our country's borders, America's biggest threat is largely homegrown and has already infiltrated most of our homes: unhealthy eating habits and no exercise.

Of all the terrorists perching at our borders, those that penetrate the barriers of our body are still our greatest threat and cause the highest numbers of casualties—roughly 2 million per year. I'm not referring to biological warfare but consumption combat. Every year more than 750,000 Americans die from cardiovascular diseases, 550,000 from cancer, and 450,000 from smoking.

A couple of years ago Dr. Richard Carmona, then Surgeon General of the United States, reported to Congress about the crisis. The facts are staggering: "[Each] year, more than 300,000 Americans will die from illnesses related to overweight and obesity. . . ."[23] Obesity contributes to the number-one cause of death in our nation: heart disease."[24] Obesity might even be a factor in the greater numbers of maternal deaths[25] and automobile accident fatalities.[26]

Carmona also noted that the fundamental reason our children are overweight is the same reason adults are: "Too many children are eating too much and moving too little."[27] He concludes by saying these nutritional habits are learned at a young age, "Our children did not create this problem. Adults did. Adults increased the portion size of children's meals, developed the games and television that children find spellbinding, and chose the sedentary lifestyles that our children emulate. So adults must take the lead in solving this problem."[28]

A NOT-SO-CLEAR BUT PRESENT DANGER

If we actually knew of terrorists trying to cross our nation's borders or even burglars breaking into our homes, we would undoubtedly do everything within our power to stop them. So why don't we prevent incoming enemies into our bodies, hearts, and minds? A good example is trans fats.

Trans fats have been proven to be terrorists to our bodies, increasing the risk of coronary heart disease, lowering levels of good cholesterol, and raising levels of bad cholesterol, among other chronic health detriments.[29] These subtle fats have been laced for decades in a host of our manufactured foods, from shortening, margarine, potato chips, cookies, crackers, buttered popcorn, snack foods, breads, breakfast cereals, and other foods made with or fried in partially hydrogenated oils, including donuts and French fries.

I'm glad to see that food industries are finally raising red flags about the not-so-clear and present danger of trans fats, most of which are commercially created when vegetable oils are hydrogenated. Government regulations have mandated industries to list trans fats separately from other fats on their product labels. Nevertheless, it's important for every consumer to know that a product with less than .5 grams can legally be advertised as "0 grams of trans fat." So read the labels for the words "partially hydrogenated." If they're there, trans fats are present, despite the label denying it.

Trans fats are only one group of terrorist cells. There are, of course, plenty of other threats we consume, breathe in, and allow to permeate nearly every organ in our bodies, some directly and some indirectly.

That's the bad news.

THE BATTLEFIELDS CALLED KITCHENS AND GYMS

The good news is that, if eating and obesity exacerbate illnesses and mortality statistics, then they also remain the most preventable causes of American deaths. We can reduce the rates of the one in five children and two out of three adults, who are overweight in our nation.[30] If we are as vigilant about attacking our bodily adversaries as we are global terrorists, we can save tens if not hundreds of thousands of Americans' lives every year—maybe your own. If we are half as tenacious about nutritional education and application as we are about e-mailing, we can reverse the trends of consumption casualties. The question is, will we be as diligent to save American lives in our kitchens as we are those on the battlefields?

If we knew more than 300,000 or 500,000 people would die from a specific type of terrorist attack this year, our government and America's citizens would move heaven and earth to deter it. Yet we know that number of people will die this next year from illnesses related to being overweight or having coronary heart disease and what are we as a nation and individuals going to do about it?

I believe the healthcare crisis in America begins with Americans, not governmental intervention and bureaucracy that mandates socialized medicine. Our Founders agreed. They also never could have imagined a government micromanaging civilian diets by creating a Food and Drug Administration or United States Department of Agriculture. Thomas Jefferson quipped, "Was the government to prescribe to us our medicine and diet, our bodies would be in such keeping as our souls are now."[31] Our Founders health care system was a very simple one: take care of your health.

We don't need to pay billions of dollars through new taxes to provide universal medical coverage. If anything, I believe the government needs to discover more ways to motivate personal responsibility and disease prevention, encourage the states' role as stages for new market-based ideas, and challenge private sectors to seek creative ways to bring down medical costs. Most of all, if we took better care of ourselves, we could reduce our personal and national medical costs and live longer and happier at the same time. If not, we will be bound to live by the words of Benjamin Franklin, "God heals and the doctor takes the fee."[32]

Unfortunately, while many conservatives quote patriots and Scriptures all Americans should live by, they often overlook our Founders' and God's commands to care for our bodies—the Bible calls our body the "temple of His spirit."[33] If we want to live at our optimum, we need to return to treating our bodies like temples instead of like trash bins. As Dr. Don Colbert says, "Eating bad is not going to keep us out of heaven, but it will get us there a lot quicker!"

The Founders of our country were generally very health conscious and in very good shape for men of their times. Benjamin Franklin shared some pithy bits of nutrition wisdom in the *Poor Richard's Almanack*. Here are a few examples:

Eat to live and not live to eat.[34]

To lengthen thy life lessen thy meals.[35]

Early to bed and early to rise, makes a man healthy, wealthy, and wise.[36]

(Many of us grew up saying those quotes, but who knew it was Benjamin Franklin who said them?!)

This type of applied wisdom is what contributed to the production and longevity of the Founders' lives. For example, it is interesting to note that the signers of the Declaration of Independence lived an average age of sixty-seven years—twenty of them in their sixties, sixteen in their seventies, five in their eighties and one (Johnson) lived to be ninety-two.[37] At seventy-six years old, Thomas Jefferson remained health conscious and healthy:

> I use spectacles at night, but not necessarily in the day unless in reading small print. My hearing is distinct in particular conversation, but confused when several voices cross each other, which unfits me for the society of the table. I have been more fortunate than my friend [Dr. Rush] in the article of health. So free from catarrhs[38] that I have not had one (in the breast, I mean) on an average of eight or ten years through life. I describe this exemption partly to the habit of bathing my feet in cold water every morning, for sixty years past. A fever of more than twenty-four hours I have not had above two or three times in my life. A periodical headache has afflicted me occasionally. . . . Perhaps, in six or eight years, for two or three weeks at a time, which now seems to have left me; and except on a late occasion of indisposition, I enjoy good health.[39]

EDUCATE YOURSELF ON HEALTH AND NUTRITION

If we are sick and tired of being sick and tired, or just want to better protect the borders of our bodies, then the first thing we must do is schedule some time to educate ourselves and our loved ones on habits of healthiness and nutrition. I would also recommend you purchase Dr. Don Colbert's book, *Seven Pillars of Health*. Dr. Colbert has been a medical doctor since 1984 and board certified in family practice since 1987, and has a great educational Web site.[40] Colbert's book gives a thorough and excellent treatise about the seven pillars for a healthy body and soul. What I love about his approach and materials is that he too simplifies complex matters and boils down the web of healthy lifestyle tips into simple steps.

If you can't afford a book, check one out at your local library or go to Web sites like the American Academy of Family Physicians[41] and the American Heart Association,[42] where you'll find loads of free information about nutrition and healthy living. The American Heart Association has some fantastic suggestions for reducing health risks and obtaining a more vigorous lifestyle,[43] even for children.[44]

Pillar #1: Drink sufficient amounts of water

Dr. Colbert says the journey to a better you starts with simply drinking water. Being made up of roughly 70 percent water, drinking water makes sense. It is the most foundational aspect of life and the single-most important nutrient. It is used in every bodily function.

The fact is you can live five to seven weeks without food, but only five days without water. Dr. Colbert says that, "Many Americans live in a mildly dehydrated state with various irritating symptoms and never realize it."[45] Some signs or symptoms of a lack of hydration include headaches, skin problems, digestion problems, back pain, arthritis, dry skin, overweight, high blood pressure, asthma, memory loss, and other ailments. Colbert says checking for sufficient amounts of water is one of his first medical checks when a patient comes to his office for medical treatment. Many people have actually experienced relief and even been cured through proper hydration.[46]

The doctor recommends you don't wait until you're thirsty to drink water. Because the average body loses about two quarts through organ functions, perspiration, filtration, and secretion, it is important to rehydrate regularly. Use a filtration system or drink good bottled water, because contaminants are plenty in much of our tap water.

The equation to figure the recommended amount of water your body needs is: your weight divided by two equals the ounces of water you need to consume daily. And not all of that needs to be drunk, as much of your food intake provides the liquid (e.g., bananas are 70 percent water, apples contain 80 percent, tomatoes and watermelons 90 percent, and lettuce 95 percent).

Pillar #2: Get adequate amounts of sleep

Dr. Colbert says that getting adequate amounts of sleep is necessary if you expect to function properly. Adequate amounts of sleep are generally seven to nine hours a day. A good night's sleep restores, repairs, and rejuvenates the body. It is vital for the immune system and slows the aging process. Dr. Mark Stibich has also studied sleep extensively and shares ten benefits of a good night's sleep: keeps your heart healthy, may prevent cancer, reduces stress, reduces inflammation, enhances alertness, bolsters memory, may help you lose weight, makes you smarter, reduces risks of depression, [and] helps the body make repairs.[47]

We all know what it's like to not get enough sleep. The causes of insomnia can range from anxiety to medical ailments. But one doesn't always need to be dependent upon sleep medications, which are now a multi-billion dollar business. There are different natural alternatives and strategies you can use to get more sleep or cure slight cases of insomnia, including taking herbs to making practical changes like learning to handle stress better, changing behaviors or patterns, or getting counseling.

Here again, Thomas Jefferson gave us glimpses into his sleep patterns, "I am not so regular in my sleep as the Doctor [Rush] says he was, devoting to it from five to eight hours, according as my company or the book I am reading interests me; and I never go to bed without an hour, or half hour's previous reading of something moral, whereon to ruminate in the intervals of sleep. But whether I retire to bed early or late, I rise with the sun."[48]

Consult a health practitioner and check reputable guides[49] to test and see if you are getting sufficient hours of sleep for your age, or for advice on how to sleep a few more hours or overcoming sleep obstacles.[50] Of course Dr. Colbert's chapter on sleep provides some wonderful counsel too.

Pillar #3: Eat living foods

You may be daily getting full from food, but, if you're like most Americans, your body is likely deprived of the nutrients it needs to be healthy. Foods with the vitamins, minerals, fiber, and other nutrients you need are what Dr. Colbert calls "live foods," which are fruits, vegetables, grains, seeds, and nuts. He says that we all generally have two shelves in our pantry: one for living foods and one for dead foods. You'll know them by their "fruit" or what they produce:

> [Dead] foods will make you disease-prone, will cause degenerative diseases such as diabetes, cardiovascular disease, and arthritis, and will make you overweight. They will also make you fatigued and prone to develop hypertension and high cholesterol.
>
> [Living] foods will protect your body from cancer, heart disease, all degenerative diseases, and obesity, and they will sharpen your mind, energize you, and enliven you.[51]

It is important that you eat a variety from the five basic food groups.[52] The American Heart Association even offers a grocery list of more than eight hundred foods from those five groups that are low in saturated fat and cholesterol.[53] Similarly, the American Academy of Family Physicians offers some excellent tips for a heart-healthy diet.[54]

It's often been said you'll know the living or good foods in your grocery store because they are along the outside parameters inside the store. Most of the processed, salt- and sugar-filled products are on the inside aisles. Once upon a time, long before the world of fast-food restaurants, live foods were not always fresh, and they were sometimes scarce, but they were the only foods that were consumed in most cultures. Even back in Jesus' day, daily bread was good bread:

> At the two meals each day, bread was the main food [for Jews of Jesus' time]. The light breakfasts—often flat bread, olives, and cheese (from goats or sheep)—were carried to work and eaten at mid-morning. Dinners were more substantial, consisting of vegetable (lentil) stew, bread (barley for the poor, wheat for the rich), fruit, eggs, and/or cheese. Fish was a common staple, but red meat was reserved for special occasions. Locusts were a delicacy and reportedly taste like shrimp. (Jews wouldn't have known that, however, since shrimp and all other crustaceans were "unclean.")[55]

If you want to live optimally, you need to consume fruits, vegetables, and whole-grain and low-fat dairy products daily. Walnuts and almonds are the king and queen of the nuts. And try to eat fish twice a week, especially salmon (which contains omega-3 fatty acids that lowers the risks of coronary artery disease). Reduce foods and beverages that are high in calories, salt, sugars, trans fats, and saturated fats. Stop to read the labels. If you can't even pronounce the ingredients going into your body, then why are you putting them in there?

Of course America's Founders knew nothing of our processed foods, rather they lived on fresh fruits, vegetables, meats, etc.[56] Here's a little insider and even humorous information about Thomas Jefferson's diet at seventy-six years of age, as he detailed to Dr. Vine Utley:

> The request of the history of my physical habits would have puzzled me not a little, had it not been for the model with which you accompanied it, of Doctor Rush's answer to a similar

inquiry. I live so much like other people, that I might refer to ordinary life as the history of my own. I have lived temperately, eating little animal food, and that not as an ailment, so much as a condiment for the vegetables which constitute my principal diet. I double, however, the Doctor's glass and a half of wine, and even treble it with a friend; but halve its effects by drinking the weak wines only. The ardent wines I cannot drink, nor do I use ardent spirits in any form. Malt liquors and cider are my table drinks, and my breakfast is of tea and coffee. I have been blest with organs of digestion which accept and concoct, without ever murmuring, whatever the palate chooses to consign to them, and I have not yet lost a tooth by age.[57]

About the only place I disagree with our Founders was their use of tobacco. Of course they were not as aware of the extensive cancer-causing risks and other debilitating diseases and conditions associated with smoking. My father was addicted to cigarettes. He contracted throat cancer and had to have a metal tracheotomy placed in his throat. I always thought he would die from alcoholism, but cigarettes did the job first.

It is very sad to see that four thousand more adolescents ages twelve to seventeen begin smoking every day.[58] We need to oppose cigarette marketing to youth through such ploys as "flavored tobacco"[59] and pseudo-healthy alternatives like "clove cigarettes."[60]

To be honest with you, Gena is the one who keeps our family on a healthy diet. But I do make a mean peanut butter and banana sandwich! She is an avid reader on health and nutrition.

We eat lots of whole foods, mostly organic. I realize it is more costly to buy foods of this kind, but, when you consider the cost of long-term disease and health care, it is a much smaller investment in the long run and you will feel better for it. Prevention is the key and should be your mind-set.

For breakfast, we try to eat a balanced diet of protein and whole grains. It is important to start the day off with something very healthy and not skipping that meal. Breakfast jump-starts your metabolism, feeds your brain, balances out your blood sugar and will supply you with sustained energy. It is typical for our family to eat a peanut butter and banana sandwich on sprouted grain bread for breakfast. This provides lots of energy and our twins love it too.

I might add that our children, Dakota and Danilee, have been taught from the time they could understand, that what you put in your mouth should have purpose for their health. Not that they aren't like other kids wanting ice cream. It is like anything else that is learned by what their parents do and are teaching them. Like my kids, I like a good bowl of Blue Bell ice cream!

We keep fresh fruit and vegetables readily available to snack on. Lunch is usually tuna fish in moderation because of mercury levels, or avocado sandwiches. We try and have dinner by 5:00 or 5:30 p.m., and no later than 6:00 p.m. By doing this we have been able to maintain our weight and feel better the next morning by not waking up sluggish. We try not to eat too many complex carbohydrates at night either: a small red baked potato or about a half cup of brown rice would be about max. We try to eat a lot of steamed, rich green vegetables, or fresh romaine salads with lots of color, along with a six-ounce piece of baked skinless chicken breast or wild salmon. Gena cooks with virgin olive oil. All oils should be cold expeller pressed (just check the label before you buy one). We don't use much sugar in our home. If we do, it is sugar in the raw. We use Stevia for a sugar substitute; it is natural and a great replacement for sugar. I would recommend checking with your doctor before you try it. And don't forget the water. I try to carry a bottle with me all the time. Drink lots.

Again, eating with a purpose is key. I will say again. I do my best to eat healthily and in moderation. I have to confess that when Gena and I see a movie, I can't watch it without a bag of popcorn (non-buttered of course). And every now and then I do splurge, but I know the importance of keeping my tank (body) fueled with the right kind of gas.

Gena has a philosophy she uses on herself. She will say, "If I eat that, how is it going to make me feel afterward?" Again it is a mind set. But, before you know it, the more you stick with it, the better you will start feeling.

Pillar #4: "Stir the waters"

Dr. Colbert refers to exercise as "stirring the waters" because we're made mostly from water. And because we all know that stagnant water like ponds only fester with fungus and disease.

I challenge you with a simple goal of daily "stirring the waters." To be like a mountain stream instead of a pond—moving, fresh, and vibrant. Ever noticed even among the elderly, those who look the best are often those who keep moving? Movement reduces the risks of stagnation and decay. Even the Bible says, "For physical training is of some value. . . ."[61] When my mom, Wilma Knight, was eighty-six years old, her hands and hips were arthritic, and she could only get around by using a cane. Then she started exercising, "stirring the waters," and a year later she no longer has arthritis in her hands, little in her hips, and no longer needs her cane, as well as possesses more energy and better spirits. Mom even motivates the other elderly residents in her assisted-living home to "stir the waters" too.

Dr. Colbert gives a list of proven physical benefits of daily stirring the waters. It reduces the risks of cancer, prevents heart attacks and heart disease, improves lymphatic flow, lowers stress, promotes weight loss, decreases appetite, increases perspiration (which eliminates toxins), slows down the aging process, builds strong bones and muscles, improves your digestion, reduces depression, improves memory retention and reaction time, slows Alzheimer's disease and may help prevent Parkinson's, increases lung capacity, alleviates pain, and increases energy levels.

I don't want to oversimplify exercise, but it is basically whatever gets your heart pumping and uses major muscle groups. Physical employment, playing with your kids, walking your dogs, working in the yard, dancing, biking, hiking, etc., are all good.[62]

Make sure to check with your health practitioner about what exercise is best for you.

Our Founders often worked hard, hiked, and walked lots. Thomas Jefferson was a huge advocate of walking and spoke about others who were as well. At forty-three years old, Jefferson wrote:

> Of all the exercises walking is best. . . . No one knows, till he tries how easily a habit of walking is acquired. A person who never walked three miles will in the course of a month become able to walk fifteen or twenty [miles] without fatigue. I have known some great walkers and had particular accounts of many more; and I never knew or heard of one who was not healthy and long lived. This species of exercise therefore is much to be advised.[63]

And when he couldn't walk great distances any longer at seventy-six years old, Jefferson jumped on his horse: "I enjoy good health; too feeble, indeed, to walk much, but riding without fatigue six or eight miles a day, and sometimes thirty or forty."[64]

Brisk walking is also one of Dr. Colbert's favorite recommended activities. If there is one universal exercise, walking has got to be it.[65] Dr. Kenneth Cooper, founder of the Cooper Institute in Dallas, Texas, and famed "father of aerobics," states:

> We know from research that if you walk two miles in thirty minutes, three times a week, the chances of dying from any cause is reduced by 58 percent and your life span increases by six years. The health and fitness of our youth are rapidly declining. We are seeing unprecedented levels of obesity and type 2 diabetes among children and adolescents. If this continues, we are living in the first generation in which parents will outlive their children. Healthy children think and learn better. The areas most profuse with blood and oxygen in the brain after

exercise are areas responsible for creativity and memory. We know from existing FITNESS GRAM data that the more physically fit students are the better they perform academically and have fewer discipline problems.[66]

I can attest to that from my KickStartKids (www.KickStart Kids.org) program, in which we teach the martial arts to middle school kids in lieu of the physical education class. The kids in our martial arts program get better grades and there are fewer discipline problems than the other kids in the school. And these are inner-city schools, with many at-risk children.

As I mentioned in the beginning of the chapter, exercise is very important to me. I will now share with you the things I do to keep this sixty-eight-year-old body in optimal condition. Actually, my wife Gena is my workout partner. I would suggest you get a workout partner, who will help you stay motivated.

Here is my weekly workout schedule. You can use part of it, all of it, or none of it!

Monday-Wednesday-Friday:

Total Gym—I do a routine that takes me exactly fifteen minutes.

Fast Walk—Then we will fast walk two miles or use one of our elliptical machines for thirty minutes.

Crunches—I will do ten minutes of crunches for my abs.

Stretching—I will finish with a few minutes of stretching. That's it!

Tuesday-Thursday-Saturday:

Martial Arts—I start by stretching, then move on to isolated kicks in slow motion. Then I will do hand and feet combination strikes on a heavy bag. If I have someone to work out with, I will practice my jujitsu. Gena doesn't like me getting her into chokeholds or arm bars!

Pool exercise—We finish by doing kicks in the pool. Why do I use the pool? It has numerous benefits: low impact water workouts combine cardiovascular exercises with strength training, with little risk of injury. Even though you might feel lighter, the added resistance of water makes the aerobics challenging. Water provides twelve times the resistance of air, because of its increased density. As water pushes against the body, the movements become more difficult, requiring muscles to work harder. I strongly recommend it.

Many of you know that I endorse the Total Gym,[67] but what you might not know is that I've also been working out on it for thirty-two years. I actually learned about the Total Gym by chance. I pulled a rotator cuff lifting weights and I was going to have it operated on when I got a call from Larry Westfall and Tom Campanaro,[68] who had just developed this machine for rehab centers. They told me the Total Gym could rehab[69] my shoulder and I wouldn't need the operation. I was skeptical, but I decided to give it a try.

Tom and Larry came to my home, set up the machine, and showed me the exercises they wanted me to do. They said to try it for six weeks and see how I feel. I did. In six weeks, my shoulder was healed and I was able to resume my jujitsu training. While I was grappling, I thought to myself, "I feel stronger and more flexible." I finally realized it was my exercising on the Total Gym that did it. I called Tom and Larry and told them that it not only rehabbed my rotator cuff but also increased my strength. They said, "Sure, because of the elongated movements on the Total Gym, it not only builds up muscle strength, but tendon strength as well." That was 1976. And the Total Gym is as much a part of my life as my martial arts training has been since 1960.

Whatever your particular exercise of choice,[70] the ideal is to hit your target heart rate[71] for twenty to thirty minutes at least four times a week. To figure out your target heart rate (during exercise): subtract your age from 220. Multiply that number by .6

(60 percent). Multiply the original number again by .9 (90 percent). The range between those two numbers is your target heart rate.

So keep moving! Or as Dr. Colbert says, "Keep stirring the waters!" Or do as sisters Bessie and Saddie Delany recommended a few years before they died (Bessie at 104 and Saddie at 109): "God only gave you one body, so you better be nice to it. Exercise, because if you don't, by the time you're our age, you'll be pushing up daisies."

Pillar #5: Detoxify

That is a big word that basically means, "Get rid of the toxins in your body." It is a word that was once reserved for drug treatment centers. Now it is used in mainstream society because our air, water, food, and household products are streaming with contaminants.

According to Dr. Colbert, we all have toxins in our bodies. Believe it or not, there are about 80,000 chemicals registered in the United States, with 2,000 new being added each year. They are used for everything from food additives to prescriptions drugs, supplements, personal products like makeup and lotions, to cleaning supplies and lawn care, etc.

Most people are aware that our food supply is polluted by herbicides, pesticides, and chemicals, but not everyone knows that up to 2,100 chemicals are present in most municipal water supplies. Is it any wonder that an American Red Cross sample study of babies' umbilical cords discovered an average of 287 contaminants, of which 180 are carcinogenic?

Some ailments caused or exacerbated by these toxins include chronic fatigue, heart disease, memory loss, premature aging, skin disorders, arthritis, hormone imbalances, anxiety, headaches, emotional disorders, cancers, and autoimmune diseases.

While we cannot completely avoid toxicity, we can reduce the number of contaminants we put into our bodies. Here are Dr. Colbert's suggestions for how to do that:

- Drinking adequate amounts of water (for flushing and filtering your body's systems)
- Eating green foods and taking specific nutritional supplements to keep your liver (the body's main detoxifying organ) healthy
- Eating plenty of fiber—25 to 30 grams per day
- Eating living, organic (chemical-free) foods
- Sweating and brushing your skin—and using sauna therapy
- Using natural products (and gloves when you're not)[72]
- Cleaning the air in your home with air purifiers and live plants
- Fasting using fresh, juiced organic fruits and vegetables.[73]

God created an awesome toxin and waste management system in our bodies, with our liver, lungs, skin, colon, urinary tract, lymphatics, and sweat glands. But our organs are being tapped out by the extensive use of chemicals throughout our society. If we plan to be around to fight the culture war in the next generation, we must detoxify!

Pillar #6: Take nutritional supplements

In 2002 the prestigious *Journal of the American Medical Association* shocked the medical world by publishing a study that recommended all adults take a multi-vitamin supplement for the purpose of helping to prevent chronic diseases.[74] Their recommendation was so shocking because for years before the medical fields continually reported that we could get all the vitamins and minerals we need from the food we consume.

Because of overused soils, contaminants, and additives, our foods have been depleted of their nutrients. You've heard it said that "God made dirt, and dirt won't hurt." Well it can now, especially when it's been stripped of its nutrients from excessive use and tampering.[75] Our fruits and vegetables might shine more in the markets, but they offer less to your body as far as nourishment.

It is estimated that we can only acquire 50 to 70 percent of our body's nutrients, even if we eat very well. But most Americans don't eat well, so those percentages are much less. Specifically, Dr. Colbert believes most Americans are deficient of vitamins and minerals, including the basic vitamins A, B, C, D, E, and K, magnesium, calcium, fiber, and potassium.

You need supplemental vitamins and minerals, but, before you purchase and take them, discuss your body's requirements with a health practitioner. Excessive dosages can be detrimental to your health and are often marketed in those amounts even in the best nutritional stores. You and your physician (not those marketing the products) should monitor your proper intake of supplements. At very least, because you can over-take some, I recommend you consult a reputable guide to supplements like Berkeley's "Wellness Guide to Dietary Supplements."[76]

Our Founders knew nothing of our processed foods. They again could never have even imagined a Twinkie or its shelf life. Most were hunters, raised their own animals, and grew gardens and orchards, from which came a rich variety of fresh foods. They would have acquired much higher dosages of nutrients from their foods than ours today, so of course they would not have needed supplements.

Pillar #7: Reduce stress

Dr. Colbert cites a June 2005 *Wall Street Journal* article about how to live longer, which concludes that stress "kills" people as much as poor health habits such as smoking, drinking alcohol, and not exercising. Similarly, a multiple-year study at the University of London showed that unmanaged stress was six times more predictive of cancer and heart disease than smoking, high cholesterol levels, and high blood pressure. And in a Mayo Clinic study of people with heart disease, stress was the strongest predictor of future cardiac problems.

Of course stress can be caused by everything from medical ailments, financial difficulties, relational problems, retirement, or just trying to relax. Some stresses are triggered by outside sources, while others we bring on ourselves. Some stresses are good, such as a wedding or a promotion. Other stresses are bad, such as the loss of employment or a loved one.

Whatever the case, Dr. Colbert recommends particular practices to lower stress:

- **Mindfulness.** Letting go of present negative thoughts and finding something to enjoy or think positively about in the present moment.
- **Reframing.** This is learning to see the past and the future in a more positive light. Even when negative things happen, God can take those and turn them around for the good. Reframing gives us the power to see the past and future in light of what good can come from them. Scriptural reframing is one of the most powerful ways to relieve stress. It is simply replacing our fears, worries, failures, grief, sorrows, and shame with God's promises.
- **Laughing.** Laughter is still the best medicine. more than two thousand years ago the Bible said, "A merry heart is good medicine, but depression drains one's strength."[77] Laughter lowers stress hormones and increases feel-good hormones.
- **Forgiving.** When you are hurt, intentionally or unintentionally, offering mercy (undeserved favor) and forgiveness (pardonable favor) will always lower stress. To the contrary, harboring bitterness actually produces stress chemicals within us.
- **Practicing stress-reducing habits.** No one is a master of stress. Practice makes perfect. Practice these above techniques, as well as others like deep breathing, sitting in serene locations, working on behavioral

modifications, and choosing to maintain a positive and optimistic attitude.[78]

No prescription on stress would be finished without mentioning that God wants to help us bear our burdens. Jesus said, "Come to me, all of you who are weary and loaded down with burdens, and I will give you rest."[79] He has helped me manage stress more than anything or anyone in this life. In fact, there's simply no way that I could handle the pressures of this life without Him. And I know He can help you too. He's always just a prayer away.

Pillar #8 (my additional pillar): Feed yourself spiritually

In thanks and tribute to Doctors Colbert, Mitchell, and Cooper, who all believe in the power of spirituality, I'm going to add an eighth pillar to my list. We are more than physical beings. We are holistic creatures. Your body is more than a shell. It houses an eternal spirit, and how you nourish it affects your mind, body, and soul. They are all interrelated. Each affects the other in some way. And we need to nourish each in a balanced way. Thomas Jefferson echoed the connection when he said, "Health must not be sacrificed to learning. A strong body makes the mind strong."[80]

Thousands of healthcare professionals concur about the power one's religious practice plays on our total wellbeing, including the National Cancer Institute,[81] the Mayo Clinic,[82] and the National Center for Complementary and Alternative Medicine.[83] More than two thousand years ago the Scriptures again proclaimed, "[Faith] will bring health to your body and nourishment to your bones."[84] Even Jesus Himself said, "Man shall not live by bread alone, but by every Word that proceeds from the mouth of God."[85]

When I first met Gena, now my wife, I had drifted from God and was living the secular life of a celebrity. I had fame and fortune, but I also had a giant hole in my heart. Gena brought me back to my faith by morning Bible reading. At first, she did all the reading, but soon after the Holy Spirit grabbed me and filled the hole in my heart, I took over the reading. To this day, as soon as we get up, we start the day reading a chapter from the Bible. For us, it helps us start the day on the right foot.

If you'd like to begin a spiritual exercise, I recommend that you read a chapter a day from the Book of Proverbs (in the Bible)—there is one for every day of the month. We like to read a Proverb in the morning and a Psalm at night, because Proverbs gives daily wisdom and life application and Psalms are soothing for the soul and a good night's sleep. The Bible version we like to read from is the *New International Version Life Application Study Bible*, for its simple readability. And lastly, I recommend a daily serving of the "Daily Bread" devotional,[86] which is now available online and is a great source of inspiration for successful living.

A FINAL FITNESS ENCOURAGEMENT

In my newest book, *The Official Chuck Norris Fact Book* (released on 11/1/09 by Tyndale Publishing), I gave my top 101 Chuck Norris Facts and favorite subsequent stories about them. For those who have somehow not heard of the Chuck Norris Facts, they are mythical expressions of my life and abilities, a collection of sayings, quips, and quotes, created by young and old alike around the country and world, that have elevated my character and personhood to almost legendary, Paul Bunyan-like dimensions. One of those 101 favorite Facts is "Chuck Norris can eat just one Lay's potato chip."

Whoever wrote that fact has not seen me when I am watching a football game at home. I can tear the bag open during the first quarter and ask myself by half time while licking the salt from my finger tips, "What's this empty bag doing in my hand?" I won't even tell you how quick a bowl of Blue Bell ice cream can disappear in the second half!

I'm a believer in new beginnings. That is why I'm an advocate of New Year's resolutions, fresh starts or do-overs, as my wife and I call them. The potential to fail is always present. But so is the potential to succeed and soar to the next level. And studies show that our successes actually happen more often than we think.

A University of Washington survey[87] conducted several years ago shows that 63 percent of the people questioned were still keeping their number one resolution after two months. That's great hope-filled news.

"The keys to making a successful resolution are a person's confidence that he or she can make the behavior change and the commitment to making that change," said the survey. "Resolutions are a process, not a one-time effort that offer people a chance to create new habits."

So don't ever stop trying, even if it's mid-July. Don't ever stop growing. Or as I say and live by in my principles for life, "Develop yourself to the maximum of your potential in all ways."

Whether you want to exercise more,[88] eat better,[89] lose weight,[90] stop smoking,[91] cut down on alcohol,[92] get out of debt,[93] build up your marriage or family,[94] make a new spiritual commitment,[95] make new friends,[96] don't ever quit striving to better yourself each and every year.

Or as Benjamin Franklin put it, "Be always at war with your vices, at peace with your neighbors, and let each new year find you a better man." Or woman!

If you do, I believe you too will find the power and discipline to eat just one Lay's potato chip! Of course—except during football games!

CHAPTER TEN

Reawaken the American Dream

LAST YEAR *Forbes* magazine produced a column in which they asked over sixty of us celebrities and other notables to answer one question: "What is the American Dream?"[1]

The answers were fascinating and showed just how diverse we are in our approach to the purpose of America.

There were those who defined the American Dream as freedom. Tom Brokaw replied, "To me, the American Dream is the freedom to choose to live how and where you want, to determine how you'll be governed and to provide your children with even more choices than you had." Similarly, Kurt Russell believes, "the American Dream has changed—now I believe it's a wish for freedom at no cost, an existence devoid of scarcity and free from judgment of any kind."

Many others defined the dream as a quality of life not yet obtained. Nancy Pelosi said, "The American Dream is the hope for a better future with equal opportunity for all to participate in the prosperity and success of our great nation."

Some defined the dream as being treated fairly or maximizing your personal potential. Condoleezza Rice said, "The American Dream is being dealt with and considered on your own merits."

Colin Powell said, "The American Dream is something that every immigrant brought to this country, as my parents did, and that is the ability to go as far as you can in life, limited only by your own dreams and willingness to work hard." And Tiki Barber simply said, "The American Dream is opportunity."

There were a few expected responses. Martha Stewart defined the dream in terms of quality of life "spent at home with my friends, family members and pets." Oliver Stone defined it as a type of corporate and government conspiracy or takeover, "The American Dream is a rigged, corporate-controlled monetary system, which encourages just enough market force and cash liquidity for a newcomer to achieve his vision of the American Dream—despite our Soviet-style corruption at the top, our maze of regulatory behaviors and the onerous dislocations of the military-industrial complex."

My favorite was Mel Brooks's explanation, "When I was a little kid fifty years ago, in 1946, I had just got out of the army after two years fighting in the war. The American Dream was a house and a car. Today, the American Dream is winning *American Idol*. It's changed slightly. In another fifty years from now, when the economy collapses and everything is in threads and torn, the American Dream then, in twenty-whatever, will be a house and a car."

The most prevalent definition of the American dream, however, circled around material prosperity. Donald Trump gave the all-purpose response, "The American Dream is freedom, prosperity, peace—and liberty and justice for all." But Ted Turner probably put it best for the materialist, "The American Dream is very similar to the dream of people all over the world who dare to dream of prosperity and a high consumption lifestyle, a dream which has become very difficult if not impossible to sustain."

For most responders, the American Dream is to get what you want, be who you want to be, and do what you want to do. In almost every case, the dream is about ourselves rather than others.

OUR FOUNDERS' DREAM

Personally, I think the American Dream is much more meaning-ful than making money and collecting material goods. In *Forbes* I was limited to about 250 words. But there's a whole lot more I'd like to say.

I believe the American dream is not something we've invented but inherited. When our Founding Fathers created our country, Thomas Jefferson penned that dream in the Declaration of Independence, "We hold these truths to be self-evident, that all men are created equal, that they are endowed by their Creator with certain unalienable Rights, that among these are Life, Liberty and the pursuit of Happiness."

"Life, liberty, and the pursuit of happiness" is so much more than fulfilling our own dreams, doing what we want, and feel-ing good. It's about living and experiencing life to the fullest, as our Creator intended, including using our God-given potential to make a positive difference on this planet. Notice in the Declaration that life and liberty are coupled with happiness, not money, status, or materialism. Why not the latter? Because they are fleeting and fluctuating, just like the stock market. I used to think the American dream could be obtained through the accumulation of possessions, positions, and prestige. The "truths self evident" to our Founding Fathers eluded me for too long.

Scholar A. N. Wilson said it well, "One sees what happens when the hearts of individuals, and of societies, become seduced by money. It is an ugly, but also completely pathetic sight. Is it sane that one's happiness should depend on the strength of the dollar, or the price of gold, or the mystic number of the Dow Jones index? If . . . money worries are allowed to be dominant in our lives, we shall always be the prisoner of our treasure."[2]

Our Founders didn't put their dreams or security in material abundance. George Washington had to borrow money to get to his own inauguration. Thomas Jefferson died $100,000 in debt. Most of our Founders lived modestly and were willing to share what they had, and even contribute to government, to build up other Americans.

Though many of the Founders were well off, they despised greed. They valued service more than securities. They were more enamored with morals than money, more in love with liberty than lucre. That is why Samuel Adams wrote, "If ye love wealth greater than liberty, the tranquility of servitude greater than the animating contest for freedom, go home from us in peace. We seek not your counsel, nor your arms. Crouch down and lick the hand that feeds you; and may posterity forget that ye were our countrymen."[3]

What our Founders valued above all else was "their Creator" who had endowed them with their unalienable rights. God is our national treasure. He is at the heart of our Founders' dream for this country. When you've got God, you've got the gold—and all you need to achieve and experience the American Dream.

There's a verse in the Bible that summarizes it for me, "Instruct those who are rich in this present world not to be conceited or to fix their hope on the uncertainty of riches, but on God, who richly supplies us with all things to enjoy."[4]

LOSING THE MEMORY OF FREEDOM

During the Revolutionary era, the English historian Edward Gibbon wrote in his six-volume classic work published between 1776 and 1788, *The History of the Decline and Fall of the Roman Empire*, "A nation of legislators and conquerors might assert their claim to the harvests . . . which had been purchased with their blood; and . . . that, in the enjoyment of plenty, the Romans should lose the memory of freedom."[5] That's exactly the way free individuals and nations collapse: humans sacrifice for freedom, humans overindulge in freedom, men forget what freedom truly means, and the infrastructure of society breaks down.

The question is, will America's "enjoyment of plenty" cause us to "lose the memory of freedom" and self-implode like Rome did? Could we be at DEFCON one in our political amnesia and demise?

Our Founders feared we would forget what freedom was all about and stray toward selfishness and greed, that we would forget the necessity of morality, integrity, and service to others. Has their fear not materialized in our day?

For too many, the American dream has indeed turned into an enjoyment of plenty rather than the responsibilities of liberty. They have fallen for the delusion that a surplus of stuff can buy us life, liberty, and happiness. That's a lesson I had to learn the hard way.

If you've read this far in the book, you know how to restore the American Dream. You know the eight major obstacles that threaten our nation's existence and what we need to do to overcome them and reawaken America. Now it's time to let others know.

I fully realize that I alone can't wake up America. It's going to take an army of us to get word out to every household, neighborhood, work place, community, county, and state. It's going to take you. Will you help me? You don't need to know everything. I don't. Once you finish this book, you can hand it off to a friend to read. Or you can buy a copy for someone. Maybe instead of buying your child or grandchild another electronic gadget for a birthday or Christmas, you could give them this book and write them a note inside about what America means to you. Or just sit down and talk to them about it. Whatever means you use, tell them the story about our nation and how they can keep the story going. Share with them how God moved upon the valiant men of old to start this nation and what they wanted for this country. Then tell them how we can get back to their principles and policies and recreate this nation into what it was always intended to be.

There is still hope for America. There can be brighter days ahead. We can still be that "City on a Hill" that provides a bright light to the world. The final chapter of our history hasn't been written.

Carpe Diem! Seize the day!

TOO OLD TO FIGHT?

In chapter five, I called the Millennials to action. Now I'm calling the rest of you to action. I know some of you might think you're too old for the culture wars. But this sixty-eight-year-old veteran is here to tell you that you're not.

An elderly friend joked around with me one day, when he was depressed about growing older, and I replied to him, "Seize the day." He said, "I'll be lucky if I don't 'Seizure the day'!"

Unfortunately too many of us retire from the culture wars instead of reenlist in them. Who better to show the way than we who know the way and go the way?

In March I passed another birthday. To be honest, some birthdays arrive like a Carnival cruise. Others pass like kidney stones. That same elderly friend gave me a card with several funny, lighthearted quips about aging, completions to the adage: "You know you're getting older, when . . ."

(Can you relate with any of these?)

- You feel like the night after, and you haven't been anywhere
- Those issues of *Reader's Digest* just can't come fast enough
- Everything hurts and what doesn't hurt doesn't work
- All you want for your birthday is to not be reminded of your age
- You actually want socks for Christmas
- You and your teeth don't sleep together
- You remember when the Dead Sea was only sick
- Your address book has mostly names that start with "Dr."
- People call at 9:00 p.m. and ask, "Did I wake you?"
- You take a metal detector to the beach

As hilarious as some of those sayings are, I actually agree with Jack Benny, who once said, "Age is strictly a case of mind over matter. If you don't mind, it doesn't matter." I truly believe that. You are only as old as you feel.

I found another proof of that adage when I stumbled on an *L.A. Times* article about ninety-two-years-young Kirk Douglas, who is now blogging on the Internet.[6] I might not agree with Kirk on politics, but I highly respect the man for his stamina, career, and activism. Not only has he won every award Hollywood offers, but he has been a goodwill ambassador for the United States to at least forty countries.

Kirk has also just come out with a new book, *Let's Face It: 90 Years of Living, Loving, and Learning.* In his pre-centennial decade, Douglas is still using his stardom to make a difference and striving to better himself and the world around him. He even has his own MySpace page and enjoys chatting online. I've always loved to watch Kirk on screen. Some of my favorite films include *20,000 Leagues Under the Sea, Gunfight at the O.K. Corral, Dr. Jekyll and Mr. Hyde* (which he did for television), and, of course, *Spartacus.*

Douglas says he is grateful for the favorable media attention he has received through the years, but he now "resents the attitude of the media," because they don't give a fair hearing to celebrity activists. I'm not sure about the accuracy of his sentiments there, since Bono, George Clooney, Sean Penn, and Brad Pitt always seem to be headlining some humanitarian cause. If, however, Kirk is referring to the media's disdain for conservative celebrity activists, I would amen his antipathy.

Another great example of optimistic aging and activism was the towering figure and icon Charlton Heston. Outside of his monumental contributions to stage and screen, the media had only given scant mention to his activism through the years, largely because it was tenaciously conservative. I remember during the Gulf War, when Heston attacked CNN for "sowing doubts" about the allied efforts. As one news report conveyed, "With age, he grew more conservative and campaigned for conservative candidates. . . . His latter-day activism almost overshadowed his achievements as an actor, which were considerable."[7] One of his most notable jabs was delivered in 1998 as the president of the NRA to President Clinton: "America doesn't trust you with our twenty-one-year-old daughters, and we sure, Lord, don't trust you with our guns."[8] In 2003 he was awarded the Presidential Medal of Freedom, the nation's highest civilian honor. Heston, like Douglas, understood we're called to use who we are to serve the greater good.

Kirk recounts how someone once told him, "Be ashamed to die before doing something for humanity." That is why he says: "As you get older you must think more of other people. You must strive to help other people." Then he offers this generational plea: "Who needs the most help but the young? What kind of a world are we leaving them?"

Dr. Anthony Campolo once did a study in which fifty people over the age of ninety-five were asked, "If you could live your life over again, what would you do differently?" An array of responses came from these eldest of senior citizens. However, three answers constantly surfaced far more than others. (1) If I had it to do over again, I would reflect more. (2) If I had it to do over again, I would risk more. (3) If I had it to do over again, I would do more things that would live on after I am dead. It's great to see people like Kirk Douglas still reflecting, risking, and advancing his legacy. He's a good model for all of us in this respect.

Our pastor once preached, "As far as the Bible is concerned, life begins at seventy-five." He even cited many biblical leaders who experienced their greatest fulfillments after that crest. For example, Abraham and Sarah bore a child and a nation; Moses led Israel out of captivity into a promised land; Joshua led military conquests; and Simeon and Anna saw the fulfillment of the promised Messiah. If it's true that life begins at seventy-five, I can't wait to see what God has in store for me seven years from now! The way I see it, God willing, I have roughly three decades ahead to continue to serve this country and world, and I plan to make them my best and most productive. If Bob Hope supported our troops until 100, George Burns made us laugh until 100, Charlton Heston showed us what conservative activism looks like at eighty-four, and Kirk Douglas is still writing and being an activist at ninety-two, then you and I have the second half of our lives to continue to make an impact on this planet. Abraham Lincoln was correct: "In the end, it's not the years in your life that count. It's the life in your years."

I don't believe we should ever stop growing, ever stop trying to improve, or ever stop trying to make a difference on this planet. As Thomas Jefferson testified, despite his aching bones at an old age, "I was a hard student until I entered on the business of life, the duties of which leave no idle time to those disposed to fulfill them and now, retired, and at the age of seventy-six, I am again a hard student."[9]

I try to be a hard student too—always learning, always growing. That is why I developed decades ago my "Principles for Life," so I would continually keep striving to better myself. I encourage you to make a list of your own, or feel free to use mine. Of course I'm not perfect at all of these—no one could be. But when I fail, I honestly do my best to stand up with God's help and start afresh on a new day. They include these commitments:

- I will develop myself to the maximum of my potential in all ways.
- I will forget the mistakes of the past and press on to greater achievements.
- I will always be in a positive frame of mind and convey this feeling to every person that I meet.
- I will continually work at developing love, happiness, and loyalty in my family and acknowledge that no other success can compensate for failure at home.
- I will work for the good in all people and make them feel worthwhile.

- If I have nothing good to say about a person, I will say nothing.
- I will give so much time to the improvement of myself that I will have no time to criticize others.
- I will always be enthusiastic about the success of others as I am about my own.
- I will maintain an attitude of open-mindedness toward another person's viewpoint while still holding fast to what I know to be true and honest.
- I will maintain respect for those in authority and demonstrate this respect at all times.
- I will always remain loyal to God, my country, my family, and my friends.
- I will remain highly goal-oriented throughout my life because that positive attitude helps my family, my country, and myself.

Of course some of these principles are more challenging than others at different times of life. Probably one of the most challenging right now is to "develop myself to the maximum of my potential in all ways." Admittedly that is not always easy, especially at sixty-eight years old, but I continue to try and press on for the prize of the upward calling.

Two years ago, at sixty-six, at the end of a *Nightline* interview with ABC host Bill Weir, he asked me my age, and I proudly told him. Then I added with a smile, "I like to say I'm thirty-nine with twenty-seven years of experience!" I loved his response even more. Quoting one of those thousands of "Chuck Norris Facts" circulating the Internet, Bill said, "Well, according to the Chuck Norris Fact Generator, 'Chuck Norris doesn't age. He roundhouse kicks time in the face!'"

After a huge laugh, I sincerely thought about it and replied, "That's exactly what I do!" That's exactly what I believe we all should do.

PASSING THE BATON OF FREEDOM TO OTHERS

Our Founders fought for our freedom until their dying breath.[10] I believe that's the way we ought to fight for the freedom of others. Freedom was not intended to stop with you and me. James C. Dobson said, "Human freedom is a precious thing and we react decisively against those who would restrict it or take it from us."[11]But would we do the same for others, those in future generations? How about those alive today, living in our land, but being restricted by our own government's regulations?

I know you know the words of John F. Kennedy, when he said, "My fellow Americans: ask not what your country can do for you—ask what you can do for your country." But do you recall or did you know that he completed his thoughts with these words, "My fellow citizens of the world: ask not what America will do for you, but what together we can do for the freedom of man"?

Even our own Liberty Bell is inscribed with these words, "Proclaim liberty throughout the land to all its inhabitants."[12] But if we don't ring the bell, who will? The government? I believe we who possess freedom have a responsibility to give and assure the same gift to others, especially those who are oppressed.

We must not allow an age of tolerance and political corruption to prevent us from sharing the truth and remaining in the fight. It might be safer, more politically correct, and cost us a whole lot less to keep to ourselves, but political and religious abstinence and seclusion doesn't exactly demonstrate a true love for our neighbors. We must not go Missing in Action!

The only question that remains is: will we bear the baton of liberty and pass it to another? Will we remind others of the grand old story about old glory? Or will we forget our history and who we are as a nation? Will we wallow in affluence and lose our memory of freedom? I plead with you to pass on the baton of freedom, to do what you can in your family and neighborhood to expand an appreciation of what America is and should be.

Great men have always stayed the course in their fight for freedom and liberty. Abraham Lincoln once said, "Those who deny freedom to others, deserve it not for themselves; and, under a just God, cannot long retain it."[13] And Daniel Webster concluded, "God grants liberty only to those who love it, and are always ready to guard and defend it." In my opinion, Lincoln and Webster are examples of past crusaders for freedom. I believe examples of modern crusaders for freedom are those like Glenn Beck, Bill O'Reilly, Sean Hannity, Rush Limbaugh, and Frank Pastore, just to name a few.

We can no longer passively sit back and just criticize government officials. We must fight for our Bill of Rights or we will most assuredly lose them to a system of bureaucratic control. As Charles Péguy once said, "Tyranny is always better organized than freedom."[14] Boy, is that the truth! The question still stands: Are we willing to sacrifice to assure not only our freedom but the freedom of future generations? Patrick Henry asked a similar question, "Is life so dear, or peace so sweet, as to be purchased at the price of chains and slavery? Forbid it, Almighty God! I know not what course others may take but as for me; give me liberty or give me death."

We must never forget that freedom (even ours) was bought at a price. It is sacrifice that sustains the continuance of freedom. This is why John Quincy Adam's challenge still beckons us from across the years, "You will never know how much it has cost my generation to preserve your freedom. I hope you will make good use of it."

What is "good use"? Keeping it only to ourselves, or assuring its preservation for future generations? I believe, along with so many others, that our abundance of liberties should overflow to help others, not be hoarded to ourselves. Even Jesus said, "To whom much is given, much is required." Are those words not also true for those who have been given greater degrees of freedom?

More than ever before, our country needs a new generation of patriots. You will know them by the fact that they will still be the ones born in the trenches of life—in the midst of adversity. Their courage is like a tea bag: you never know its strength until it's in hot water. In other words, it still takes guts to leave the ruts! But I know we can do it. We know where we started. We know what doesn't work. And now we know what will.

Thomas Paine could be speaking to us today, when he said to the revolutionists in 1776, "These are the times that try men's souls. The summer soldier and the sunshine patriot will, in this crisis, shrink from the service of their country, but he that stands it now, deserves the love and thanks of man and woman. Tyranny, like hell, is not easily conquered; yet we have this consolation with us, that the harder the conflict, the more glorious the triumph."[15]

We must not allow the efforts of patriots past to come to naught. We must continue where they left off. We must finish their work. As Abraham Lincoln said at Gettysburg in 1863, "It is for us the living rather to be dedicated here to the unfinished work which they who fought here have thus far so nobly advanced. It is rather for us to be here dedicated to the great task remaining before us—that from these honored dead we take increased devotion to that cause for which they gave the last full measure of devotion—that we here highly resolve that these dead shall not have died in vain. . . ."[16]

I'm not willing to allow those who have sacrificed for America's freedom to die in vain. That is why I've committed the rest of my life to assure that the America of yesteryear becomes the America of tomorrow. My wish is that you will now join me, and encourage others to do the same.

THE COMING REVOLUTION

I believe a revolution is coming to America. I am more and more convinced as every year passes that a needed voter revolution is brewing and imminent to America's shores and ballot boxes.

Like the turbulent winds of a hurricane last year at my Texas ranch, you can feel the birth pains for this voter revolution through the dissatisfaction with political polarities and government solutions. I believe they were felt through the surge of the constitutional community supporting presidential candidate Ron Paul. I believe they were felt in evangelicals' and conservatives' frustration with a lack of leadership. I believe they are felt in Americans' virtually unanimous disapproval rating (roughly 91 percent) for Congress.[17]

Most Americans have grown cold over partisan politics. They cringe over the political power plays and pollution emitting from Washington. They expect that their representatives will stand for special interests or their own, rather than the people's. Americans are sick and tired of politics as usual. And the fact is: only a voter revolution is strong enough to change the current tides of corruption.

Of course America has some good congressmen, like Ron Paul, Randy Forbes, Senator Jim DeMint, and others. But the fact is those good congressmen are few and far between. The majority need to be replaced and the minority need our help to do it.

So how do we do it? By a voter revolution. By discovering, raising up, equipping and electing great Americans who truly represent average America.

The way I see it, there are three major commonsense steps toward a voter revolution:

First, examine your representatives, from the top down, and ask yourself: do they represent the people? Do they stand by the Constitution and Bill of Rights? Do they reduce big government and taxes? Do they reduce the deficit? Are they working toward protecting our borders and sovereignty? Will they stand up to governmental status quo and gridlock? Do they have the type of character that can resist the temptations of political power and special interests?

Second, if your answer is "no" to any of the preceding, get them out of office. Petition their dismissal, publicize their political problems, and muster community consent in order to vote others in. Call them by name on blogs, and explain to people why they should be ousted—then do it. No more talk. Stay the course—no matter how long it takes.

Third, fight to vote in solid, reputable, law-abiding, constitutional-honoring citizens and representatives. Could you be one? I'm talking about those who first have a long track record of possessing an upright and moral character and standing, and those who clearly take care of their marriages and families first. Half of our problem today is that we have been duped to vote into office individuals who have no integrity. Scrutinize their records and characters more carefully. Politicians' integrity must precede our interests. And if you can't find a better upstanding citizen then yourself, then consider running for public service. It's time for many of us to get out of the bleachers and onto the battlefield.

I bring you back to that timeless truth of English orator Edmund Burke: "Evil flourishes when good men do nothing." Well, evil has flourished for too long. It's time for the good people to rise up again in another voter revolution. Don't wait out the voter revolution and let it pass by. We must prepare now. Get involved. Start in your community. Fight for your county and state. And together we can reawaken our country. It's time for spring cleaning in winter politics.

It's time we all revive the revolutionary spirit of our Founders and reinvigorate their legacy. I heard it said once that it only took 2 percent of our population to create our nation. That it still would only take 2 percent to change it today. Like me, if you don't like what you see today in America, then join me by being a part of the new 2 percent. If you're with me, then you know the road ahead will not be easy and the war will not be won easily, but the rewards (I promise you) will be ultimately glorious.

Lastly, as we go back into the cultural battlefield, let me have you ponder one more time those great words from Thomas Paine from his now-famous rallying call to the Continental Army on December 23, 1776:

> These are the times that try men's souls. The summer soldier and the sunshine patriot will, in this crisis, shrink from the service of their country, but he that stands it now, deserves the love and thanks of man and woman. Tyranny, like hell, is not easily conquered; yet we have this consolation with us, that the harder the conflict, the more glorious the triumph.

Acknowledgments

I would like to thank Gary A. Terashita, Kim Stanford, Tim Jordan, and others at Fidelis Books, an imprint of B&H Publishing Group (Nashville, TN), for providing the means and assistance to make this expanded paperback version a printed reality for the reading world. Equally, I thank Mark Sweeney, the finest of literary agents, for his continued wisdom and assistance. To my friends and associates, Mike Forshey, Bill Hickl, Lloyd Ford, and Jeff Duclos, for your constant counsel and support. And thanks to our loyal staff (Kim, Marie, Laura, among others), who handle a host of details in our lives each and every day. Mostly, I give thanks to God, who has granted this once simple country boy the platform to proclaim these principles of a patriot's life.

Special Acknowledgment

This book could not have been written with the insight I believe it offers without the help of Todd DuBord (www.National Treasures.org). I have written several books over the years, but nothing of this depth. Mission completed. Thank you, Todd! You're the best!

The Declaration of Independence

IN CONGRESS, July 4, 1776.

The unanimous Declaration of the thirteen united States of America,

When in the Course of human events, it becomes necessary for one people to dissolve the political bands which have connected them with another, and to assume among the powers of the earth, the separate and equal station to which the Laws of Nature and of Nature's God entitle them, a decent respect to the opinions of mankind requires that they should declare the causes which impel them to the separation.

We hold these truths to be self-evident, that all men are created equal, that they are endowed by their Creator with certain unalienable Rights, that among these are Life, Liberty and the pursuit of Happiness.—That to secure these rights, Governments are instituted among Men, deriving their just powers from the consent of the governed,—That whenever any Form of Government becomes destructive of these ends, it is the Right of the People to alter or to abolish it, and to institute new Government, laying its foundation on such principles and organizing its powers in such form, as to them shall seem most likely to effect their Safety and Happiness. Prudence, indeed, will dictate that Governments long established should not be changed for light and transient causes; and accordingly all experience hath shewn, that mankind are more disposed to suffer, while evils are sufferable, than to right themselves by abolishing the forms to which they are accustomed. But when a long train of abuses and usurpations, pursuing invariably the same Object evinces a design to reduce them under absolute Despotism, it is their right, it is their duty, to throw off such Government, and to provide new Guards for their future security.—Such has been the patient sufferance of these Colonies; and such is now the necessity which constrains them to alter their former Systems of Government. The history of the present King of Great Britain is a history of repeated injuries and usurpations, all having in direct object the establishment of an absolute Tyranny over these States. To prove this, let Facts be submitted to a candid world.

He has refused his Assent to Laws, the most wholesome and necessary for the public good.

He has forbidden his Governors to pass Laws of immediate and pressing importance, unless suspended in their operation till his Assent should be obtained; and when so suspended, he has utterly neglected to attend to them.

He has refused to pass other Laws for the accommodation of large districts of people, unless those people would relinquish the right of Representation in the Legislature, a right inestimable to them and formidable to tyrants only.

He has called together legislative bodies at places unusual, uncomfortable, and distant from the depository of their public Records, for the sole purpose of fatiguing them into compliance with his measures.

He has dissolved Representative Houses repeatedly, for opposing with manly firmness his invasions on the rights of the people.

He has refused for a long time, after such dissolutions, to cause others to be elected; whereby the Legislative powers, incapable of Annihilation, have returned to the People at large for their exercise; the State remaining in the mean time exposed to all the dangers of invasion from without, and convulsions within.

He has endeavoured to prevent the population of these States; for that purpose obstructing the Laws for Naturalization of Foreigners; refusing to pass others to encourage their migrations hither, and raising the conditions of new Appropriations of Lands.

He has obstructed the Administration of Justice, by refusing his Assent to Laws for establishing Judiciary powers.

He has made Judges dependent on his Will alone, for the tenure of their offices, and the amount and payment of their salaries.

He has erected a multitude of New Offices, and sent hither swarms of Officers to harrass our people, and eat out their substance.

He has kept among us, in times of peace, Standing Armies without the Consent of our legislatures.

He has affected to render the Military independent of and superior to the Civil power.

He has combined with others to subject us to a jurisdiction foreign to our constitution, and unacknowledged by our laws; giving his Assent to their Acts of pretended Legislation:

For Quartering large bodies of armed troops among us:

For protecting them, by a mock Trial, from punishment for any Murders which they should commit on the Inhabitants of these States:

For cutting off our Trade with all parts of the world:

For imposing Taxes on us without our Consent:

For depriving us in many cases, of the benefits of Trial by Jury:

For transporting us beyond Seas to be tried for pretended offences

For abolishing the free System of English Laws in a neighbouring Province, establishing therein an Arbitrary government, and enlarging its Boundaries so as to render it at once an example and fit instrument for introducing the same absolute rule into these Colonies:

For taking away our Charters, abolishing our most valuable Laws, and altering fundamentally the Forms of our Governments:

For suspending our own Legislatures, and declaring themselves invested with power to legislate for us in all cases whatsoever.

He has abdicated Government here, by declaring us out of his Protection and waging War against us.

He has plundered our seas, ravaged our Coasts, burnt our towns, and destroyed the lives of our people.

He is at this time transporting large Armies of foreign Mercenaries to compleat the works of death, desolation and tyranny, already begun with circumstances of Cruelty & perfidy scarcely paralleled in the most barbarous ages, and totally unworthy the Head of a civilized nation.

He has constrained our fellow Citizens taken Captive on the high Seas to bear Arms against their Country, to become the executioners of their friends and Brethren, or to fall themselves by their Hands.

He has excited domestic insurrections amongst us, and has endeavoured to bring on the inhabitants of our frontiers, the merciless Indian Savages, whose known rule of warfare, is an undistinguished destruction of all ages, sexes and conditions.

In every stage of these Oppressions We have Petitioned for Redress in the most humble terms: Our repeated Petitions have been answered only by repeated injury. A Prince whose character is thus marked by every act which may define a Tyrant, is unfit to be the ruler of a free people.

Nor have We been wanting in attentions to our Brittish brethren. We have warned them from time to time of attempts by their legislature to extend an unwarrantable jurisdiction over us. We have reminded them of the circumstances of our emigration and settlement here. We have appealed to their native justice and magnanimity, and we have conjured them by the ties of our common kindred to disavow these usurpations, which, would inevitably interrupt our connections and correspondence. They too have been deaf to the voice of justice and of consanguinity. We must, therefore, acquiesce in the necessity, which denounces our Separation, and hold them, as we hold the rest of mankind, Enemies in War, in Peace Friends.

We, therefore, the Representatives of the united States of America, in General Congress, Assembled, appealing to the Supreme Judge of the world for the rectitude of our intentions, do, in the Name, and by Authority of the good People of these Colonies, solemnly publish and declare, That these United Colonies are, and of Right ought to be Free and Independent States; that they are Absolved from all Allegiance to the British Crown, and that all political connection between them and the State of Great Britain, is and ought to be totally dissolved; and that as Free and Independent States, they have full Power to levy War, conclude Peace, contract Alliances, establish Commerce, and to do all other Acts and Things which Independent States may of right do. And for the support of this Declaration, with a firm reliance on the protection of divine Providence, we mutually pledge to each other our Lives, our Fortunes and our sacred Honor.

Georgia
Button Gwinnett
Lyman Hall
George Walton

North Carolina
William Hooper
Joseph Hewes
John Penn

South Carolina
Edward Rutledge
Thomas Heyward, Jr.
Thomas Lynch, Jr.
Arthur Middleton

Massachusetts
John Hancock

Maryland
Samuel Chase
William Paca
Thomas Stone
Charles Carroll of Carrollton

Virginia
George Wythe
Richard Henry Lee
Thomas Jefferson
Benjamin Harrison
Thomas Nelson, Jr.
Francis Lightfoot Lee
Carter Braxton

Pennsylvania
Robert Morris
Benjamin Rush
Benjamin Franklin
John Morton
George Clymer
James Smith
George Taylor
James Wilson
George Ross

Delaware
Caesar Rodney
George Read
Thomas McKean

New York
William Floyd
Philip Livingston
Francis Lewis
Lewis Morris

New Jersey
Richard Stockton
John Witherspoon
Francis Hopkinson
John Hart
Abraham Clark

New Hampshire
Josiah Bartlett
William Whipple
Matthew Thornton

Massachusetts
Samuel Adams
John Adams
Robert Treat Paine
Elbridge Gerry

Rhode Island
Stephen Hopkins
William Ellery

Connecticut
Roger Sherman
Samuel Huntington
William Williams
Oliver Wolcott

The Constitution
of the United States

We the People of the United States, in Order to form a more perfect Union, establish Justice, insure domestic Tranquility, provide for the common defence, promote the general Welfare, and secure the Blessings of Liberty to ourselves and our Posterity, do ordain and establish this Constitution for the United States of America.

ARTICLE I
Section 1
All legislative Powers herein granted shall be vested in a Congress of the United States, which shall consist of a Senate and House of Representatives.
Section 2
The House of Representatives shall be composed of Members chosen every second Year by the People of the several States, and the Electors in each State shall have the Qualifications requisite for Electors of the most numerous Branch of the State Legislature.

No Person shall be a Representative who shall not have attained to the Age of twenty five Years, and been seven Years a Citizen of the United States, and who shall not, when elected, be an Inhabitant of that State in which he shall be chosen.

Representatives and direct Taxes shall be apportioned among the several States which may be included within this Union, according to their respective Numbers, which shall be determined by adding to the whole Number of free Persons, including those bound to Service for a Term of Years, and excluding Indians not taxed, three fifths of all other Persons. The actual Enumeration shall be made within three Years after the first Meeting of the Congress of the United States, and within every subsequent Term of ten Years, in such Manner as they shall by Law direct. The Number of Representatives shall not exceed one for every thirty Thousand, but each State shall have at Least one Representative; and until such enumeration shall be made, the State of New Hampshire shall be entitled to chuse three, Massachusetts eight, Rhode-Island and Providence Plantations one, Connecticut five, New-York six, New Jersey four, Pennsylvania eight, Delaware one, Maryland six, Virginia ten, North Carolina five, South Carolina five, and Georgia three.

When vacancies happen in the Representation from any State, the Executive Authority thereof shall issue Writs of Election to fill such Vacancies.

The House of Representatives shall chuse their Speaker and other Officers; and shall have the sole Power of Impeachment.
Section 3
The Senate of the United States shall be composed of two Senators from each State, chosen by the Legislature thereof for six Years; and each Senator shall have one Vote.

Immediately after they shall be assembled in Consequence of the first Election, they shall be divided as equally as may be into three Classes. The Seats of the Senators of the first Class shall be vacated at the Expiration of the second Year, of the second Class at the Expiration of the fourth Year, and of the third Class at the Expiration of the sixth Year, so that one third may be chosen every second Year; and if Vacancies happen by Resignation, or otherwise, during the Recess of the Legislature of any State, the Executive thereof may make temporary Appointments until the next Meeting of the Legislature, which shall then fill such Vacancies.

No Person shall be a Senator who shall not have attained to the Age of thirty Years, and been nine Years a Citizen of the United States, and who shall not, when elected, be an Inhabitant of that State for which he shall be chosen.

The Vice President of the United States shall be President of the Senate, but shall have no Vote, unless they be equally divided.

The Senate shall chuse their other Officers, and also a President pro tempore, in the Absence of the Vice President, or when he shall exercise the Office of President of the United States.

The Senate shall have the sole Power to try all Impeachments. When sitting for that Purpose, they shall be on Oath or Affirmation. When the President of the United States is tried, the Chief Justice shall preside: And no Person shall be convicted without the Concurrence of two thirds of the Members present.

Judgment in Cases of Impeachment shall not extend further than to removal from Office, and disqualification to hold and enjoy any Office of honor, Trust or Profit under the United States: but the Party convicted shall nevertheless be liable and subject to Indictment, Trial, Judgment and Punishment, according to Law.

Section 4

The Times, Places and Manner of holding Elections for Senators and Representatives, shall be prescribed in each State by the Legislature thereof; but the Congress may at any time by Law make or alter such Regulations, except as to the Places of chusing Senators.

The Congress shall assemble at least once in every Year, and such Meeting shall be on the first Monday in December, unless they shall by Law appoint a different Day.

Section 5

Each House shall be the Judge of the Elections, Returns and Qualifications of its own Members, and a Majority of each shall constitute a Quorum to do Business; but a smaller Number may adjourn from day to day, and may be authorized to compel the Attendance of absent Members, in such Manner, and under such Penalties as each House may provide.

Each House may determine the Rules of its Proceedings, punish its Members for disorderly Behaviour, and, with the Concurrence of two thirds, expel a Member.

Each House shall keep a Journal of its Proceedings, and from time to time publish the same, excepting such Parts as may in their Judgment require Secrecy; and the Yeas and Nays of the Members of either House on any question shall, at the Desire of one fifth of those Present, be entered on the Journal.

Neither House, during the Session of Congress, shall, without the Consent of the other, adjourn for more than three days, nor to any other Place than that in which the two Houses shall be sitting.

Section 6

The Senators and Representatives shall receive a Compensation for their Services, to be ascertained by Law, and paid out of the Treasury of the United States. They shall in all Cases, except Treason, Felony and Breach of the Peace, be privileged from Arrest during their Attendance at the Session of their respective Houses, and in going to and returning from the same; and for any Speech or Debate in either House, they shall not be questioned in any other Place.

No Senator or Representative shall, during the Time for which he was elected, be appointed to any civil Office under the Authority of the United States, which shall have been created, or the Emoluments whereof shall have been encreased during such time; and no Person holding any Office under the United States, shall be a Member of either House during his Continuance in Office.

Section 7

All Bills for raising Revenue shall originate in the House of Representatives; but the Senate may propose or concur with Amendments as on other Bills.

Every Bill which shall have passed the House of Representatives and the Senate, shall, before it become a Law, be presented to the President of the United States: If he approve he shall sign it, but if not he shall return it, with his Objections to that House in which it shall have originated, who shall enter the Objections at large on their Journal, and proceed to reconsider it. If after such Reconsideration two thirds of that House shall agree to pass the Bill, it shall be sent, together with the Objections, to the other House, by which it shall likewise be reconsidered, and if approved by two thirds of that House, it shall become a Law. But in all such Cases the Votes of both Houses shall be determined by yeas and Nays, and the Names of the

Persons voting for and against the Bill shall be entered on the Journal of each House respectively. If any Bill shall not be returned by the President within ten Days (Sundays excepted) after it shall have been presented to him, the Same shall be a Law, in like Manner as if he had signed it, unless the Congress by their Adjournment prevent its Return, in which Case it shall not be a Law.

Every Order, Resolution, or Vote to which the Concurrence of the Senate and House of Representatives may be necessary (except on a question of Adjournment) shall be presented to the President of the United States; and before the Same shall take Effect, shall be approved by him, or being disapproved by him, shall be repassed by two thirds of the Senate and House of Representatives, according to the Rules and Limitations prescribed in the Case of a Bill.

Section 8

The Congress shall have Power To lay and collect Taxes, Duties, Imposts and Excises, to pay the Debts and provide for the common Defence and general Welfare of the United States; but all Duties, Imposts and Excises shall be uniform throughout the United States;

To borrow Money on the credit of the United States;

To regulate Commerce with foreign Nations, and among the several States, and with the Indian Tribes;

To establish an uniform Rule of Naturalization, and uniform Laws on the subject of Bankruptcies throughout the United States;

To coin Money, regulate the Value thereof, and of foreign Coin, and fix the Standard of Weights and Measures;

To provide for the Punishment of counterfeiting the Securities and current Coin of the United States;

To establish Post Offices and Post Roads;

To promote the Progress of Science and useful Arts, by securing for limited Times to Authors and Inventors the exclusive Right to their respective Writings and Discoveries;

To constitute Tribunals inferior to the supreme Court;

To define and punish Piracies and Felonies committed on the high Seas, and Offences against the Law of Nations;

To declare War, grant Letters of Marque and Reprisal, and make Rules concerning Captures on Land and Water;

To raise and support Armies, but no Appropriation of Money to that Use shall be for a longer Term than two Years;

To provide and maintain a Navy;

To make Rules for the Government and Regulation of the land and naval Forces;

To provide for calling forth the Militia to execute the Laws of the Union, suppress Insurrections and repel Invasions;

To provide for organizing, arming, and disciplining, the Militia, and for governing such Part of them as may be employed in the Service of the United States, reserving to the States respectively, the Appointment of the Officers, and the Authority of training the Militia according to the discipline prescribed by Congress;

To exercise exclusive Legislation in all Cases whatsoever, over such District (not exceeding ten Miles square) as may, by Cession of particular States, and the Acceptance of Congress, become the Seat of the Government of the United States, and to exercise like Authority over all Places purchased by the Consent of the Legislature of the State in which the Same shall be, for the Erection of Forts, Magazines, Arsenals, dock-Yards, and other needful Buildings;— And

To make all Laws which shall be necessary and proper for carrying into Execution the foregoing Powers, and all other Powers vested by this Constitution in the Government of the United States, or in any Department or Officer thereof.

Section 9

The Migration or Importation of such Persons as any of the States now existing shall think proper to admit, shall not be prohibited by the Congress prior to the Year one thousand eight hundred and eight, but a Tax or duty may be imposed on such Importation, not exceeding ten dollars for each Person.

The Privilege of the Writ of Habeas Corpus shall not be suspended, unless when in Cases of

Rebellion or Invasion the public Safety may require it.

No Bill of Attainder or ex post facto Law shall be passed.

No Capitation, or other direct, Tax shall be laid, unless in Proportion to the Census or enumeration herein before directed to be taken.

No Tax or Duty shall be laid on Articles exported from any State.

No Preference shall be given by any Regulation of Commerce or Revenue to the Ports of one State over those of another; nor shall Vessels bound to, or from, one State, be obliged to enter, clear, or pay Duties in another.

No Money shall be drawn from the Treasury, but in Consequence of Appropriations made by Law; and a regular Statement and Account of the Receipts and Expenditures of all public Money shall be published from time to time.

No Title of Nobility shall be granted by the United States: And no Person holding any Office of Profit or Trust under them, shall, without the Consent of the Congress, accept of any present, Emolument, Office, or Title, of any kind whatever, from any King, Prince, or foreign State.

Section 10

No State shall enter into any Treaty, Alliance, or Confederation; grant Letters of Marque and Reprisal; coin Money; emit Bills of Credit; make any Thing but gold and silver Coin a Tender in Payment of Debts; pass any Bill of Attainder, ex post facto Law, or Law impairing the Obligation of Contracts, or grant any Title of Nobility.

No State shall, without the Consent of the Congress, lay any Imposts or Duties on Imports or Exports, except what may be absolutely necessary for executing it's inspection Laws: and the net Produce of all Duties and Imposts, laid by any State on Imports or Exports, shall be for the Use of the Treasury of the United States; and all such Laws shall be subject to the Revision and Controul of the Congress.

No State shall, without the Consent of Congress, lay any Duty of Tonnage, keep Troops, or Ships of War in time of Peace, enter into any Agreement or Compact with another State, or with a foreign Power, or engage in War, unless actually invaded, or in such imminent Danger as will not admit of delay.

ARTICLE II
Section 1

The executive Power shall be vested in a President of the United States of America. He shall hold his Office during the Term of four Years, and, together with the Vice President, chosen for the same Term, be elected, as follows:

Each State shall appoint, in such Manner as the Legislature thereof may direct, a Number of Electors, equal to the whole Number of Senators and Representatives to which the State may be entitled in the Congress: but no Senator or Representative, or Person holding an Office of Trust or Profit under the United States, shall be appointed an Elector.

The Electors shall meet in their respective States, and vote by Ballot for two Persons, of whom one at least shall not be an Inhabitant of the same State with themselves. And they shall make a List of all the Persons voted for, and of the Number of Votes for each; which List they shall sign and certify, and transmit sealed to the Seat of the Government of the United States, directed to the President of the Senate. The President of the Senate shall, in the Presence of the Senate and House of Representatives, open all the Certificates, and the Votes shall then be counted. The Person having the greatest Number of Votes shall be the President, if such Number be a Majority of the whole Number of Electors appointed; and if there be more than one who have such Majority, and have an equal Number of Votes, then the House of Representatives shall immediately chuse by Ballot one of them for President; and if no Person have a Majority, then from the five highest on the List the said House shall in like Manner chuse the President. But in chusing the President, the Votes shall be taken by States, the Representation from each State having one Vote; A quorum for this purpose shall consist of a Member or Members from two thirds of the States, and a Majority of all the States shall be necessary to a Choice. In every Case, after the Choice of the President, the Person having the greatest Number of Votes of the Electors shall be the Vice President. But if there should remain two or more who have equal Votes, the Senate shall chuse from them by Ballot the Vice President.

The Congress may determine the Time of chusing the Electors, and the Day on which they shall give their Votes; which Day shall be the same throughout the United States.

No Person except a natural born Citizen, or a Citizen of the United States, at the time of the Adoption of this Constitution, shall be eligible to the Office of President; neither shall any Person be eligible to that Office who shall not have attained to the Age of thirty five Years, and been fourteen Years a Resident within the United States.

In Case of the Removal of the President from Office, or of his Death, Resignation, or Inability to discharge the Powers and Duties of the said Office, the Same shall devolve on the Vice President, and the Congress may by Law provide for the Case of Removal, Death, Resignation or Inability, both of the President and Vice President, declaring what Officer shall then act as President, and such Officer shall act accordingly, until the Disability be removed, or a President shall be elected.

The President shall, at stated Times, receive for his Services, a Compensation, which shall neither be increased nor diminished during the Period for which he shall have been elected, and he shall not receive within that Period any other Emolument from the United States, or any of them.

Before he enter on the Execution of his Office, he shall take the following Oath or Affirmation:—"I do solemnly swear (or affirm) that I will faithfully execute the Office of President of the United States, and will to the best of my Ability, preserve, protect and defend the Constitution of the United States."

Section 2

The President shall be Commander in Chief of the Army and Navy of the United States, and of the Militia of the several States, when called into the actual Service of the United States; he may require the Opinion, in writing, of the principal Officer in each of the executive Departments, upon any Subject relating to the Duties of their respective Offices, and he shall have Power to grant Reprieves and Pardons for Offences against the United States, except in Cases of Impeachment.

He shall have Power, by and with the Advice and Consent of the Senate, to make Treaties, provided two thirds of the Senators present concur; and he shall nominate, and by and with the Advice and Consent of the Senate, shall appoint Ambassadors, other public Ministers and Consuls, Judges of the supreme Court, and all other Officers of the United States, whose Appointments are not herein otherwise provided for, and which shall be established by Law: but the Congress may by Law vest the Appointment of such inferior Officers, as they think proper, in the President alone, in the Courts of Law, or in the Heads of Departments.

The President shall have Power to fill up all Vacancies that may happen during the Recess of the Senate, by granting Commissions which shall expire at the End of their next Session.

Section 3

He shall from time to time give to the Congress Information of the State of the Union, and recommend to their Consideration such Measures as he shall judge necessary and expedient; he may, on extraordinary Occasions, convene both Houses, or either of them, and in Case of Disagreement between them, with Respect to the Time of Adjournment, he may adjourn them to such Time as he shall think proper; he shall receive Ambassadors and other public Ministers; he shall take Care that the Laws be faithfully executed, and shall Commission all the Officers of the United States.

Section 4

The President, Vice President and all civil Officers of the United States, shall be removed from Office on Impeachment for, and Conviction of, Treason, Bribery, or other high Crimes and Misdemeanors.

ARTICLE III
Section 1

The judicial Power of the United States shall be vested in one supreme Court, and in such inferior Courts as the Congress may from time to time ordain and establish. The Judges, both of the supreme and inferior Courts, shall hold their Offices during good Behaviour, and shall, at stated Times, receive for their Services a Compensation, which shall not be diminished during their Continuance in Office.

Section 2

The judicial Power shall extend to all Cases, in Law and Equity, arising under this Constitution, the Laws of the United States, and Treaties made, or which shall be made, under their Authority;—to all Cases affecting Ambassadors, other public Ministers and Consuls;—to all Cases of admiralty and maritime Jurisdiction;—to Controversies to which the United States shall be a Party;—to Controversies between two or more States;—between a State and Citizens of another State;—between Citizens of different States;—between Citizens of the same State claiming Lands under Grants of different States, and between a State, or the Citizens thereof, and foreign States, Citizens or Subjects.

In all Cases affecting Ambassadors, other public Ministers and Consuls, and those in which a State shall be Party, the supreme Court shall have original Jurisdiction. In all the other Cases before mentioned, the supreme Court shall have appellate Jurisdiction, both as to Law and Fact, with such Exceptions, and under such Regulations as the Congress shall make.

The Trial of all Crimes, except in Cases of Impeachment, shall be by Jury; and such Trial shall be held in the State where the said Crimes shall have been committed; but when not committed within any State, the Trial shall be at such Place or Places as the Congress may by Law have directed.

Section 3

Treason against the United States, shall consist only in levying War against them, or in adhering to their Enemies, giving them Aid and Comfort. No Person shall be convicted of Treason unless on the Testimony of two Witnesses to the same overt Act, or on Confession in open Court.

The Congress shall have Power to declare the Punishment of Treason, but no Attainder of Treason shall work Corruption of Blood, or Forfeiture except during the Life of the Person attainted.

ARTICLE IV

Section 1

Full Faith and Credit shall be given in each State to the public Acts, Records, and judicial Proceedings of every other State. And the Congress may by general Laws prescribe the Manner in which such Acts, Records and Proceedings shall be proved, and the Effect thereof.

Section 2

The Citizens of each State shall be entitled to all Privileges and Immunities of Citizens in the several States.

A Person charged in any State with Treason, Felony, or other Crime, who shall flee from Justice, and be found in another State, shall on Demand of the executive Authority of the State from which he fled, be delivered up, to be removed to the State having Jurisdiction of the Crime.

No Person held to Service or Labour in one State, under the Laws thereof, escaping into another, shall, in Consequence of any Law or Regulation therein, be discharged from such Service or Labour, but shall be delivered up on Claim of the Party to whom such Service or Labour may be due.

Section 3

New States may be admitted by the Congress into this Union; but no new State shall be formed or erected within the Jurisdiction of any other State; nor any State be formed by the Junction of two or more States, or Parts of States, without the Consent of the Legislatures of the States concerned as well as of the Congress.

The Congress shall have Power to dispose of and make all needful Rules and Regulations respecting the Territory or other Property belonging to the United States; and nothing in this Constitution shall be so construed as to Prejudice any Claims of the United States, or of any particular State.

Section 4

The United States shall guarantee to every State in this Union a Republican Form of Government, and shall protect each of them against Invasion; and on Application of the Legislature, or of the Executive (when the Legislature cannot be convened), against domestic Violence.

ARTICLE V

The Congress, whenever two thirds of both Houses shall deem it necessary, shall propose Amendments to this Constitution, or, on the Application of the Legislatures of two thirds of the several States, shall call a Convention for proposing Amendments, which, in either Case, shall be valid to all Intents and Purposes, as Part of this Constitution, when ratified by the Legislatures of three fourths of the several States, or by Conventions in three fourths thereof, as the one or the other Mode of Ratification may be proposed by the Congress; Provided that no Amendment which may be made prior to the Year One thousand eight hundred and eight shall in any Manner affect the first and fourth Clauses in the Ninth Section of the first Article; and that no State, without its Consent, shall be deprived of its equal Suffrage in the Senate.

ARTICLE VI

All Debts contracted and Engagements entered into, before the Adoption of this Constitution, shall be as valid against the United States under this Constitution, as under the Confederation.

This Constitution, and the Laws of the United States which shall be made in Pursuance thereof; and all Treaties made, or which shall be made, under the Authority of the United States, shall be the supreme Law of the Land; and the Judges in every State shall be bound thereby, any Thing in the Constitution or Laws of any State to the Contrary notwithstanding.

The Senators and Representatives before mentioned, and the Members of the several State Legislatures, and all executive and judicial Officers, both of the United States and of the several States, shall be bound by Oath or Affirmation, to support this Constitution; but no religious Test shall ever be required as a Qualification to any Office or public Trust under the United States.

ARTICLE VII

The Ratification of the Conventions of nine States, shall be sufficient for the Establishment of this Constitution between the States so ratifying the Same.

The Word, "the," being interlined between the seventh and eighth Lines of the first Page, the Word "Thirty" being partly written on an Erazure in the fifteenth Line of the first Page, The Words "is tried" being interlined between the thirty second and thirty third Lines of the first Page and the Word "the" being interlined between the forty third and forty fourth Lines of the second Page.

Attest William Jackson Secretary

Done in Convention by the Unanimous Consent of the States present the Seventeenth Day of September in the Year of our Lord one thousand seven hundred and Eighty seven and of the Independence of the United States of America the Twelfth In witness whereof We have hereunto subscribed our Names,

G°. Washington
Presidt and deputy from Virginia

Delaware
Geo: Read
Gunning Bedford jun
John Dickinson
Richard Bassett
Jaco: Broom

Maryland
James McHenry
Dan of St Thos. Jenifer
Danl. Carroll

Virginia
John Blair
James Madison Jr.

North Carolina
Wm. Blount
Richd. Dobbs Spaight
Hu Williamson

South Carolina
J. Rutledge
Charles Cotesworth Pinckney
Charles Pinckney
Pierce Butler

Georgia
William Few
Abr Baldwin

New Hampshire
John Langdon
Nicholas Gilman

Massachusetts
Nathaniel Gorham
Rufus King
Connecticut
Wm. Saml. Johnson
Roger Sherman

New York
Alexander Hamilton

New Jersey
Wil: Livingston
David Brearley
Wm. Paterson
Jona: Dayton

Pennsylvania
B Franklin
Thomas Mifflin
Robt. Morris
Geo. Clymer
Thos. FitzSimons
Jared Ingersoll
James Wilson
Gouv Morris

AMENDMENT I

Congress shall make no law respecting an establishment of religion, or prohibiting the free exercise thereof; or abridging the freedom of speech, or of the press; or the right of the people peaceably to assemble, and to petition the Government for a redress of grievances.

AMENDMENT II

A well regulated Militia, being necessary to the security of a free State, the right of the people to keep and bear Arms, shall not be infringed.

AMENDMENT III

No Soldier shall, in time of peace be quartered in any house, without the consent of the Owner, nor in time of war, but in a manner to be prescribed by law.

AMENDMENT IV

The right of the people to be secure in their persons, houses, papers, and effects, against unreasonable searches and seizures, shall not be violated, and no Warrants shall issue, but upon probable cause, supported by Oath or affirmation, and particularly describing the place to be searched, and the persons or things to be seized.

AMENDMENT V

No person shall be held to answer for a capital, or otherwise infamous crime, unless on a presentment or indictment of a Grand Jury, except in cases arising in the land or naval forces, or in the Militia, when in actual service in time of War or public danger; nor shall any person be subject for the same offence to be twice put in jeopardy of life or limb; nor shall be compelled in any criminal case to be a witness against himself, nor be deprived of life, liberty, or property, without due process of law; nor shall private property be taken for public use, without just compensation.

AMENDMENT VI

In all criminal prosecutions, the accused shall enjoy the right to a speedy and public trial, by an impartial jury of the State and district wherein the crime shall have been committed, which district shall have been previously ascertained by law, and to be informed of the nature and cause of the accusation; to be confronted with the witnesses against him; to have compulsory process for obtaining witnesses in his favor, and to have the Assistance of Counsel for his defence.

AMENDMENT VII

In Suits at common law, where the value in controversy shall exceed twenty dollars, the right of trial by jury shall be preserved, and no fact tried by a jury, shall be otherwise re-examined in any Court of the United States, than according to the rules of the common law.

AMENDMENT VIII

Excessive bail shall not be required, nor excessive fines imposed, nor cruel and unusual punishments inflicted.

AMENDMENT IX

The enumeration in the Constitution, of certain rights, shall not be construed to deny or disparage others retained by the people.

AMENDMENT X

The powers not delegated to the United States by the Constitution, nor prohibited by it to the States, are reserved to the States respectively, or to the people.

AMENDMENT XI

Passed by Congress March 4, 1794. Ratified February 7, 1795.

The Judicial power of the United States shall not be construed to extend to any suit in law or equity, commenced or prosecuted against one of the United States by Citizens of another State, or by Citizens or Subjects of any Foreign State.

AMENDMENT XII

Passed by Congress December 9, 1803. Ratified June 15, 1804.

The Electors shall meet in their respective states and vote by ballot for President and Vice-President, one of whom, at least, shall not be an inhabitant of the same state with themselves; they shall name in their ballots the person voted for as President, and in distinct ballots the person voted for as Vice-President, and they shall make distinct lists of all persons voted for as President, and of all persons voted for as Vice-President, and of the number of votes for each, which lists they shall sign and certify, and transmit sealed to the seat of the government of the United States, directed to the President of the Senate;—the President of the Senate shall, in the presence of the Senate and House of Representatives, open all the certificates and the votes shall then be counted;—The person having the greatest number of votes for President, shall be the President, if such number be a majority of the whole number of Electors appointed; and if no person have such majority, then from the persons having the highest numbers not exceeding three on the list of those voted for as President, the House of Representatives shall choose immediately, by ballot, the President. But in choosing the President, the votes shall be taken by states, the representation from each state having one vote; a quorum for this purpose shall consist of a member or members from two-thirds of the states, and a majority of all the states shall be necessary to a choice. [And if the House of Representatives shall not choose a President whenever the right of choice shall devolve upon them, before the fourth day of March next following, then the Vice-President shall act as President, as in case of the death or other constitutional disability of the President.] The person having the greatest number of votes as Vice-President, shall be the Vice-President, if such number be a majority of the whole number of Electors appointed, and if no person have a majority, then from the two highest numbers on the list, the Senate shall choose the Vice-President; a quorum for the purpose shall consist of two-thirds of the whole number of Senators, and a majority of the whole number shall be necessary to a choice. But no person constitutionally ineligible to the office of President shall be eligible to that of Vice-President of the United States.

AMENDMENT XIII

Passed by Congress January 31, 1865. Ratified December 6, 1865.

Section 1

Neither slavery nor involuntary servitude, except as a punishment for crime whereof the party shall have been duly convicted, shall exist within the United States, or any place subject to their jurisdiction.

Section 2

Congress shall have power to enforce this article by appropriate legislation.

AMENDMENT XIV

Passed by Congress June 13, 1866. Ratified July 9, 1868.

Section 1

All persons born or naturalized in the United States, and subject to the jurisdiction thereof, are citizens of the United States and of the State wherein they reside. No State shall make or enforce any law which shall abridge the privileges or immunities of citizens of the United States; nor shall any State deprive any person of life, liberty, or property, without due process of law; nor deny to any person within its jurisdiction the equal protection of the laws.

Section 2

Representatives shall be apportioned among the several States according to their respective numbers, counting the whole number of persons in each State, excluding Indians not taxed. But when the right to vote at any election for the choice of electors for President and Vice-President of the United States, Representatives in Congress, the Executive and Judicial officers of a State, or the members of the Legislature thereof, is denied to any of the male inhabitants of such State, being twenty-one years of age, and citizens of the United States, or in any way abridged, except for participation in rebellion, or other crime, the basis of representation therein shall be reduced in the proportion which the number of such male citizens shall bear to the whole number of male citizens twenty-one years of age in such State.

Section 3

No person shall be a Senator or Representative in Congress, or elector of President and Vice-President, or hold any office, civil or military, under the United States, or under any State, who, having previously taken an oath, as a member of Congress, or as an officer of the United States, or as a member of any State legislature, or as an executive or judicial officer of any State, to support the Constitution of the United States, shall have engaged in insurrection or rebellion against the same, or given aid or comfort to the enemies thereof. But Congress may by a vote of two-thirds of each House, remove such disability.

Section 4

The validity of the public debt of the United States, authorized by law, including debts incurred for payment of pensions and bounties for services in suppressing insurrection or rebellion, shall not be questioned. But neither the United States nor any State shall assume or pay any debt or obligation incurred in aid of insurrection or rebellion against the United States, or any claim for the loss or emancipation of any slave; but all such debts, obligations and claims shall be held illegal and void.

Section 5

The Congress shall have the power to enforce, by appropriate legislation, the provisions of this article.

AMENDMENT XV

Passed by Congress February 26, 1869. Ratified February 3, 1870.

Section 1

The right of citizens of the United States to vote shall not be denied or abridged by the United States or by any State on account of race, color, or previous condition of servitude.

Section 2

The Congress shall have the power to enforce this article by appropriate legislation.

AMENDMENT XVI

Passed by Congress July 2, 1909. Ratified February 3, 1913.

The Congress shall have power to lay and collect taxes on incomes, from whatever source derived, without apportionment among the several States, and without regard to any census or enumeration.

AMENDMENT XVII

Passed by Congress May 13, 1912. Ratified April 8, 1913.

The Senate of the United States shall be composed of two Senators from each State, elected by the people thereof, for six years; and each Senator shall have one vote. The electors in each State shall have the qualifications requisite for electors of the most numerous branch of the State legislatures.

When vacancies happen in the representation of any State in the Senate, the executive authority of such State shall issue writs of election to fill such vacancies: Provided, That the legislature of any State may empower the executive thereof to make temporary appointments until the people fill the vacancies by election as the legislature may direct.

This amendment shall not be so construed as to affect the election or term of any Senator chosen before it becomes valid as part of the Constitution.

AMENDMENT XVIII

Passed by Congress December 18, 1917. Ratified January 16, 1919.

Section 1

After one year from the ratification of this article the manufacture, sale, or transportation of intoxicating liquors within, the importation thereof into, or the exportation thereof from the United States and all territory subject to the jurisdiction thereof for beverage purposes is hereby prohibited.

Section 2

The Congress and the several States shall have concurrent power to enforce this article by appropriate legislation.

Section 3

This article shall be inoperative unless it shall have been ratified as an amendment to the Constitution by the legislatures of the several States, as provided in the Constitution, within seven years from the date of the submission hereof to the States by the Congress.

AMENDMENT XIX

Passed by Congress June 4, 1919. Ratified August 18, 1920.

The right of citizens of the United States to vote shall not be denied or abridged by the United States or by any State on account of sex.

Congress shall have power to enforce this article by appropriate legislation.

AMENDMENT XX

Passed by Congress March 2, 1932. Ratified January 23, 1933.

Section 1

The terms of the President and the Vice President shall end at noon on the 20th day of January, and the terms of Senators and Representatives at noon on the 3d day of January, of the years in which such terms would have ended if this article had not been ratified; and the terms of their successors shall then begin.

Section 2

The Congress shall assemble at least once in every year, and such meeting shall begin at noon

on the 3d day of January, unless they shall by law appoint a different day.

Section 3

If, at the time fixed for the beginning of the term of the President, the President elect shall have died, the Vice President elect shall become President. If a President shall not have been chosen before the time fixed for the beginning of his term, or if the President elect shall have failed to qualify, then the Vice President elect shall act as President until a President shall have qualified; and the Congress may by law provide for the case wherein neither a President elect nor a Vice President shall have qualified, declaring who shall then act as President, or the manner in which one who is to act shall be selected, and such person shall act accordingly until a President or Vice President shall have qualified.

Section 4

The Congress may by law provide for the case of the death of any of the persons from whom the House of Representatives may choose a President whenever the right of choice shall have devolved upon them, and for the case of the death of any of the persons from whom the Senate may choose a Vice President whenever the right of choice shall have devolved upon them.

Section 5

Sections 1 and 2 shall take effect on the 15th day of October following the ratification of this article.

Section 6

This article shall be inoperative unless it shall have been ratified as an amendment to the Constitution by the legislatures of three-fourths of the several States within seven years from the date of its submission.

AMENDMENT XXI

Passed by Congress February 20, 1933. Ratified December 5, 1933.

Section 1

The eighteenth article of amendment to the Constitution of the United States is hereby repealed.

Section 2

The transportation or importation into any State, Territory, or Possession of the United

States for delivery or use therein of intoxicating liquors, in violation of the laws thereof, is hereby prohibited.

Section 3

This article shall be inoperative unless it shall have been ratified as an amendment to the Constitution by conventions in the several States, as provided in the Constitution, within seven years from the date of the submission hereof to the States by the Congress.

AMENDMENT XXII

Passed by Congress March 21, 1947. Ratified February 27, 1951.

Section 1

No person shall be elected to the office of the President more than twice, and no person who has held the office of President, or acted as President, for more than two years of a term to which some other person was elected President shall be elected to the office of President more than once. But this Article shall not apply to any person holding the office of President when this Article was proposed by Congress, and shall not prevent any person who may be holding the office of President, or acting as President, during the term within which this Article becomes operative from holding the office of President or acting as President during the remainder of such term.

Section 2

This article shall be inoperative unless it shall have been ratified as an amendment to the Constitution by the legislatures of three-fourths of the several States within seven years from the date of its submission to the States by the Congress.

AMENDMENT XXIII

Passed by Congress June 16, 1960. Ratified March 29, 1961.

Section 1

The District constituting the seat of Government of the United States shall appoint in such manner as Congress may direct:

A number of electors of President and Vice President equal to the whole number of Senators and Representatives in Congress to which the District would be entitled if it were a State, but in no event more than the least populous State; they shall be in addition to those appointed by the States, but they shall be considered, for the purposes of the election of President and Vice President, to be electors appointed by a State; and they shall meet in the District and perform such duties as provided by the twelfth article of amendment.

Section 2

The Congress shall have power to enforce this article by appropriate legislation.

AMENDMENT XXIV

Passed by Congress August 27, 1962. Ratified January 23, 1964.

Section 1

The right of citizens of the United States to vote in any primary or other election for President or Vice President, for electors for President or Vice President, or for Senator or Representative in Congress, shall not be denied or abridged by the United States or any State by reason of failure to pay poll tax or other tax.

Section 2

The Congress shall have power to enforce this article by appropriate legislation.

AMENDMENT XXV

Passed by Congress July 6, 1965. Ratified February 10, 1967.

Section 1

In case of the removal of the President from office or of his death or resignation, the Vice President shall become President.

Section 2

Whenever there is a vacancy in the office of the Vice President, the President shall nominate a Vice President who shall take office upon confirmation by a majority vote of both Houses of Congress.

Section 3

Whenever the President transmits to the President pro tempore of the Senate and the Speaker of the House of Representatives his written declaration that he is unable to discharge the powers and duties of his office, and until he transmits to them a written declaration to the contrary, such powers and duties shall be discharged by the Vice President as Acting President.

Section 4

Whenever the Vice President and a majority of either the principal officers of the executive departments or of such other body as Congress may by law provide, transmit to the President pro tempore of the Senate and the Speaker of the House of Representatives their written declaration that the President is unable to discharge the powers and duties of his office, the Vice President shall immediately assume the powers and duties of the office as Acting President.

Thereafter, when the President transmits to the President pro tempore of the Senate and the Speaker of the House of Representatives his written declaration that no inability exists, he shall resume the powers and duties of his office unless the Vice President and a majority of either the principal officers of the executive department or of such other body as Congress may by law provide, transmit within four days to the President pro tempore of the Senate and the Speaker of the House of Representatives their written declaration that the President is unable to discharge the powers and duties of his office. Thereupon Congress shall decide the issue, assembling within forty-eight hours for that purpose if not in session. If the Congress, within twenty-one days after receipt of the latter written declaration, or, if Congress is not in session, within twenty-one days after Congress is required to assemble, determines by two-thirds vote of both Houses that the President is unable to discharge the powers and duties of his office, the Vice President shall continue to discharge the same as Acting President; otherwise, the President shall resume the powers and duties of his office.

AMENDMENT XXVI

Passed by Congress March 23, 1971. Ratified July 1, 1971.

Section 1

The right of citizens of the United States, who are eighteen years of age or older, to vote shall not be denied or abridged by the United States or by any State on account of age.

Section 2

The Congress shall have power to enforce this article by appropriate legislation.

AMENDMENT XXVII

Originally proposed Sept. 25, 1789. Ratified May 7, 1992.

No law, varying the compensation for the services of the Senators and Representatives, shall take effect, until an election of representatives shall have intervened.

The Ten Commandments

I.   I am the Lord your God; you shall have no other gods before me

II.   You shall not make for yourself an idol

III.   You shall not misuse the name of your God

IV.   Remember the Sabbath and keep it holy

V.   Honor your father and mother

VI.   You shall not murder

VII.   You shall not commit adultery

VIII.   You shall not steal

IX.   You shall not bear false witness against your neighbor

X.   You shall not covet your neighbor's house; you shall not covet your neighbor's wife

Notes

INTRODUCTION

1. See http://www.foxnews.com/politics/elections/2009/03/25/report-obama-administration-backing-away-global-war-terror/and http://www.nydailynews.com/opinions/2009/08/08/2009-08-08_war_of_words_call_it_what_you_will_americas_struggle_against_terrorism_must_cont.html.

2. See http://www.boston.com/news/politics/politicalintelligence/2009/08/n_american_lead.html and http://economictimes.indiatimes.com/News/News-By-Industry/Services/Travel/Obama-says-immigration-changes-must-wait-till-2010/articleshow/4882335.cms.

3. See http://www.examiner.com/x-2154-Phoenix-Liberal-Examiner~y2009m4d8-Obama-in-Turkey-US-is-not-a-Christian-nation.

4. See http://www.wnd.com/index.php?pageId=101063.

5. See http://www.marketwatch.com/story/text-of-obama-speech-on-the-economy?dist=msr_1.

6. Bernard Goldberg, *A Slobbering Love Affair* (New York, NY: Regnery Press, 2009). This book gives a great analysis about the media's blind bias and infatuation with Obama, showing how Obama-mania, mass hysteria, and favoritism permeated our culture from political corridors to public schools.

7. See http://www.afa.net/youscareme.asp.

8. See http://www.loupritchett.com.

9. See http://www.snopes.com/politics/soapbox/youscareme.asp.

10. See http://www.google.com/hostednews/ap/article/ALeqM5j8db-x8aZtGaU-FOMlbG5cSsIRWQD98NBUE01.

11. See http://www.catholicnewsagency.com/new.php?n=14176.

12. See http://foxforum.blogs.foxnews.com/2009/06/05.obama%E2%80%99s-christian-muslim-double-standard-our-first-dhimmi-president.

13. See http://www.cnsnews.com/public/content/article.aspx?RsrcID
=49484.

14. See http://www.nationaltreasures.org.

15. See http://townhall.com/blog/g/993acf60-b2ae-4904-9d81-1a22c8ef38fa.

16. See http://www.glennbeck.com/content/articles/article/198/26445.

17. Tom Brokaw, *The Greatest Generation* (New York, NY: Random House, 1999).

18. See http://www.glennbeck.com/content/articles/article/196/22220.

CHAPTER ONE: One Nation, Divided, and Without a Clue

1. "Survey Reveals Most Americans Can't Name Nation's Founding Fathers," FOX News, August 15, 2007.

2. Treasury Direct. "Historical Debt Outstanding—Annual 1791–1849," http://www.treasurydirect.gov/govt/reports/pd/histdebt/ histdebt_histo1.htm.

3. Ibid.

4. Truth in Accounting, April 2008, http://www.truthin2008.org.

5. Sherrod Brown, "Don't call me a protectionist," *Wall Street Journal*, April 23, 2008, http://online.wsj.com/article/SB1208912234 98936727.html?mod=googlenews_wsj.

6. CardWeb.com, April 2008, http://www.cardweb.com/carddata.

7. Thomas Jefferson to Samuel Kercheval, July 12, 1816.

8. Treasury Direct. "Historical Debt Outstanding—Annual 1791–1849,"http://www.treasurydirect.gov/govt/reports/pd/histdebt/histdebt_histo1.htm.

9. Elizabeth Newell, "Homeland Security faces continued vacancies in high-level jobs," www.governmentexecutive.com http://www. govexec.com/story_page.cfm?articleid=37408&sid=60.

10. James Madison, Speech in Congress, February 3, 1790.

11. George Barna, "Barna Update," Barna Research Group, August 9, 2005, http://www.barna.org/FlexPage.aspx?Page=BarnaUpdate& BarnaUp-dateID=194.

12. George Barna, "Barna Update," Barna Research Group, February 12, 2002, http://www.barna.org/FlexPage.aspx?Page=BarnaUpdate &BarnaUpdateID=106.

13. Laurin Sydney, "Meet Brad Pitt: Actor talks traps, perfection, and honesty," CNN.com, November 13, 1998, http://www.cnn.com/ SHOWBIZ/Movies/9811/13/brad.pitt.

14. David Barton, Affidavit in Support of the Ten Commandments. Barna Research Group http://www.wallbuilders.com/LIBissues Articles.asp?id=87.

15. Thomas Jefferson to Maryland Republicans, 1809.

16. "Almost 4 in 10 U.S. children born out of wedlock in 2005," *USA*

Today, November 21, 2006, http://www.usatoday.com/news/ health/2006-11-21-births_x.htm.

17. National Association of Child Care Resource and Referral Agencies: "Executive Summary of Parents' Perceptions of Child Care in the United States," 1 (2006). Http://www.naccrra.org/policy/docs/ Execsumm.pdf.

18. Northwest Area Foundation, 2008 National Poll Results, April 16, 2008.

19. U.S. Department of Labor, *Quick Stats 2007*, http://www.dol.gov/wb/ stats/main.htm.

20. Associated Content, "Latchkey Kids: An American Epidemic," http://www.associatedcontent.com/article/73413/latchkey_kids_an_american_epidemic.html.

21. World Health Organization, http://www.who.int/en.

22. Centers for Disease Control and Prevention, http://www.cdc.gov.

23. Ibid., http://www.cdc.gov/nccdphp/dnpa/obesity.

24. Thomas Jefferson, Notes on Virginia, viii, 400. Fored Ed iii 264 (1782).

CHAPTER TWO: Go Back to Go Forward

1. Barry Gewen, "Forget the Founding Fathers," *New York Times*, June 5, 2005, http://query.nytimes.com/gst/fullpage.html? res=9C03EEDD1039F936 A35755C0A9639C8B63.

2. Samuel Adams, "Essay in the Boston Gazette," 1771.

3. Thomas G. West, *Vindicating the Founders* (New York: Rowman and Littlefield Publishers, Inc., 2001), xi.

4. Joseph Ellis, *Founding Brothers* (New York, Vintage Books), 8.

5. Thomas Jefferson, *Notes on Virginia*, viii, 390. Ford Ed., iii, 254.

6. The First Continental Congress was the collection of representatives from twelve colonies of the Kingdom of Great Britain that met from September 5, 1774, to October 26, 1774. The First and Second make up the Continental Congress.

7. Article II, section 1: "I do solemnly swear (or affirm) that I will faithfully execute the Office of President of the United States, and will to the best of my Ability, preserve, protect and defend the Constitution of the United States."

8. Ron Paul, "Unconstitutional Legislation Threatens Freedom," May 7, 2007, http://www.house.gov/paul/tst/tst2007/tst050707.htm.

9. See http://www.census.gov/population/cen2000/tab01.pdf.

10. See http://www.foxnews.com/story/0,2933,519872,00.html.

11. See http://www.heritage.org/research/regulation/em368.cfm.

12. See http://www.focusonthefamily.com/carrie_prejean_interview.aspx.

13. See http://www.youtube.com/watch?v=Zpsyf8L5GDc.

14. See http://www.rushlimbaugh.com/home/daily/site_051209.
content/01125106.guest.html.

15. See http://wiki.monticello.org/mediawiki/index.php/Quotations_on_
Jefferson_Memorial#_note-0.

16. See http://www.youtube.com/watch?v=GQ-lQMUn0xw.

17. See http://www.suntimes.com/news/politics/obama/891685,CST-NWS-
obama12.article.

18. See http://www.foxnews.com/opinion/2009/10/05/curt-levey-supreme-
court-guns-new-abortion.

19. See http://www.cbsnews.com/stories/2008/03/17/opinion/courtwatch/
main3944104.shtml.

20. See http://www.foxnews.com/opinion/2009/10/05/curt-levey-supreme-
court-guns-new-abortion.

21. See http://www.cbsnews.com/stories/2008/06/26/supremecourt/
main4211588.shtml.

22. See http://www.youtube.com/watch?v=qyoLuTjguJA.

23. See http://www.law.ucla.edu/volokh/2amteach/sources.htm#TOC1.

24. James Madison, the author of the Bill of Rights, wrote: "Besides the
advantage of being armed, which the Americans possess over the people of
almost every other nation. . . Notwithstanding the military establishments in
the several kingdoms of Europe, which are carried as far as the public
resources will bear, the governments are afraid to trust the people with
arms."—James Madison in Federalist Paper No. 46.

25. See http://www.sfgate.com/cgi-bin/article.cgi?f=/c/a/2008/03/19/
MNOOVM1PS.DTL.

26. Thomas Jefferson to William Johnson, June 12, 1823, *The Complete
Jefferson*, 322.

27. See http://www.yale.edu/lawweb/avalon/jefflett/let31.htm.

28. See http://www.brainyquote.com/quotes/quotes/t/thomasjeff157249.
html.

29. See "VI. Religion and Federal Government" at the Library of
Congress Web site: http://www.loc.gov/exhibits/religion/
rel06-2.html.

30. Roy Moore, "Files brief supporting 'In God We Trust,'" World Net
Daily, November 20, 2006. Http://worldnetdaily.com/news/article.
asp?ARTICLE_ID=53160.

31. Pastor Todd is now a chaplain in my organization and his personal Web
site and research can be found at www.nationaltreasures.org. Lake Almanor
Community Church's Web site can be found at www.lacconline.org.

32. It should be noted that the Jamestown Settlement, which is overseen by
the Jamestown Yorktown Foundation, falls under the auspices of the

Commonwealth of Virginia. Historic Jamestown is down the road from the Jamestown Settlement and is run by the National Park Service.

33. Bob Unruh, "Can't say 'Christian' at U.S. Birthplace," World Net Daily, March 15, 2007.

34. His excellent research, which reads like a mystery novel, can be read at his personal Web site: www.nationaltreasures.org. Also there you will find other research on how other historic sites are not presenting the full picture of America's religious (Judeo-Christian) history, including the Washington Monument, the U.S. Supreme Court and Monticello (the estate of Thomas Jefferson).

35. A copy of the memorandum written to the Jamestown Settlement employees can read in entirety at www.nationaltreasures.org.

36. His account and research on the Washington Monument can also be found on Todd's Web site.

37. These two photos (and others) can be seen on Todd's Web site as well.

38. Bob Unruh, "Now, God banished from Washington Monument," World Net Daily, October 26, 2008, http://www.worldnetdaily.com/news/article.asp?ARTICLE_ID=58349.

39. The FOX News broadcast and the National Park Service's faxed letter with their so-called explanation of this vanishing and reappearing Laus Deo description can be found at www.nationaltreasures.com.

40. See http://www.youtube.com/watch?v=QIVd7YT0oWA.

41. See http://www.visitthecapitol.gov/index.html.

42. See http://www.govtrack.us/congress/bill.xpd?bill=hc111-131.

43. See http://www.visitthecapitol.gov/For%20the%20Press/Press%20Materials/Press%20Releases/PDF%20-%20Capitol%20Visitor%20Center%20Welcomes%20One%20Millionth%20Visitor%20to%20U.S.%20Capitol.pdf.

44. See http://www.youtube.com/watch?v=dpQOCvthw-o.

45. See http://www.youtube.com/watch?v=eXbWyrN6BdU.

46. For more information about the Christian history and the Capitol Visitor Center and other historic monuments in Washington D.C., http://newt.org/Portals/0/Capitol%20Visitor%20Center%20Report_.pdf and www.NationalTreasures.org

47. See http://www.google.com/hostednews/ap/article/ALeqM5htxe4DfXCO-Usm3nLfXgWZmLiYTQD99EEU200.

48. See http://www.google.com/hostednews/ap/article/ALeqM5htxe4DfXCO-Usm3nLfXgWZmLiYTQD99EEU200.

49. See http://www.aoc.gov/aoc/press-room/index.cfm.

50. Architect of the Capitol Office; phone: 202-228-1793.

51. See http://www.visi.com/juan/congress.

CHAPTER THREE: Stop America's Nightmare of Debt

1. See 1 Timothy 6:10.
2. Robert Wuthnow, *Poor Richard's Principle: Recovering the American Dream through Moral Dimension of Work, Business, and Money* (Princeton, NJ: Princeton University Press, 1998), 198.
3. See www.foxnews.com/story/0,2933,501825,00.html.
4. See http://www.foxnews.com/politics/2009/02/25/house-approves-billion-spending.
5. See http://news.yahoo.com/s/ap/obama_budget.
6. See http://news.yahoo.com/s/ap/20090226/ap_on_go_pr_wh/obama_budget.
7. Ibid.
8. "Historical Debt Outstanding—Annual 1791–1849," Treasury Direct, http://www.treasurydirect.gov/govt/reports/pd/histdebt/ histdebt_histo1.htm.
9. See http://www.truthin2008.org.
10. See http://news.yahoo.com/s/nm/20090825/pl_nm/us_obama_budget.
11. "House passes bill to make coin-making cheaper," 5/8/08. Associated Press, http://ap.google.com/article/ALeqM5gQ_5aPT7vFsDV495aft27lory 8uwD90HIV2G1.
12. Ryan Grim, "You've been had! How the government wastes nearly $1 trillion of your money every year," *Reader's Digest*, January 2008, 84.
13. Ibid., 84–97.
14. Michael Crowley, "Your Taxes at Play," *Reader's Digest*, June 2008.
15. "Federal Reserve Cuts the Interest Rate, Again in New Issue of Money and Markets," 5/2/08, http://www.prweb.com/release/2008/05/ prweb907984.htm.
16. See http://money.cnn.com/2008/04/29/news/companies/retail_rebates/? postversion=2008042910.
17. See http://listen.family.org/daily/A000001588.cfm.
18. See http://www.worldmag.com/articles/13673.
19. Dave Ramsey, "A husband's guilt-free debt," World Net Daily, March 6, 2007, http://worldnetdaily.com/news/article.asp?ARTI CLE_ID=54561.
20. See http://www.daveramsey.com.
21. See http://www.daveramsey.com/etc/cms/kids_teens_money_5195.htmlc.
22. See http://www.daveramsey.com/the_truth_about/bankruptcy_3018. html.cfm.
23. Thomas Jefferson to Dr. Currie, 1787.
24. See Romans 13:8.
25. Robert E. Wright and David J. Cowen, *Financial Founding Fathers: The Men Who Made America Rich* (Chicago: University of Chicago Press, 2006).
26. Robert E. Wright, *One Nation under Debt* (Columbus, OH: McGraw-Hill, 2008),13.

27. Thomas Jefferson to Nicholas Lewis, 1792.

28. Jefferson and other citizens from the south struggled with the fact that they already began paying off their state's debt, but were supposed to be okay with other states who hadn't and were going to receive a paid-in-full receipt by the feds for all their debt.

29. Thomas Jefferson to the Commissioners of the Treasury, 1788.

30. Thomas Jefferson to George Washington, 1788.

31. Letter to Henry Lee, 1790.

32. Thomas Jefferson to James Madison, 1789.

33. See Psalm 37:21.

34. See http://www.foxnews.com/story/0,2933,531045,00.html.

35. See http://www.ronpaul.com/on-the-issues/audit-the-federal-reserve-hr-1207.

36. See http://www.foxnews.com/story/0,2933,531045,00.html.

37. See http://www.foxnews.com/story/0,2933,531045,00.html.

38. See http://www.nytimes.com/2009/07/10/business/economy/10fed.html?hp.

39. See http://washingtonpost.com/wp-dny/content/story/2009/02/26/ST2009022601696.html.

40. See http://www.tangle.com/view_video.php?viewkey=a98d163d2efea0fb7a90.

41. If you don't have contact information for your representative (s), go to http://www.americansolutions.com/TakeAction/ElectedOfficials.

42. To James Welch, 1799.

43. I'm so glad that Huckabee's political work continues through http://www.huckpac.com.

44. Thomas Jefferson to Fulwar Skipwith, 1787.

45. Thomas Jefferson to Samuel Kercheval, 1816.

46. See http://www.ronpaul2008.com/articles/104/taxes-spending-and-debt-are-the-real-issues.

47. Of course the 16th Amendment changed all that when it was ratified in 1913.

48. Ibid.

49. For great studies on taxation and the Founding Fathers see Robert E. Wright's *One Nation Under Debt*.

50. Patrick Henry, "Debates in the Virginia Convention on the adoption of the Federal Constitution," 1788.

51. "Many tax protesters claim that because the IRS itself was not created by statute and because the IRS has no legal capacity to sue or be sued, the IRS is not a federal government agency. Some claim it is a Puerto Rican trust." See http://en.wikipedia.org/wiki/Internal_ Revenue_Service#cite_note-witness-12.

52. In contrast to "external" revenues of duties and tariffs that were collected by the U.S. government.

53. "Brief History of the IRS," Internal Revenue Service Web site. See http://www.irs.gov/irs/article/0,,id=149200,00.html.

54. Michael Crowley, "Outrageous! Tax-Cheating Tycoons," *Readers Digest*, April 2007.

55. Ibid.

56. Mike Huckabee interview with Chris Wallace, FOX News, May 27, 2007.

57. James Madison "Address to the States," 1783.

58. Thomas Jefferson to A. L. C. Destutt de Tracy, 1820.

59. Washington, George. "Farewell Address—1796." The Avalon Project at Yale Law School.

60. Thomas Jefferson to C. W. F. Dumas, 1790.

61. Thomas Jefferson to Albert Gallatin, 1809.

62. "Historical Debt Outstanding—Annual 1791–1849" Treasury Direct, http·//www.treasurydirect.gov/govt/reports/pd/histdebt/histdebt_histo1.htm.

63. See 1 Timothy 6:17.

64. Thomas Jefferson to Ellicot Thomas 1807.

65. Ron Blue, *The New Master Your Money* (Chicago: Moody Publishers, 2004).

66. Randy Alcorn, *The Treasure Principle* (New York: Moltromah Books, 2005). Randy has written more than twenty-seven books on everything from giving and heaven to thriller fiction. You can read free samples at his Web site, "Eternal Perspective Ministries," http://www.epm.org.

67. See Proverbs 13:20–21

CHAPTER FOUR: SECURE AND PROTECT OUR BORDERS

1. Gerard W. Gawalt, "America and the Barbary Pirates: An International Battle Against an Unconventional Foe," Library of Congress online, http://memory.loc.gov/ammem/collections/jefferson_papers/mtjprece.html.

2. See http://en.wikipedia.org/wiki/Barbary_Pirates.

3. Thomas Jewett, "Terrorism In Early America," http://www.early america.com/review/2002_winter_spring/terrorism.htm.

4. "Barbary Pirates," *Encyclopedia Britanica*, http://penelope.uchicago.edu/Thayer/E/Gazetteer/Topics/history/American_and_Military/Barbary_Pirates/Britannica_1911*.html.

5. Ibid.

6. "Treaties with The Barbary Powers : 1786–1836," The Avalon Project at Yale Law School, http://www.yale.edu/lawweb/avalon/ diplomacy/barbary/barmenu.htm.

7. "The Barbary Treaties : Treaty of Peace and Friendship,
Signed at Tripoli November 4, 1796," The Avalon Project at Yale Law
School, http://www.yale.edu/lawweb/avalon/diplomacy/barbary/
bar1796t.htm.

8. Prior to Carter, American relations with Iran were great. In 1964 President
Lyndon Johnson described our relations when he said, "What is going on in
Iran is about the best thing going on anywhere in the world." During the
early seventies democratic-flavored reforms flourished in Iran because of the
Shah, Mohammad Reza Pahlavi, from economic and educational reforms, to
increased rights for women, religious minorities, etc. The Nixon and Ford
administrations applauded and rewarded these reforms. With Carter's induc-
tion as president and push for human rights in international affairs, the
Shah's popularity declined, because of accusations that he tortured thousands of prisoners. Carter demanded the Shah release political prisoners,
break up military trials, permit free assemblies, among other requests—all of
which only fostered political and social unrest. Carter's push for social
reform in the name of human rights prompted the further uprising of
extremists and anti-government rallies. By the fall of 1977, anti-Shah Shiite
clergy and university students conducted well-organized resistances. In
November of 1977, while visiting the White House, the Shah and his
empress were met with hostility by roughly 4,000 Iranian-Communist students. Carter's connection and influence over the Shah prompted this pro-
western leader's backlash in Iran and around the world. Instead of Carter
bringing further social reform in Iran, he fed the fire for a political revolution
and the return of Ayatollah Khomeini, who was a seventy-eight-year old
theological scholar and cleric who provided leadership to Shia Muslims. Having spent more than fourteen years in exile in Iraq, in 1978 he was kicked out
of the country by none other than Saddam Hussein (a tension that would lead
to the eight-year war between the countries from 1980-1988). Khomeini,
however, would not return to Iran until the Shah was disposed of. And so,
on January 16, 1979, the Shah left Iran "on vacation," not to return. Two
weeks later Khomeini stepped back onto Iranian soil, with six million
welcoming him and the full fanfare of even western media. In power, he
reversed many of the Shah's reforms and ushered in an era of Islamic extremism that would serve as a model and catalyst for future terrorist groups.
Eleven months after Khomeini came back to Iran, the U.S. Embassy in Tehran
was taken over by extremists and fifty-two Americans were held hostage for
444 days. It is reported that among the extremists was none other than
twenty-three-year-old Mahmoud Ahmadinejad, though he personally denied
it to *Time*. Whatever the truth, he would eventually become a Khomeini-
successor and the president of Iran—he who denies a holocaust, wants to

wipe Israel off the map, and is in the process of building a nuclear arsenal. And who's to thank for Ahmadinejad's rise to power? Among the contributors is President Jimmy Carter, for his "negotiations and intervention" with the Shah and Iran. When will we learn that intervening and negotiating with America's enemies doesn't work? (Source: Slater Bakhtavar, "Jimmy Carter's Human Rights Disaster in Iran," August 26, 2007).

9. John Dickerson, "It Just Exploded on Us," *Slate*, October 25, 2007, http://www.slate.com/id/2176629/pagenum/2.

10. Ron Paul, The Revolution, 9.

11. Thomas Jefferson to W. C. C. Claiborn, October 1808.

12. "America's Founding Fathers: Delegates to the Constitutional Convention," http://www.archives.gov/exhibits/charters/constitution_founding_fathers_overview.html.

13. If you have a spare Christmas gift this year, consider sending it to one of our active service members or their families—"America Supports You" can help you: http://www.americasupportsyou.mil/americasupportsyou/help.html. Or, thanks to Xerox and other military support groups, you can even send a free Christmas card to one of our troops by following three easy steps at "LetsSayThanks.com," http://www.letssaythanks.com. Your card will actually be sent in care packages by military support organization "Give2thetroops. org," http://www.give2thetroops.org. I can tell you personally from my two tours of Iraq, if you do, you will definitely bring joy and a smile to a homesick troop.

14. See http://www.abcnews.go.com/TheLaw/story?id=7126415&page=1.

15. See http://www.msnbc.msn.com/id/29779661.

16. See http://www.elpasotimes.com/newupdated/ci_11951528.

17. See http://www.nytimes.com/2009/03/19/us/19train.html?ref=us.

18. See http://www.google.com/hostednews/ap/article/ALeqM5iS6Ud8q-1BoxP3lYLMiI1JUXmxPOwD971DN180.

19. See http://projects.latimes.com/mexico-drug-war/#/its-a-war.

20. See http://www.stripes.com/article.asp?section=104&article=61407.

21. See http://www.google.com/hostednews/ap/article/ALeqM5jAUe T4w6h2Tf5-ToNP4zdMOljKDAD9AEUS800.

22. See http://features.csmonitor.com/globalnews/2009/08/24/mexico-quietly-decriminalizes-drug-use.

23. See http://www.kswt.com/Global/story.asp?S=10044527&nav=menu613_2_6.

24. See http://www.capsweb.org/content.php?id=595&menu_id=8.

25. See http://www.cbsnews.com/blogs/2009/03/19/world/worldwatch/entry4877436.shtml.

26. See http://www.guardian.co.uk/world/2009/mar/26/mexico-hillary-clinton-drugs-weapons.

27. See http://features.csmonitor.com/globalnews/2009/08/24/mexico-quietly-decriminalizes-drug-use.

28. See http://www.foxnews.com/politics/2009/03/14/napolitano-plan-near-dealing-mexico-border-violence.

29. See http://www.google.com/hostednews/ap/article/ALeqM5imNxm GwUQ-VtnMqGXRe2mLo1Gl0AD970GN9O0.

30. See http://www.signonsandiego.com/news/mexico/tijuana/20080814-9999-1m14rocks.html.

31. See http://www.signonsandiego.com/news/mexico/tijuana/20080814-9999-1m14rocks.html.

32. See http://www.chron.com/disp/story.mpl/metropolitan/5929096.html.

33. See http://www.signonsandiego.com/news/mexico/tijuana/20080814-9999-1m14rocks.html.

34. See http://www.cis.org/trends_and_enforcement.

35. See http://www.americanchronicle.com/articles/viewArticle.asp?article ID=41229.

36. Jeff Bingaman, Newsletter Update, April 21, 2008.

37. Ruben Casteneda, "FBI's New Division Chief to Target Terrorism, Gangs, Organized Crime," *Washington Post*, May 27, 2008.

38. See http://www.govexec.com/story_page.cfm?articleid=37408&sid=60.

39. I'm so glad that Huckabee's political work continues through http://www.huckpac.com.

40. The term "naturalization" is the process that gives to a resident alien the rights granted to a natural-born citizen.

41. Joseph Bessette, "Congress and the Naturalization of Immigrants," Heritage Foundation, December 1, 2005, http://www.heritage.org/research/governmentreform/wm926.cfm.

42. Newt Gingrich, "Ten Simple, Direct Steps to a Legal American Immigration System," *Human Events*, June 18, 2007. See http://www.humanevents.com/article.php?id=21184#1.

43. Ibid.

44. Federalists past the Naturalization Act of 1798, which extended the residency requirement from five to fourteen years. It specifically targeted Irish and French immigrants.

CHAPTER FIVE: From Here to Eternity

1. Dana Blanton, "More believe in God than Heaven," FOX News, http://www.foxnews.com/story/0,2933,99945,00.html. It appears nominal

belief is less likely on the coastal states. Another study even showed that "One out of every six residents of Massachusetts, Connecticut and Washington are atheist or agnostic—nearly double the national average. Atheists and agnostics are hardest to locate in Louisiana and Missouri." It also concluded that only seven percent were Christians. (George Barna, "Barna Update," August 23, 2005.)

2. The Pew Forum on Religion and Public Life, "2008 U.S. Religious Landscape Survey," http://religions.pewforum.org/reports.

3. Alexis de Tocqueville, *Democracy in America* (New York: Penguin Classics, 2003).

4. David L. Holmes, *The Faiths of the Founding Fathers* (London: Oxford University Press, 2006), 164.

5. For proof on God's existence I recommend Lee Strobel's The Case for a Creator or Hugh Ross's The Creator and the Cosmos: How the Latest Scientific Discoveries of the Century Reveal God. Another recent great book is Vox Day's The Irrational Atheist, which defends belief in God against the militant atheism of antagonists like Richard Dawkins, Sam Harris, and Daniel Dennett.

6. Justice James Wilson, a signer of the Constitution, explained the relation between natural law and nature's God: "As promulgated by reason and the moral sense, it has been called natural [law]; as promulgated by the Holy Scriptures, it has been called revealed law. As addressed to men, it has been denominated the law of nature; as addressed to political societies, it has been denominated the law of nations. But it should always be remembered that this law, natural or revealed, made for men or for nations, flows from the same divine source; it is the law of God. . . . What we do, indeed, must be founded on what He has done; and the deficiencies of our laws must be supplied by the perfections of His." Barton, David. "Affidavit in Support of the Ten Commandments," Wall Builders http://www.wallbuilders.com/LIBissues Articles. asp?id=87.

7. Thomas Paine, *Thoughts on Defensive War*, 1775.

8. Franklin, Ben. "Information to those who would remove to America," 1787.

9. Barton, David. "Affidavit in Support of the Ten Commandments" from Wall Builders http://www.wallbuilders.com/LIBissues Articles. asp?id=87.

10. Article VI of Constitution: ". . . no religious test shall ever be required as a qualification to any office or public trust under the United States."

11. To Jedidiah Morse on February 28, 1797. It is interesting to note that, though a majority of Americans continue to claim to be Christians, a Gallup Poll discovered 45 percent of us would support an atheist for president. Jones, Jeffrey, "Some Americans Reluctant to Vote for Mormon, 72-Year-

Old Presidential Candidates," Gallup Poll, 2/20/07, http://www.gallup.com/poll/26611/Some-Americans-Reluctant-Vote-Mormon-72YearOld-Presiden tial-Candidates.aspx.

12. Italics mine. Amendment XI in the 1797 Treaty of Tripoli. See http://www.wallbuilders.com/LIBissuesArticles.asp?id=125.

13. To Thomas Jefferson on June 28, 1813. There are many other quotes like these. For example, John Quincy Adams, America's sixth President, spoke at an Independence Day celebration in 1837, "Is it not that the Declaration of Independence first organized the social compact on the foundation of the Redeemer's mission upon earth? That it laid the corner stone of human government upon the first precepts of Christianity . . . ?" Finally, Andrew Jackson, our seventh President, pointed to a Bible as he lay sick near death in 1845 and said, "That book, sir, is the rock on which our republic rests."

14. Benjamin Franklin, *Memoirs of the Life and Writings of Benjamin Franklin*, 389. This was a motion by Franklin to start each day of the convention with daily prayers. Unfortunately, it was added by Dr. Franklin: "The convention, except for the three or four persons, thought prayers unnecessary." This may not have represented the religious temperature of the group or their passion for prayer, just their decision that daily prayers were not needed here. My concern here is not that the convention denied the motion, but that Franklin passionately pleaded and testified to an intervening God in the governing affairs of the U.S., which most (if not nearly all) believed. The remaining part of his motion was equally moving, "We have been assured, Sir, in the Sacred Writings, that 'except the Lord build the house, they labor in vain that build it.' I firmly believe this; and I also believe, that without his concurring aid, we shall succeed in this political building no better than the builders of Babel: we shall be divided by our little partial local interests, our projects will be confounded, and we ourselves shall become a reproach and a bye-word down to future ages. And what is worse, mankind may hereafter, from this unfortunate instance, despair of establishing government by human wisdom, and leave it to chance, war, and conquest. I therefore beg leave to move, that henceforth prayers, imploring the assistance of Heaven, and its blessing on our deliberations, be held in this assembly every morning before we proceed to business; and that one or more of the clergy of this city be requested to officiate in that service."

15. For youngsters, I recommend they read what even fourteen-year-old George Washington wrote out in freehand by his own volition, http://www.amazon.com/Civility-Decent-Behavior-Company-Conversation/dp/9562911772/ref=sr_1_1?ie=UTF8&s=books&qid=1234024867&sr=1-1 110 Rules of Civility & Decent Behavior in Company and Conversation. To everyone else, I recommend http://www.amazon.com/Ethics-American-Handbook-Jacob-Abbott/dp/0925279722/ref=sr_1_1?ie=UTF8&s=book

s&qid=1234019709&sr=1-1 Jacob Abbott's "Ethics: An Early American Handbook"—a reprint of an 1890 study on ethics. And stay attuned to ethical issues in politics by frequenting the "Citizens for Responsibility and Ethics in Washington" Web site at www.citizensforethics.org.

16. See http://www.barackobama.com/issues/ethics.

17. See http://www.youtube.com/watch?v=EroItoazpiA&feature =related.

18. See http://news.yahoo.com/s/ap/20090109/ap_on_go_ca_st_pe/obama_defense.

19. See http://voices.washingtonpost.com/44/2009/02/05/solis_senate_session_canceled.html?hpid=topnews.

20. There are other Obama appointees who worked as lobbyists and are now located among his administration, like Mark Patterson, who represented Goldman Sachs and is now chief of staff to Treasury Secretary Timothy Geithner.

21. See http://www.nytimes.com/2009/02/04/technology/internet/04myspace.html?ref=technology

22. I'd recommend Ogden and indeed everyone else watch the DVD, http://www.christianbook.com/Christian/Books/product?item_no=012841&netp_id=535659&event=ESRCN&item_code=WW&view=covers "Someone's Daughter—A Journey to Freedom from Pornography" (distributed by www.VisionVideo.com).

23. See http://www.cnn.com/2009/POLITICS/09/06/obama.adviser.resigns/index.html.

24. See http://www.foxnews.com/politics/2009/09/06/jones-resignation-embolden-administration-critics.

25. Maxwell, John, *The 21 Irrefutable Laws of Leadership* (Nashville, TN: Thomas Nelson, 2007).

26. See http://www.washingtonpost.com/wp-dyn/content/article/2009/02/03/AR2009020304112_pf.html.

27. "George Washington's Rules of Civility—110 Maxims Helped Shape and Guide America's First President," NPR news, 5/11/03 notes: "But in the introduction to the newly published *Rules of Civility: The 110 Precepts That Guided Our First President in War and Peace*, Brookhiser warns against dismissing the maxims as 'mere' etiquette. 'The rules address moral issues, but they address them indirectly,' Brookhiser writes. 'They seek to form the inner man (or boy) by shaping the outer.' Brookhiser says the advice the rules offer, though often outlandish in detail, is still applicable in our day and age: 'Maybe they can work on us in our century as the Jesuits intended them to work in theirs—indirectly—by putting us in a more ambitious frame of mind.'

28. See http://www.myfoxtampabay.com/dpp/news/hernando_sexting_ arrest_030409.

29. Benjamin Rush to John Armstrong, March 19, 1783.

30. John Quincy Adams, *Letters of John Quincy Adams to His Son on the Bible and Its Teachings*. David Barton, Original Intent (Aledo, TX: Wall-Builder Press, 2004) 319–20.

31. Patrick Henry to Archibald Blair on January 8, 1799.

32. To James McHenry, on November 4, 1800.

33. George Washington, Farewell Address, 1796, http://www.yale.edu/law-web/avalon/washing.htm.

34. See Psalm 33:12.

35. Even the architect of the U.S. Supreme Court planned for the Ten Commandments to be displayed seven times on its Building. That includes the 9th Commandment, "Thou shall not lie," written out in Hebrew and being held by Moses for all to see (including the Justices at their Bench) above the court on the South Wall Frieze.

36. Of course our Founders and Framers were merely passing along the religious and moral baton, as the Colonialists handed it to them. The proof of that is found in the fact that every early American colony (all thirteen except Rhode Island under Roger Williams) incorporated the Ten Commandments into its own civil code of laws.

For example, the Fundamental Orders of Connecticut, established in 1638–1639 as the first written constitution in America and the direct predecessor of the U. S. Constitution, stated that the Governor and his council of six elected officials would "have power to administer justice according to the laws here established; and for want thereof according to the rule of the word of God."

Also in 1638, the Rhode Island government adopted "all those perfect and most absolute laws of His, given us in His holy word of truth, to be guided and judged thereby. Exod. 24. 3, 4; 2 Chron. II. 3; 2 Kings. II. 17."

The following year, in 1639, the New Haven Colony adopted its "Fundamental Articles" based upon the Scriptures, just as Connecticut reaffirmed its commitment to the sacred scriptures when it revised its laws in 1672.

Barton, David. Affidavit in Support of the Ten Commandments. See http://www.wallbuilders.com/LIBissues Articles.asp?id=87.

37. Pullella, Philip. "US among most bible-literate nations: poll," Reuters, April 20, 2008.

38. John Witherspoon, 1776.

CHAPTER SIX: Reclaim the Value of Human Life

1. See Genesis 1:26–28. Such words would have been regarded as revolutionary in ancient Middle East civilizations (as in many still today), as only kings

and pharaohs (and the like) were created in the image of the gods. To include all men in such a pool would have been bold. To include all women among those created in the image of God was simply radical and gutsy! Most societies then were of course male-dominated and treated females as possessions. Genesis, however, calls men and women to rule over creation, not one another.

2. John Adams to Dr. Price, 1785. "Americans are so enamored of equality that they would rather be equal in slavery than unequal in freedom." Alexis de Tocqueville.

3. To John Jay, August 1, 1786.

4. "Abigail Adams writes to her husband, John, who is attending the Continental Congress in Philadelphia, asking that he and the other men— who were at work on the Declaration of Independence—'Remember the Ladies.' John responds with humor. The Declaration's wording specifies that "all men are created equal." See http://lcweb2.loc.gov/ammem/naw/nawstime.html.

5. To Patrick Henry, June 3, 1776.

6. George Washington also demonstrated the value of women for many, "Nor would I rob the fairer sex of their share in the glory of a revolution so honorable to human nature, for, indeed, I think you ladies are in the number of the best patriots America can boast." From George Washington to Annie Boudinot Stockton, August 31, 1788.

7. Thomas G. West, *Vindicating the Founders*, 5.

8. Randy Alcorn, *Why Pro-Life?* (New York: Multnomah Books, 2003), 53.

9. Thomas Jefferson to Maryland Republicans, 1809.

10. See http://www.youtube.com/watch?v=pf0XIRZSTt8&feature=related.

11. See http://www.nrlc.org/FOCA/LawmakersProposeFOCA.html.

12. See http://www.christiannewswire.com/news/298859085.html.

13. See http://lauraetch.googlepages.com/thefreedomofchoiceact.

14. See http://www.nrlc.org/ObamaBAIPA/WhitePaperAugust28 2008.html.

15. See http://www.youtube.com/watch?v=pf0XIRZSTt8&feature= related">.

16. See http://www.lifesitenews.com/ldn/2009/jan/09010503.html.

17. Before FOCA flies onto the Congressional floor in the upcoming days, sign the online petition at http://www.fightfoca.com/to fight FOCA and then contact your representatives and Senators to tell them how you expect them to vote on the bill. You can write them online by simply entering your zip code at http://www.capwiz.com/nrlc/issues/bills/?bill=9668701.

18. See http://www.nrlc.org/Election2008/Release101608.html.

19. See http://blogs.cbn.com/thebrodyfile/archive/2008/03/31/obama-says-he-doesnt-want-his-daughters-punished-with-a.aspx.

20. See http://abcnews.go.com/Politics/International/
story?id=6716958&page=1.
21. See http://www.worldnetdaily.com/index.php/index.
php?pageId=85874">.
22. On the evolution debate, I recommend the works of Dr. Philip E.
Johnson of the University of California at Berkeley.
23. "To the citizens of Philadelphia: A Plan for Free Schools," on March 28,
1787.
24. "For example, Anaximander (610–546 BC) introduced the theory of
spontaneous generation; Diogenes (412–323 BC) introduced the concept of
the primordial slime; Empedocles (495–455 BC) introduced the theory of the
survival of the fittest and of natural selection; Deomocritus (460–370 BC)
advocated the mutability and adaptation of species; the writings of Lucretius
(99–55 BC) announced that all life sprang from "mother earth" rather than
from any specific deity; Bruno (1548-1600) published works arguing against
creation and for evolution in 1584-85; Leibnitz (1646–1716) taught the theory of intermedial species; Buffon (1707–1788) taught that man was a quad-
ruped ascended from the apes, about which Helvetius also wrote in 1758;
Swedenborg (1688–1772) advocated and wrote on the nebular hypothesis
(the early "big bang") in 1734, as did Kant in 1755; etc. It is a simple fact
that countless works for (and against) evolution had been written for over
two millennia prior to the drafting of our governing documents and that
much of today's current phraseology surrounding the evolution debate was
familiar rhetoric at the time our documents were framed." As quoted in
Barton, David. "The Founding Fathers on Creation and Evolution,"
2008. See http://www.wallbuilders.com/LIBissuesArticles.asp?id=
7846.
25. Thomas Paine, "The Existence of God: A Discourse at the Society of
Theophilanthropists, Paris." As quoted in Barton, David. "The Founding
Fathers on Creation and Evolution," 2008, http://www.wallbuilders.com/
LIBissuesArticles.asp?id=7846.
26. Benjamin Franklin, "A Lecture on the Providence of God in the Govern-
ment of the World." As quoted in Barton, David. "The Founding Fathers on
Creation and Evolution," 2008, http://www.wallbuilders.com/LIBissues
Articles.asp?id=7846.
27. John Quincy Adams, "Letters of John Quincy Adams to His Son on the
Bible and Its Teachings" Letter II, 23–24. As quoted in Barton, David. "The
Founding Fathers on Creation and Evolution," 2008, http://www.wallbuilders.
com/LIBissuesArticles. asp?id=7846.
28. John Quincy Adams, "Letters of John Quincy Adams to His Son on the
Bible and Its Teachings" Letter II, 27–28. As quoted in Barton, David. "The

Founding Fathers on Creation and Evolution," 2008, http://www.wallbuilders.
com/LIBissuesArticles.asp? id=7846.

CHAPTER SEVEN: CALLING ALL MILLENNIALS!

1. C. Brian Kelly, *Best Little Stories from the American Revolution*
(Nashville, TN: Cumberland House Publishing, 1999), 275–80.
2. Dr. Meg Meeker's book *Epidemic: How Teen Sex Is Killing Our Kids*
(Washington, D.C.: Regnery, 2002).
3. For a great article on the Millennials, see Carl M. Cannon's article in
June 2008, *Reader's Digest*.
4. See Proverbs 16:21.
5. Alex and Brett Harris, Do Hard Things: *A Teenage Rebellion against Low
Expectations* (New York: Multnomah Books, 2008).
6. Alex and Brett Harris, *Do Hard Things*, 25.
7. The Harris's book and other resources, including upcoming conferences,
can be found at their Web site www.therebelution.com.
8. "Medals for Rescuers of 26 Sailors," Aircrewman's Association,
http://www.aircrewman.org.uk/qgm.html.
9. Ibid.
10. The latter two citations read: "Awarded for their outstanding flying
skills in atrocious conditions during the rescue of the crew from the stricken
MSC Napoli on 18 January 2007. Norris and Rhodes were the Aircraft
Commanders at the same incident. Their actions resulted in all crew members being rescued and flown to safety." "It is extremely gratifying to be recognized in this way," said Lieutenant Norris. Op. Cit.
11. Address to the annual meeting of the Phoenix Chamber of Commerce,
March 30, 1961.
12. *Benjamin Rush, Medical Inquiries and Observations* (Philadelphia:
Published by J. Conrad & Co., Printed by T. & G. Palmer, 1805), Vol. II,
4–46, "An Inquiry into the Influence of Physical Causes upon the Moral
Faculty, Delivered before the American Philosophical Society, held at
Philadelphia, on the 27th of February, 1786." As quoted in David Barton,
Benjamin Rush: Signer of the Declaration of Independence (Aledo, TX: Wall-
Builder Press, 1999).
13. Thomas Paine, *Dissertations on First Principles of Government*, 1795.
14. As of July 2007. "Online sexual predators on the rise, U.S. officials say,"
CBC News, July 25, 2007, http://www.cbc.ca/technolo gy/story/2007/07/25/
onlinepredators.html.
15. Noted in its "Net Threats" (September 2007), "Why going online remains
risky" http://www.consumerreports.org/cro/electronics-computers/computers/
internet-and-other-services/net-threats-9-07/overview/0709_net_ov.htm.

16. Arnold Bell, "Internet Safety for the wired generation," http://www.fbi. gov/page2/sept04/cac090104.htm.

17. "Justice Department Ignores Citizen Obscenity Complaints," 8/15/07. Citizen Link online, http://www.citizenlink.org/content/ A000005273.cfm.

18. "Chat rooms help FBI hunt for pedophiles," *USA Today*, May 15, 2006, http://www.usatoday.com/tech/news/2006-05-15-fbi-chat-rooms_x.htm.

19. "A Parent's Guide to Internet Safety," FBI, http://www.fbi.gov/ publications/pguide/pguidee.htm.

20. See http://www.fbi.gov/publications/pguide/pguide.htm. Also helpful is the information at: http://obscenitycrimes,org/helpparents.cfm.

21. Other resources can also be found at Obscenity Crimes Web site: http://obscenitycrimes.org/helpparents.cfm.

22. See http://www.webwisekids.org.

23. See http://obscenitycrimes.org.

24. See http://www.fbi.gov/contactus.htm.

25. See http://www.missingkids.com/missingkids/servlet/PageServlet? LanguageCountry=en_US&PageId=169.

26. See http://www.nsopr.gov.

27. See http://www.fbi.gov/hq/cid/cac/states.htm.

28. See http://www.usatoday.com/tech/wireless/2009-03-11-sexting_N.htm.

29. See http://wearecentralpa.com/content/fulltext/news/?cid=74631.

30. See http://www.thenationalcampaign.org/sextech/PDF/SexTech_ Summary.pdf.

31. See http://community.norton.com/t5/Ask-Marian/quot-Sexting-quot-and-quot-The-Talk-quot-Revised-for-Cellphones/ba-p/72099#A270.

32. See http://www.msnbc.msn.com/id/29613192.

33. See http://community.norton.com/t5/Ask-Marian/quot-Sexting-quot-and-quot-The-Talk-quot-Revised-for-Cellphones/ba-p/72099#A270.

34. New York University Child Study Center, http://www.aboutour kids.org/ aboutour/articles/latchkey.html.

35. Alex Kingsbury, "After Columbine, School Shootings Proliferate," *U.S. News and World Report*, April 17, 2007, http://www.usnews. com/usnews/ news/articles/070417/17shootings.htm.

36. You can start by learning specific ways to fight crime via Web sites like the National Council on Crime and Delinquency (http://www.nccd-crc.org) and Fight Crime: Invest in Kids (http://www.fightcrime.org). And rather than just sit around and watch crimes on YouTube, teach your children and grandchildren to report them to your local authorities and even the FBI, http://www.fbi.gov/hq/cid/cac/crimesmain.htm.

37. The Web site securityinfowatch.com has information worth sharing with your school's principals and vice-principals about school safety measures,

http://www.securityinfowatch.com/online/The-Latest/School-shootings—
What-can-be-done/14302SIW306.

38. Samuel Adams to James Warren, 1775.

39. James Madison, Federalist No. 63., 1788.

40. See http://www.standardnewswire.com/news/59949946.html.

41. While signers of the Declaration like Dr. Rush were outspoken about their
Christian belief, they were also gratified with the religious respect exercised in
America. For example, in Dr. Rush's description of the federal parade in Philadelphia following the adoption of the Constitution, he joyously declared: "The
rabbi of the Jews locked in the arms of two ministers of the Gospel was a most
delightful sight. There could not have been a more happy emblem." I concur.

42. Benjamin Rush, *Essays, Literary, Moral and Philosophical* (Philadelphia:
Thomas & Samuel F. Bradford, 1798), 8, "Of the Mode of Education Proper
in a Republic." As quoted in David Barton's *Original Intent* (Aledo, TX:
WallBuilder Press, 2002), 31.

43. Rod Dreher,, "Newsletters," *Dallas Morning News*, May 6, 2006, http://
www.dallasnews.com/sharedcontent/dws/du/opinion/columnists/all/stories/
DN-amish_06edi.ART.State.Edition1.3dce193.html.

44. See http://www.rachelschallenge.com.

45. See for instance Bethlehem Books at http://www.bethlehembooks.com.

46. As the Library of Congress Web site says, "Although not accepted these
drafts reveal the religious temper of the Revolutionary period. Franklin and
Jefferson were among the most theologically liberal of the Founders, yet they
used biblical imagery for this important task." http://www.loc.gov/exhibits/
religion/rel04.html.

47. Samuel Adams, *The Writings of Samuel Adams*, Harry Alonzo Cushing,
editor (New York: G. P. Putnam's Sons, 1908), Vol. IV, 401, to the Legislature
of Massachusetts on January 27, 1797. As quoted in David Barton's *Original
Intent*, 153.

48. Journals of Congress, Vol. 8, 734-735. See http://memory.loc.gov/cgi-bin/
ampage?collId=lljc&fileName=008/lljc008.
db&recNum=360&itemLink=r?ammem/hlaw:@field(DOCID 1 @lit
(jc00897))%230080361&linkText=1.

49. See http://www.heritage.org/Research/Education/bg2257.cfm.

50. See http://www.usnews.com/blogs/peter-roff/2009/04/22/obama-wrong-
on-dc-school-vouchers-and-hypocritical-just-like-congress.html.

51. See http://ies.ed.gov/ncee/pubs/20094050/pdf/20094050.pdf.

52. See http://www.findingdulcinea.com/features/profiles/m/thurgood-
marshall.html.

53. See http://online.worldmag.com/2009/08/28/homeschooler-ordered-to-
school.

54. Miya Shay, "Houston parents keeping an eye on CA court," ABC Eyewitness News, March 7, 2008. Http://abclocal.go.com/ktrk/story?section=news/local&id=6006264.

55. Http://www.parentalrights.org/learn/the-attack-on-parental-rights/international-law.

56. Bartlby.com, http://bartelby.org/cgi-bin/texis/webinator/sitesearch?filter=colQuotations&query=stalin.

57. See http://www.brainyquote.com/quotes/authors/t/thomas_jefferson.html.

58. See http://www.hslda.org/laws/default.asp.

59. See http://www.parentalrights.org.

60. See http://www.homeschoolfoundation.org/default.asp.

61. Thomas Jefferson wrote William Roscoe, http://www.loc.gov/exhibits/jefferson/jeffrep.html#75.

62. See http://cms.studentsforacademicfreedom.org//index.php?option=com_content&task=view&id=1925&Itemid=43.

63. See http://cms.studentsforacademicfreedom.org//index.php?option=com_content&task=view&id=1922&Itemid=43.

64. See http://www.christiancollegeguide.net/. See also the Intercollegiate Studies Institute guides to *Choosing the Right College and All-American Colleges*.

65. See http://www.kick-start.org.

66. See http://thinkexist.com/quotation/i_am_only_one-but_i_am_one-i_can-t_do_everything/205060.html. Http://www.brainyquote. com/quotes/authors/e/edward_everett_hale.html.

CHAPTER EIGHT: Honor and Care for the Family

1. C. Brian Kelley, *Best Little Stories from the American Revolution* (Nashville, TN: Cumberland House Publishing, 1999),89–95.

2. "Most of the delegates married and raised children. Sherman fathered the largest family: 15 children by 2 wives. At least nine (Bassett, Brearly, Johnson, Mason, Paterson, Charles Cotesworth Pinckney, Sherman, Wilson, and Wythe) married more than once. Four (Baldwin, Gilman, Jenifer, and Alexander Martin) were lifelong bachelors." Http://www.archives.gov/exhibits/charters/constitution_founding_fathers_overview.html.

3. The number of unmarried couples living together increased 72 percent between 1990 and 2000. The number of unmarried couples living together has increased tenfold between 1960 and 2000 (U.S. Census Bureau, 2000).

4. See http://www.unmarried.org/unmarried-people.html.

5. I support the passage of a federal constitutional amendment that defines marriage as a union between one man and one woman.

6. Family Process, vol. 41, no. 2, 2002, http://www.familyprocess.org.

7. Rush, Letters, Vol. I, 132, to Julia Rush on January 31, 1777. As quoted by Barton, David. "Benjamin Rush: Signer of the Declaration of Independence," in chapter on "His Private Life," 209–12.

8. Thomas Jefferson to Mary Jefferson, 1799.

9. Thomas Jefferson to Mary Jefferson, 1800.

10. Thomas Jefferson to William. Clarke, 1809.

11. *Poor Richard's Almanck*, 1738.

12. See Ed Cole's Web site, "The Man," at http://www.edcole.org/edcole.

13. Ibid.

14. See http://www.edcole.org.

15. Austin L. Sorensen, "These Time" *Christianity Today*, Vol. 32, no. 13, June 1979.

16. David Kupelan, "The War on Fathers," World Net Daily, October 9, 2006, http://worldnetdaily.com/news/ artcle.asp?ARTICLE_ID=52314.

17. David Barton, *Original Intent* (Aledo, TX: WallBuilder Press, 2002),136.

18. Letters of the Delegates to Congress: 1774-1789, Paul H. Smith, editor (Washington, D. C.: Library of Congress, 1992), Vol. XIX, 325, from a letter of Elias Boudinot to his daughter, Susan Boudinot, on October 30, 1782; see also, Elias Boudinot, *The Life, Public Services, Addresses, and Letters of Elias Boudinot, LL.D., President of Continental Congress* (Boston and New York: Houghton, Mifflin, and Company, 1896), Vol. I, 260–62. As quoted in David Barton's *Original Intent*, 136.

19.See http://www.nobleinstitute.org.

20.See http://www.btea.org/aboutus.asp.

21. David Ramsay, An Oration Delivered in St. Michael's Church Before the Inhabitants of Charleston, South Carolina, on the Fourth of July 1794 (Charleston: W. P. Young, 1794), 19. As quoted in David Barton's *Original Intent*, 174, 2002.

22. Rush, Letters, Vol. II, 776, to John Rush on May 18, 1796. As quoted by David Barton, *Benjamin Rush: Signer of the Declaration of Independence* (Aledo, TX: WallBuilder Press, 1999), 209–12.

23. See Matthew 20:28.

24. See Hebrews 3:13.

25. Autobiography, 299, June 11, 1812.

CHAPTER NINE: Be Fit for the Fight

1. See http://www.mensfitness.com/fitness/415.

2. See http://ifitandhealthy.com/barack-obama-diet.

3. See http://obamafoodorama.blogspot.com.

4. See http://www.southtownstar.com/news/1315515,120508food.article.

5. See http://www.connpost.com/ci_11279182.

6. See http://www.csmonitor.com/2008/1226/p09s02-coop.html.

7. See http://newmexicoindependent.com/13305/obamas-choice-of-vilsack-risks-agribusiness-as-usual.

8. See http://www.foxnews.com/story/0,2933,534385,00.html.

9. See http://www.nytimes.com/2008/12/24/dining/24food.html?_r=1&pagewanted=2&hp.

10. See http://www.baltimoresun.com/news/health/bal-te.fda22dec22,0,917401.story.

11. See http://www.washingtonpost.com/wp-dyn/content/article/2008/12/23/AR2008122302423.html?hpid=topnews.

12. See http://www.examiner.com/x-867-LowCarb-Lifestyle-Examiner~y2008m12d10-Oprahs-Weight-Struggles-A-Microcosm-Of-Americas-Obesity-Epidemic.

13. See http://topics.nytimes.com/topics/reference/timestopics/subjects/o/organic_food/index.html.

14. World Health Organization, http://www.who.int/en.

15. Centers for Disease Control and Prevention, http://www.cdc.gov.

16. Department of public relations and Marketing Communications for the University of Michigan Health System, "Kids' obesity not weighing on their parents' minds," online report: http://www.med.umich.edu/opm/news-page/2007/poll6.htm.

17. Ibid., http://www.cdc.gov/nccdphp/dnpa/obesity.

18. "U.S. Physical Activity Statistics," Centers for Disease Control and Prevention, http://apps.nccd.cdc.gov/PASurveillance/DemoComparev. asp.

19. Mike Huckabee, *Quit Digging Your Grave with a Knife and Fork* (New York: Center Street, 2005).

20. See http://www.cdc.gov/nccdphp/dnpa/obesity.

21. See http://www.cooperaerobics.com/default.aspx.

22. See http://www.cdc.gov/nccdphp/dnpa/obesity.

23. "Overweight," National Center for Health Statistics, http://www.cdc.gov/nchs/fastats/overwt.htm. Studies still show that obesity contributes to the number-one cause of death in our nation: cardiovascular disease (the leading cause of death since 1900). It includes stroke, heart disease, high blood pressure, heart failure and several other conditions.

24. Richard H. Carmona, M.D., M.P.H., F.A.C.S., "The Obesity Crisis in America: Testimony Before the Subcommittee on Education Reform Committee on Education and the Workforce United States House of Representatives," United States Dept. of Health and Human Services, July 16, 2003, http://www.surgeongeneral.gov/news/testimony/obesity07162003.htm.

25. Branwen Jeffreys, "Maternal deaths linked to obesity," BBC News, http://news.bbc.co.uk/2/hi/health/7121566.stm.

26. David Schlundt, "Study: Lack Of Seat Belt Use By The Obese Puts Them At Greater Risk In A Car Crash," http://livinlavidalocarb. blogspot. com/2007/12/study-lack-of-seat-belt-use-by-obese.html.

27. "Understanding Adult Obesity," Weight Control Information Network, http://win.niddk.nih.gov/publications/understanding.html.

15. Carmona, op. cit, http://www.surgeongeneral.gov/news/testimony/ 28.htm.

29. "Trans-formed My Diet," *Prevention*, December 2006.

30. Sally Pipes, "Brave New Diet," *Washington Post*, December 26, 2007, http://www.washingtonpost.com/wp-dyn/content/article/2007/12/25/ AR2007122500862.html.

31. Jefferson, Thomas, Notes on Virginia, viii, 400. Fored Ed iii 264, (1782).

32. *Poor Richard's Almanack*, 1736.

33. See 1 Corinthians 3:16–17; 6:19.

34. *Poor Richard's Almanack*, 1733.

35. Ibid.

36. Ibid., 1735.

37. "For their era, the delegates to the convention (like the signers of the Declaration of Independence) were remarkably long-lived. Their average age at death was almost 67. Johnson reached the age of 92, and Few, Franklin, Madison, Williamson, and Wythe lived into their eighties. Fifteen or sixteen (depending on Fitzsimmon's exact age) passed away in their eighth decade, and twenty or twenty-one in their sixties. Eight lived into their fifties; five lived only into their forties, and two of them (Hamilton and Spaight) were killed in duels. The first to die was Houston in 1788; the last, Madison in 1836." See http://www.archives.gov/exhibits/charters/constitution_founding_ fathers_overview.html.

38. "Inflammation of a mucous membrane; *especially*: one chronically affecting the human nose and air passages," *Webster's Dictionary*.

39. To Doctor Vine Utley (1819).

40. See http://www.drcolbert.com.

41. See http://familydoctor.org/online/famdocen/home/healthy/ food.html.

42. See http://www.americanheart.org/presenter.jhtml?identifier=1200010.

43. The American Heart Association has some great readings on what a "Healthy Lifestyle" is. See http://www.americanheart.org/presenter. jhtml?identifier=1200009.

44. See http://www.americanheart.org/presenter.jhtml?identifier=3028650.

45. Colbert, Don., M.D., "Seven Pillars of Health."

46. Ibid., See pages 8–9 for benefits of water.

47. Dr. Mark Stibich, "10 Health Benefits of a Good Night Sleep," About.com: Longevity http://longevity.about.com/od/lifelongenergy/tp/healthy_sleep.htm.

48. To Doctor Vine Utley (1819).

49. See "Understanding Sleep: Sleep needs, cycles, and stages," http://www. helpguide.org/life/sleeping.htm.

50. For ideas how to sleep better, see Dr. Mark Stibich's "Understanding Sleep," About.com: Longevity, http://longevity.about.com/od/sleep/a/sleep_ facts.htm.

51. Colbert, *Seven Pillars of Health*.

52. See http://www.americanheart.org/presenter.jhtml?identifier=851.

53. See http://checkmark.heart.org.

54. See http://familydoctor.org/online/famdocen/home/common/heartdisease/ risk/288.html.

55. "The Life and Times of Jesus of Nazareth," *Christian History*, Issue 59.

56. Thomas Jefferson: "The wealthy people in Virginia are attentive to the raising of vegetables, but very little so to fruits. The poorer people attend to neither, living principally on milk and animal diet. This is the more inexcusable, as the climate requires indispensably a free use of vegetable food, for health as well as comfort." (Notes on Virginia—1782.)

57. To Doctor Vine Utley (1819).

58. See http://www.tobaccofreekids.org.

59. "Fruity tobacco faces ban to protect young," *Sydney Morning Herald*, December 27, 2007, http://www.smh.com.au/news/national/fruity-tobacco- faces-ban-to-protect-young/2007/12/26/1198345080910.html.

60. "Questions About Smoking, Tobacco, and Health," American Cancer Society, http://www.cancer.org/docroot/PED/content/ PED_ 10_2x_Questions_ About_Smoking_Tobacco_and_Health.asp.

61. See 1 Timothy 4:8.

62. Dr. Colbert gives a great list of fun activities to burn calories and get your heart pumping on pages 142–43.

63. To Thomas Man Randolph, Jr., 1786.

64. To Doctor Vine Utley (1819).

65. Granted walking was the main mode of land mobility for most 2000 years ago, it has been estimated that Jesus walked roughly 21,595 miles in his life—based upon multiple religious pilgrimages a year as well as other local travel. The distance around the earth is 24,901 miles. There are 1,440 minutes in every day. Do you think you can find 30 of them for physical activity? See "Exercise and Phyiscal Fitness" at http://www.nlm.nih.gov/ medlineplus/ exerciseandphysicalfitness.html.

66. Tedd Mitchell, *Move Yourself* (Hoboken, NJ: John Wiley & Sons, Inc., 2008).

67. See http://www.chucknorris.com/html/fitness.html.

68. See http://www.efisportsmedicine.com.

69. See http://www.efisportsmedicine.com/rehab.

70. "The Exercise Habit," http://familydoctor.org/online/famdocen/ home/ healthy/physical/basics/059.html.

71. "Target Heart Rate," American Heart Association, http:// www.americanheart.org/presenter.jhtml?identifier=4736.

72. Women can check out natural products for make-up at http://safecosmetics.org.

73. Colbert, op. cit.

74. Their decision was based upon the review of studies from 1966-2002, in which those who did not take supplements were at increased risk for heart disease, cancer, and other chronic diseases.

75. The conditions of our soils make us consider the curse of the soil in Genesis as a result of man's sin, as well as a reason for God requirement in Leviticus 25:1–7 that soil rest every seventh year to replenish itself.

76. Berkeley's "Wellness Guide to Dietary Supplements," http:// www.wellnessletter.com/html/ds/dsSupplements.php.

77. See Proverbs 17:22.

78. Colbert, op. cit.

79. See Matthew 11:28.

80. To Peter Carr, 1785.

81. See http://www.cancer.gov/cancertopics/pdq/supportivecare/spirituality/ Patient/page3.

82. See http://www.mayoclinic.com/health/stress-relief/SR00035.

83. See http://nccam.nih.gov/news/newsletter/2005_winter/ prayer.htm.

84. See Proverbs 3:8.

85. See Matthew 4:4.

86. You can daily read the "Daily Bread" online at http://www.rbc.org/odb/ odb.shtml.

87. University of Washington. "How to keep up with those New Year's resolutions, researchers find commitment is the secret of success," Dec. 23, 1997, http://www.washington.edu/newsroom/news/1997archive/12-97archive/k122397.html.

88. See http://health.yahoo.com/experts/gabbyguide/9331/get-a-head-start-on-your-new-years-resolution.

89. See http://www.healthnews.com/blogs/susan-brady/nutrition-diet/new-years-resolution-2009-one-small-step-toward-healthy-eating-2345.html.

90. See http://www.bestsyndication.com/?q=taxonomy/term/24.

91. See http://www.smokefree.gov.

92. See http://alcohol-abuse.suite101.com/article.cfm/how_to_reduce_or_stop_drinking.

93. See http://www.daveramsey.com/etc/cms/index.cfm?intContentID=4055.

94. See http://www.smalleyonline.com.

95. See http://www.focusonthefamily.com/faith/becoming_a_christian.aspx.

96. See http://www.wikihow.com/Make-Friends.

CHAPTER TEN: REAWAKEN THE AMERICAN DREAM

1.David M. Ewalt and Michael Noer, eds., "The White Picket Fence," *Forbes*, June 26, 2007, http://www.forbes.com/2007/06/26/ame rican-dream-suburbs-biz-cx_de_dream0607_0626picket_land.html.

2.Christianity Today, Vol. 36, no. 4.

3."The Rights of the Colonists," *The Report of the Committee of Correspondence to the Boston Town Meeting*, November 20, 1772, http://www.crispinsartwell.com/adams.htm.

4.See 1 Timothy 6:17.

5.Edward Gibbon, *The History of the Decline and Fall of the Roman Empire*, chapter XVII, http://www.ccel.org/g/gibbon/decline/vol ume1/chap17.htm.

6.Tina Duant, "Kirk Douglas hits cyberspace for another facet of his legacy," *Los Angeles Times*, April 4, 2008.

7.See http://www.starpulse.com/news/index.php/2008/04/06/hollywood_legend_conservative_activist_c.

8.NRA Convention, June 6, 1998, http://www.nrawinningteam. com/hest-quot.html.

9.To Doctor Vine Utley, 1819.

10.See "The Founding Fathers: A Brief Overview" on the National Archives Web site: *"Post-Convention Careers: "The delegates subsequent careers reflected their abilities as well as the vagaries of fate. Most were successful, although seven (Fitzsimons, Gorham, Luther Martin, Mifflin, Robert Morris, Pierce, and Wilson) suffered serious financial reverses that left them in or near bankruptcy. Two, Blount and Dayton, were involved in possibly treasonous activities. Yet, as they had done before the convention, most of the group continued to render outstanding public service, particularly to the new government they had helped to create.*

"Washington and Madison became President of the United States, and King and Charles Cotesworth Pinckney were nominated as candidates for the office. Gerry served as Madison's Vice President. Hamilton, McHenry, Madison, and Randolph attained Cabinet posts. Nineteen men became U.S.

senators: Baldwin, Bassett, Blount, Butler, Dayton, Ellsworth, Few, Gilman, Johnson, King, Langdon, Alexander Martin, Gouverneur Morris, Robert Morris, Paterson, Charles Pinckney, Read, Sherman, and Strong. Thirteen served in the House of Representatives: Baldwin, Carroll, Clymer, Dayton, Fitzsimons, Gerry, Gilman, Madison, Mercer, Charles Pinckney, Sherman, Spaight, and Williamson. Of these, Dayton served as Speaker. Four men (Bassett, Bedford, Brearly, and Few) served as federal judges, four more (Blair, Paterson, Rutledge, and Wilson) as Associate Justices of the Supreme Court. Rutledge and Ellsworth also held the position of Chief Justice. Seven others (Davie, Ellsworth, Gerry, King, Gouverneur Morris, Charles Pinckney, and Charles Cotesworth Pinckney) were named to diplomatic missions for the nation.

"Many delegates held important state positions, including governor (Blount, Davie, Franklin, Gerry, Langdon, Livingston, Alexander Martin, Mifflin, Paterson, Charles Pinckney, Spaight, and Strong) and legislator. And most of the delegates contributed in many ways to the cultural life of their cities, communities, and states. Not surprisingly, many of their sons and other descendants were to occupy high positions in American political and intellectual life." See http://www.archives.gov/exhibits/charters/constitution_founding_fathers_overview.html.

11. James Dobson, *Love Must Be Tough* (Carol Stream, IL: Tyndale House Publishers, 2007).

12. These words were derived from the Bible in Leviticus 25:10.

13. Abraham Lincoln in a letter to Henry L. Pierce and others, April 6, 1859.

14. See http://www.fdrs.org/against_tyranny.html.

15. Thomas Paine, *The Crisis*, December 23, 1776.

16. Abraham Lincoln, The Gettysburg Address, November 19, 1863.

17. See http://www.rasmussenreports.com/public_content/politics/mood_of_america/congressional_performance/congressional_performance.

Index

A

Academic Bill of Rights, 154
academic institutions, 154.
  See also schools
acting, 107–08, 155–56
activism, 211–13
Adams, Abigail, 162
Adams, John, 15, 19, 98, 103,
  113–14, 122
Adams, John Quincy, 104–05, 123
Adams, Samuel, 25, 103, 146, 208
Adelaja, Sunday, 164
Afghanistan, 128
Africa, 123–24
Against All Odds, 144, 165
Ahmadinejad, Mahmoud, 76
al Qaeda, 87
Alamo, The, 145
alcohol, 107–08, 157, 172–73, 191,
  199
Alcorn, Randy, 71, 117
alternative education, 150–53.
  See also homeschooling; private
  education
America
  direction of, 13–14
  problems of, 13–24
  reawakening, 13–24, 130–31,
    205–20
American Academy of Family
  Physicians, 187, 189
American Civil Liberties Union
  (ACLU), 19, 36–37, 101
American dream, describing, 205–06
American dream, reawakening,
  205–20
American Heart Association, 187,
  189
American Revolution, 17, 53–54,
  66, 73, 127–28, 145. See also
  Revolutionary era
Ames, Fisher, 121
Anti-Federalists, 15, 54
apathy, 22, 26, 37, 181–82
Articles of Confederation, 15, 27, 89
atheism, 19–20, 44, 96
Atwater, Lee, 108

B

Baby-Boomer generation, 13, 129,
  156
bank, creating, 53
Barbary Pirates, 17–18, 70, 73–74,
  78
Barbary Powers Conflict, 73–78
Barber, Tiki, 206
Barna, George, 18
Barriger, Robert, 164
Beck, Glenn, 11, 216
Bell, Arnold, 136, 139
Benny, Jack, 211
*Best Little Stories from the Ameri-
  can Revolution*, 127

Bible
  abiding by, 128, 167
  banning of, 145–46
  men of, 105, 112–13, 121
  reading, 105, 108–09, 145–47,
    155, 169, 171, 202
  teaching from, 106–07, 120–21,
    145–47
Biddle, Nicholas, 54
Big Bang theory, 93–94
big government, 2, 8, 15, 59, 70,
  106, 115, 218
Bill of Rights, 15, 27, 34–35, 66, 85,
  117, 154, 167, 216, 218
Bingaman, Jeff, 87
bisexuality, 128–30
Black, Jim Nelson, 153
Blue, Ron, 71
Bono, 211
border agents, 83–86, 88
Border Patrol, 17, 81, 84–85, 87–88,
  182
borders, flying along, 83–84
borders, protecting, 74, 78, 88, 218
Boudinot, Elias, 99, 169
Boyd, James, 145
Briner, Bob, 169
Brokaw, Tom, 10, 205
broken homes, 147
Brooks, Mel, 206
Bureau of Internal Revenue, 66
Burke, Edmund, 142, 219
Burkett, Larry, 52
Burns, George, 213
Burr, Aaron, 55
Bush, George H. W., 16, 108, 157

C
Campanaro, Tom, 196–97
Campolo, Anthony, 212
cancer, 8, 181–82, 188–89, 191,
  193, 197, 199, 201

cardiovascular diseases, 177,
  182–83, 189–90, 197–99
Carmona, Richard, 182
Carroll, Charles, 104
Carroll, Daniel, 95
Carter, Jimmy, 76
censorship, 25–45
Centers for Disease Control and
  Prevention, 22, 179–81
challenges, analyzing, 13–24
child rights, 136, 151
children, failing, 20–21.
  See also youth
cholesterol, 177, 181, 183, 189, 199
Christian education, 154–55
Christianity, 19, 38, 94, 98.
  See also religion
Chronicles of Narnia series, 124
"Chuck Norris Facts," 214
Church and State, separation of,
  35–36
CIA, 182
Civil War, 42, 66, 145
civility, 19, 99, 103–04, 115, 120,
  124
Clarke, William, 163
Clinton, Bill, 5, 51, 153
Clooney, George, 211
Colbert, Don, 185–89, 193–94, 197,
  199–201
Cole, Edwin Louis, 163–66, 169,
  174
college, 153–54. See also education
Columbine High School, 141–43
Coming Economic Earthquake, The,
  52
Constitution of the United States
  abiding by, 26–27, 29, 167
  content of, 229–41
  framers of, 16, 36
  understanding, 15

Constitutional Chaos, 27
Constitutional Convention, 26–27,
    79, 89, 98, 121
consumer debt, 17
consumption war, 179–82
Continental Congress, 27, 160,
    170–71
Coolidge, Calvin, 172
Cooper Aerobics Center, 181
Cooper Institute, 194
Cooper, Kenneth, 194, 201
Copeland, Kenneth, 164
Corbett, Nancy, 164
Corbin, Margaret, 162
corruption, 28–29, 45, 51, 59, 70,
    102, 135, 206, 215, 218
Cosby, Bill, 173
Cowen, David, 54
Cox, Andrew, 116–17
Coxe, Tench, 54
Creator
    belief in, 20, 36, 44, 70, 94–98,
        106–07, 113–14, 116, 120,
        122–23, 146, 165, 171
    and unalienable rights, 20, 36,
        96, 112–14, 225–26. See also
        religion
crime, 21, 139
culture wars, 119, 170, 179, 210
curriculum, 121, 155–56. See also
    education

D
Daniel Boone, 145
Darwinism, 20, 120, 122
Daugherty, James, 145
dead-beat dads, 21, 160
debt, as bondage, 17–18, 53
debt, of nation, 16–17, 47–71
Declaration of Independence
    abiding by, 26–27, 167
    adopting, 27

content of, 225–27
    and human value, 20, 111–25
    understanding, 15
Democracy in America, 94
Democrats, 153
Department of Agriculture, 23, 185
Department of Homeland Security,
    17, 87–88
detoxify, 197–98
diabetes, 181, 189, 194
diet, 184–203
discipline, 134–35, 158, 195
disconnection, 128–29
diseases, 180–81
disrespect, 13, 115, 142
division of nation, 13–24
divorce, 20–21, 160
*Do Hard Things: A Teenage Rebel-
    lion against Low Expectations*,
    131
Dobson, James C., 215
Douglas, Kirk, 211–13
Dred Scott v. Sandford, 20
Dreher, Rod, 143
drug cartels, 17, 83–84, 87
drugs, 14, 47, 58, 87, 157, 197
Drums, 145
DuBord, Todd, 37–41
Duer, William, 54

E
earmarks, 49, 62
eating habits, 177–82
Eaton, William, 77
economy
    problems with, 13, 48–49,
        65–68, 78, 90–91, 206
    stimulating, 48–49, 68
    and taxes, 65–70
    education, 120–21, 146–56,
        150–52, 170–71. See
        also homeschooling; schools

Ellis, Joseph, 26
equality, 20, 26, 95, 112–20, 161,
    207
euthanasia, 20, 117
evolution, 116, 120, 122
exercise, 177–203
extremists, 73–80, 96–97

F
Fair Tax, 65–68
faith, 93–109, 201–02
Falwell, Jerry, Jr., 154
family
    breakdown of, 20–21, 147,
        161–62
    honoring, 159–76
    relations within, 159–76
    unifying, 163–64
    values of, 21–22
"Father of the Christian Men's
    Movement," 163
fathers, 160, 165–68, 172–74
FBI, 136–39, 182
federal crimes, 28
Federal Reserve, 17, 51, 55–58, 60
Federalists, 15, 27
Ferguson, Catherine, 162
Financial Founding Fathers: The
    Men Who Made America Rich,
    54
financial system, 54–55
First Amendment, 28, 30–32, 35–36,
    42, 120–21
fiscal prudence, 17, 62
fitness, 177–203
Fitzsimons, Thomas, 95
Fontaine, Leon, 164
Food and Drug Administration, 23,
    185
food consumption, 177–82
Forbes, 205, 207
Forbes, Esther Hoskins, 145

foreign policy, 74, 76, 78–80
Founding Brothers, 26
founding documents
    abiding by, 167
    Constitution of the United States,
        229–41
    Declaration of Independence,
        225–27
    and education, 147
    framers of, 15–16
    and human value, 111–25
    and tyranny, 215–17, 225–27
    understanding, 5, 25–45, 66–67
Founding Fathers
    achievements of, 26
    beliefs of, 95, 121–22
    dreams of, 207–08
    expectations of, 28–29, 207–08
    labeling, 25
    learning from, 21
Franklin, Benjamin
    beliefs of, 94–95, 98, 122
    and family, 159
    on slavery, 113–14
    wisdom by, 185–86
    on youth, 20–21
Franklin, William (Billy), 159–60
freedom
    basis for, 95–99
    baton of, 215–17
    extinction of, 134–35
    See also liberty
Freefall of the American University,
    153

G
Gallatin, Albert, 54, 58
gangs, 87, 157
gasoline crisis, 17, 22–23
Generation X, 129
Gibbon, Edward, 208
Gingrich, Newt, 61, 90

Girard, Stephen, 54
giving to others, 70–71
God
    belief in, 19–20, 70–71, 93–110,
        112–13, 116–23, 164–67
    and unalienable rights, 20, 36,
        96, 112–14, 225–26
    See also religion
government
    big government, 2, 8, 15, 59, 70,
        106–07, 115, 218
    and education, 150–52
    purpose of, 60–61
    reconstructing, 27–30
    remedying, 29–30
    restraining, 29–30, 48–49, 64, 66
    roots of, 15–16
Great Depression, 7–8, 10, 57, 59,
    61
greed, 13, 21, 47–48, 58–59, 70–71,
    208–09
Greed, 47
gun sprees, 141–42

H
Hale, Edward Everett, 158
Hamas, 76
Hamilton, Alexander, 54, 114
Hannity, Sean, 216
happiness, pursuit of, 6, 20, 29–45,
    70–71, 95, 113, 207
Harris, Alex, 131–33, 156, 170
Harris, Brett, 131–33, 156, 170
Harris, Gregg, 170
Harris, Sono, 170
hate crimes, 28
healthcare crisis, 184
healthy lifestyles, 177–203
healthy tips, 186–203
heart disease, 181–84, 186, 189,
    193, 197, 199
Hee, Kong, 164

Henry, Patrick, 29, 66, 104, 172,
    216
Hensley, John, 85
Herbert, George, 166
heritage
    appreciating, 13–14
    censoring, 25–45
Heston, Charlton, 211–13
historical adventures, 145
history
    erasing, 25–45
    learning from, 13–15, 26, 74–75,
        78
    teaching, 144–47
History of the Decline and Fall of the
    Roman Empire, The, 208
Hitler, Adolf, 151
Holmes, David, 95
Homeland Security Department, 17,
    87–88
homeschooling, 149–52, 156, 170
homosexuality, 128–29
Hope, Bob, 213
housing market, 48
Huckabee, Mike, 22, 28, 63, 67, 88,
    142, 180
human life, in Early America,
    112–14
human life, value of, 20, 111–25
human rights, 76, 98, 116–17
Hussein, Saddam, 31, 85

I
illnesses, 182–84
immigration problems, 17–18,
    85–91
immorality, 21, 103, 107, 128, 142,
    147
inflation, 51
"Information to those who would
    remove to America," 21
Institute for Truth in Accounting, 16

Internal Revenue Service (IRS),
    65–66
Internet safety, 137, 140
Iran, 76
Iraq, 31–32, 80–82, 85, 116, 128
Islamic extremists, 73–80

J

Jackson, Andrew, 54
Jamestown Settlement, 37–39, 41
Jay, John, 97
Jefferson, Thomas
    on American dream, 207
    on Bill of Rights, 35
    on Church and State, 35–36
    on debts, 17, 53–65, 69–70,
        207–08
    on diet, 22, 190–91
    on education, 151–53, 213
    on exercise, 194
    on family, 161–62
    on foreign policy, 78–79
    on government, 22
    on health, 185–86, 188, 201
    on history, 26
    on human life, 17, 117
    on peace, 70–71
    on power, 172
    as president, 15
    on taxes, 64–65
    on tyranny, 151–52
    and U.S. seal, 145–46
Jesus, 23, 107, 116, 120, 125, 146,
    169, 171–72, 190, 201, 216
Johnny Tremain, 145
*Journal of the American Medical
    Association*, 198
Judeo-Christian faith, 6, 19, 36,
    42–43, 45, 107, 128, 147
judges, 150–51
juvenile crime, 21, 139

K

Kelly, C. Brian, 127
Kennedy, John F., 215
Khomeini, Ayatollah, 76–77
KickStartKids, 87, 155–58, 195
Kids Who Kill, 142
Knight, Wilma, 193
Kurulo, Suliasi, 164

L

L.A. Times, 211
Lafayette, Marquis de, 127–28
Language of Love, The, 174
latchkey kids, 22
leadership, 78, 168–69.
    See also mentoring
Leadership Lessons of Jesus, The,
    169
Ledyaev, Alexey, 164
Lee, Bruce, 23
legacy, 15–16, 129–30, 168, 170,
    212, 219
Leo, Eddy, 164
lethargic, 182
*Let's Face It: 90 Years of Living,
    Loving, and Learning*, 211
Lewis, C. S., 124
liberal judges, 150–52
liberty, 6, 15, 20, 25, 29, 33, 35–36,
    44, 60, 64, 66, 70, 78, 84, 95–96,
    107, 113–14, 142, 152, 162, 166,
    180, 206–09, 215–16.
    See also freedom
Liberty Bell, 215
Limbaugh, Rush, 31, 216
Lincoln, Abraham, 213, 216–17
*Lion, the Witch, and the Wardrobe,
    The*, 125
longevity, 181, 186
Louisiana Purchase, 17, 55

M

MacArthur, Douglas, 168
Madison, Dolly, 162
Madison, James, 15, 18, 36, 55, 68, 114, 142
Mae, Fannie, 5, 51
Mae, Freddie, 5, 52
man, descent of, 115–17
martial arts, 23, 87, 108, 155, 157, 172, 195–96
martial arts program, 87, 157, 195
materialism, 13, 129, 207
Maxwell, John, 102, 164
McCartney, Bill, 164
McPherson, Aimee Semple, 164
mentoring, 142, 163, 169–70
Mexican Mafia, 87
Middle East, 76, 80–82.
    See also Iran; Iraq
Millennials, 127–58, 210
Mitala, Alex, 164
Mitchell, Tedd, 181, 201
monetary system, 54, 60, 206
Moore, Roy, 37
moral compass, 13, 18, 104
moral lives, 129, 135.
    See also morality
Morales, Larry, 108
morality
    basis for, 18, 103–07
    and laws, 103
    loss of, 13–14, 18–19, 208–09
    and parents, 168–69
    and religion, 19, 146
Morris, Gouverneur, 121
Morris, Robert, 54
motivator, 172–76
Move Yourself, 181
movies, 101, 108, 145
MS-13, 87

murder, 34, 78, 87, 125, 142–44, 160
Muslim extremists, 73–75, 77–78
MySpace, 101, 136, 211
"Myths and Truths of Personal Finance," 53–54

N

NAFTA, 17
Napolitano, Andrew P., 27–28, 55–56
nation, division of, 13–24
"National Council of Bible Curriculum in Public Schools, The," 121
national debt, 16–17, 47–71
national deficit, 16–17, 63, 70
national legacy, 15–16
National Park Service, 39–41
national security, 18, 86, 130
naturalization, 18, 89–91.
    See also immigration problems
Naturalization Act, 89–91
New York Times, 1, 3, 25
Nightline, 214
Noble Institute for Leadership Development, 170
Norris, Aaron, 82–83
Norris, Dakota, 112, 192
Norris, Danilee, 112, 192
Norris, Gena
    and education, 121
    and faith, 108–09, 169, 201–02
    and fitness, 195–96
    and healthy diet, 191–93
    and homeschooling, 150, 156, 170
    on human life, 111–12
    meeting, 108, 201
    as mentor, 170
Norris, Guy "Chuck," 133–34
Norris, Wieland, 82
North American Union, 17

North, Oliver, 164
Northwest Ordinance, 15
nutrients, 189–90, 198–99
nutritional supplements, 189–91

O
Obama, 2–3, 5, 7, 33, 49–50, 52, 56, 58, 62, 84, 99–102,118–19, 149, 178–79
obesity, 20–21, 179–84, 190, 194–95
O'Donnell, Jay, 133–34
oil prices, 17, 48–49
online safety, 135–39
open-door policy, 89–90.
    See also immigration problems
O'Reilly, Bill, 216
overweight society, 20–21, 24, 179–84, 190

P
Paine, Thomas, 96, 122, 136, 217, 220
parenting, 147–48, 158, 165–68, 170–71, 182–83. See also youth
past, learning from, 13–16, 26, 75
Pastore, Frank, 216
Paul, Ron, 28, 56–57, 65, 67, 130, 218
peace, cultivating, 69–70
Péguy, Charles, 216
Pelosi, Nancy, 58, 205
Penn, Sean, 211
Penn, William, 167
physical activity, 181, 195–203
Pinsof, William, 161
Pitcher, Molly, 162
Pitt, Brad, 18, 211
Poor Richard's Almanack, 185
pornography, 20–21, 101, 128, 137–41
Powell, Colin, 206
power, 22–23

prayer and school, 13, 19.
    See also education
presidents, naming, 14
Prince Caspian, 124–25
"Principles for Life," 213–14
private education, 148, 151–52.
    See also education
promiscuity, 13, 21
prudence, 17, 62–63, 70, 114
public schools, 38, 120–21, 145, 148–49, 152–53, 156.
    See also education

R
Rachel's Challenge, 144
Ramsay, David, 170–71
Ramsey, Dave, 53
Randazzo, Marisa, 141
Read, Deborah, 159
Reagan, Ronald, 50, 86, 134, 153
real estate market, 17, 48
reawakening, 13–24, 130–31, 205–20
rebelution, 132, 156–57
reconnecting, 129–32, 144–47
religion
    and beliefs, 93–110, 121–23
    and civility, 19, 103–07
    and education, 115–21
    and law, 96–97
    and morality, 18–19, 99, 103–05
    See also God
Republicans, 11, 101, 153
responsibility, 19, 64, 88, 91, 107, 120, 145, 162, 168, 185, 215
revolution, fostering, 23, 54, 131, 156–57
Revolutionary Era, 170, 208
Revolutionary War, 17, 53–54, 66, 73, 127
Rhodes, Martin "Oz," 134
Rice, Condoleezza, 205

"right to life," 117–18
Rights of the Child, 151
Robertson, Pat, 164
Roe v. Wade, 6, 20, 117–19
Roosevelt's New Deal, 9, 61
Ross, Betsy, 162
Rules of Civility & Decent Behavior
    in Company and Conversation,
    103
Rush, Benjamin, 104, 120, 135, 143,
    161, 174
Rush, John, 171
Russell, Kurt, 205
Russert, Tim, 173

S
Schenck, Rob, 142
school and prayer, 14, 19, 105–06
school shootings, 139–41
schools, 38, 120–21, 144–56. See
    also education; homeschooling
Scott, Craig, 143
Scott, Darrell, 143
Scott, Rachel, 143
seal of the United States, 146
Second Continental Congress, 27
Secret Service, 141
senior citizens, 120, 212–14
separation of Church and State, 35
Seven Pillars of Health, 186
sex, 14, 128
sex offenders, 101, 136
sexual predators, 101–02
sexuality, 127–28, 161
sexually transmitted diseases, 21,
    128
Shaw, George Bernard, 47
Sherman, General, 80
sickness, 180–82
Sixteenth Amendment, 66
slavery, 19–20, 26, 112–14, 237–38
sleep requirements, 188–89

Smalley, Gary, 124, 174
smoking, 135, 182, 191, 199, 203
smuggling operations, 17, 87
soldiers, supporting, 80–82, 127–28
spending, curbing, 69–70
spending habits, 47–51
spirituality, 201–02, 93–109
Stalin, Joseph, 151
Stamp Act, 160
Stewart, Martha, 206
Stibich, Mark, 188
stimulus program, 48–49
"stirring the waters," 193, 197
stock market, 16, 48, 207–08
Stockton, Richard, 167
Stone, Oliver, 206
Stossel, John, 47
street gangs, 87, 157
strength training, 196–97
stress, reducing, 199–201
Student's Bill of Rights, 154
success, 22, 47–48, 90, 107–09,
    213–14
suicide, 19–20, 135–36

T
taxes, 63–70
TBN, 62
Tebow, Bob, 170
Tebow, Pam, 170
Tebow, Tim, 156, 170
teen pregnancy, 21
teen violence, 142–44
television shows, 107–08, 211
Ten Commandments, 19, 38, 99,
    105–06, 145, 167
Tenth Amendment, 28, 57, 60
terror threats, 17–18, 80–81.
    See also terrorism
terror, war on, 73–78
terrorism, 17–18, 73–78, 87,
    182–86

Tocqueville, Alexis de, 94
Total Gym, 195–97
toxins, 193, 197–98
trade deficit, 16
trans fats, 183–84, 190
transgender sexuality, 128
treason, 28, 160
Treasure Principle and Money, Possessions, and Eternity, The, 71
Treaty of Paris, 160
Treaty of Tripoli, 74, 97–98
Trent, John, 174
troops, supporting, 80–81, 213
Trump, Donald, 32, 47, 206
Turner, Ted, 47, 206
tyranny, 32–33, 106, 149, 151–52, 177, 180, 216–17, 220

U

United Nations Convention on the Rights of the Child, 151
U.S. Constitution
    abiding by, 26, 167
    content of, 229–41
    framers of, 15–16, 37–38
    understanding, 15
Utley, Vine, 190

V

Vietnam War, 8, 82
Vindicating the Founders, 25
violence, 22, 83, 128, 132, 144
vitamin supplements, 198–99
voting, 28, 119

W

Walker, Texas Ranger, 108, 164
walking, 193–94
Wall Street Journal, 16, 199
Warren, Mercy, 162
Washington, George
    and debts, 16, 50, 55, 63, 207
    on foreign policy, 78–79
    on morality, 19, 103, 105
    on peace, 69–70
    on perfection, 112–13
    as president, 15
    on religion, 97, 105, 120
    and revolution, 23
    on slavery, 113–14
    on taxes, 64
Washington, Martha, 162
Washington Monument, 37, 39, 41
Washington Times, 87
water, drinking, 187–88, 192, 197–98
Wayne, John, 145
Webster, Daniel, 216
Webster, Noah, 105
Weir, Bill, 214
"Wellness Guide to Dietary Supplements," 199
West, Thomas G., 25
Westfall, Larry, 196
Willing, Thomas, 54
Wilson, A. N., 207
Wilson, Earl, 53
Wilson, James, 96
Wisdom of our Fathers: Lessons and Letters from Daughters and Sons, 173
Witherspoon, John, 94,106–07
workout schedule, 195–96
World Health Organization, 22, 179
Wright, Robert, 54

Y

youth
    assisting, 133–34
    failing, 20–21
    influence of, 127–58
    protecting, 132–44, 191
    providing for, 147–56
    reconnecting, 144–47